The Batsford Book of
Practical Dressmaking

Amanda Stevenson

B.T. Batsford Ltd, London

ACKNOWLEDGMENT

To Kitty Todor and staff at Barnfield College, Luton, especially the late Ann Hornblow; to Ann Smith, my mother; to Jo Waters and to Richard and Alexander – my grateful thanks.

ISBN 0 7134 1436 7

Typeset by Tradespools Ltd., Frome, Somerset
and printed in Great Britain by
R.J. Acford Ltd, Chichester, Sussex
for the publishers
B.T. Batsford Ltd.
4 Fitzhardinge Street
London W1H 0AH

Contents

Preface

Dressmaking has suffered for a long time from an unimaginative and boring image. This is directly due to old-fashioned and time-consuming ideas, presented to the beginner by 'home dressmaking' methods linked to the commercial paper pattern.

This book seeks to present a method that offers useful and relevant information for cutting and making up garments to fit, whether they be original designs, adaptations or copies. This is no over-simplified short-cut or unnecessarily complicated or unexplained gimmickry; the basic methods shown have a sound, professional basis, with excellence of workmanship and high standards of quality the main priorities.

The presentation of this information should be acceptable to a complete beginner as well as being informative to the dressmaker with experience. It is better for the experienced to cover the basics, at the risk of possible boredom, so that logical progression may be followed through and a clearer picture of the systems described might emerge. To avoid rep-etition, each section covered appears isolated, but each area influences and is influenced by others, so a constant overlap of thought must occur. For this reason, the greatest advantage will be gained by not fragmenting the information too much, but absorbing it as a whole.

It is sincerely hoped that this book will give dressmaking a more exciting and creative image. Those who are uninterested or disillusioned may then be encouraged to acquire the skills and know-ledge that, together with the ability to apply individual ideas, will lead to enthusiasm, pleasure, satisfaction and a sense of achievement.

Individual thinking is encouraged throughout. All the instructions and examples serve to illustrate a principle, to be used as a lead for the imaginative, 'thinking' person. The more that individual deviation and development arise, the greater the success of the book will be, as its main aim will have then been truly achieved.

Part I:

General information

CHAPTER ONE

Design

In recent years the whole fashion industry has, in order to survive, found the need to diversify and satisfy a wider range of individual tastes rather than dictate 'one look for all'. Many different looks are now acceptable at any one time and, while some may find this confusing, it allows for so much more individuality, variety and interest.

Most people have quite strong ideas about their likes and dislikes and personal circumstances affect the type of clothing worn by each person: life-style, figure type and personal taste are things that most people consider automatically when choosing clothes in the shops. The thoughts that run through your mind as you search rail after rail for 'that dress', eliminating unsuitable details and wishing this dress had sleeves of that blouse, are often those needed to design your perfect garment.

There is no reason why anybody with the determination to dress well should not be able to make their own clothes with style and quality and, at the same time, enjoy considerably such creativity.

Designing your own clothes need not be a frightening struggle for originality but merely a matter of choosing and putting together, with discernment, those details which appeal most to you. As all your ideas must be practicable, a basic understanding of the cut and construction of clothing and an appreciation of the various qualities of fabric are both vital. It is hoped that the information included here will provide much of the knowledge needed to turn design ideas into reality and to introduce a way of thinking that will bring confidence by destroying some of the mystery and over-complication so often associated with dressmaking.

My personal view is that, in most cases, it is better to buy your fabric before completing any design ideas. Every fabric has different qualities and designing with these specifically in mind will enable you to use the fabric to greatest advantage. A variety of good quality, exciting fabrics are increasingly available and the wider the choice, the better. A particular fabric may suggest design ideas to you which you can explore and develop.

The most important reason for appreciating fully the qualities of the fabric you wish to use is that you will be able to calculate the necessary size and shape of each cut piece to achieve the exact finished look you require. It is important that the proportions of a design are decided upon at an early stage and controlled throughout the work. The finished silhouette must have been carefully contrived, rather than appear of its own accord, and consideration of this point will result in a strong statement that is unquestionably 'you'. You must have the confidence to control your work. At every stage of the design and cut of the garment, question every decision you make, for the finished garment you create will simply convey the result of these decisions.

Often a degree of exaggeration is necessary to state an intention clearly. This is preferable to a rather apologetic design feature which might even be thought by others to be a mistake. Place extra emphasis on features of the design by cutting dainty, extra narrow cuffs and collar to make more of huge, puffed sleeves, for instance. Extravagance of design alone is obviously not what makes a design succeed, but it is important to make a strong statement of whatever it is that you wish your design to include. The character of your work is not incidental, but exactly what you make it. This is true whatever style of clothing you wish to make even if you have a simple or classic taste.

Some people will tend to 'over design'; they must learn to exercise restraint. A multitude of ideas are better spread over a number of garments than crammed together on just one, resulting in a confused mess. Other people may be more tentative; they should learn new processes to give them confidence to try out new ideas and bring excitement and interest to their work. If you have very little experience, but many ideas, try and begin either with very simple garments or with an adaptation of something you have already seen made up. It can be extremely disheartening to imagine a design which you then find is too complicated or impossible to create.

Have the courage to try out new ideas. If you have no extra fabric to spare, make up any area you are uncertain about using a similar fabric. Not only does this mean that you can sort out any complications in the construction and simplify and alter as necessary, but you can see the effect made up and check its success on the body in a mirror. You will undoubtedly find that while working through a trial process, your mind will wander and lead to many alternative ideas and possibilities. Also, having worked through a method once, you will then achieve a much better finish when you come to make up the garment.

If you are not so prone to wild flashes of imagination you will probably find it easier to work in a logical, orderly manner. Again, develop any particular idea you are unfamiliar with by working with scraps of fabric at the machine. As problems arise, you will search for alternatives and these minor adjustments may well lead on to new and unrelated developments. Trial and error is also marvellous for the confidence, for the more you cut a shape and see the instant result of it made up, the more you learn about the relationship between scissor and cloth and the less you will fear chopping into the fabric.

Gaining inspiration from fabric lengths and realising innovations by playing with scraps at the machine may not fuel the imagination sufficiently. You don't have to be a gifted designer to gain pleasure and benefit from making your own clothes; often those who are less ambitious, although sometimes less inclined to try in the first place, will achieve a greater rate of immediate success as they are less likely to tear their hair out in their efforts to make a wide ruffle collar poke out in particular places.

Magazines, pattern books, shops and the clothes other people wear are all rich sources of information. Keep your eyes open and you will never be short of ideas. There is nothing that has not been done in some form or other before and by using your own fabric and making a garment up with your own hands, you will have a finished garment that is individual enough to be 'yours'. The idea of adapting something that already exists in some form is an important point to remember when looking through the section on cutting. A little knowledge can go a long way and by using information from, among other things, your existing wardrobe, you can begin to cut your own designs.

Wherever inspiration comes from, you will need some way of recording your ideas. A good eye for detail will mean you will retain much of what you see when you are out and about, and the greater your understanding of the construction of clothing, the easier this will become. The best way to keep track of your thoughts is to make small sketches. These need not remotely resemble professional fashion drawings but merely be enough to jog your memory. When helpful, add descriptive notes and jot any other thoughts that may spring to mind alongside. If you enjoy sketching, you will probably do most of your designing with a pencil. More important than flamboyant fashion drawing is an accurate recording of proportion and detail and a good 'working drawing' is ideal to work from. If you despair of ever being able to put what is in your mind down on paper, rather than giving up completely, try a more diagrammatical style. This, too, will become easier as you understand the construction of what you are trying to represent.

Collect cuttings of details and shapes that appear to you for reference and inspiration. Photographs and drawings from magazines and newspapers are always useful. Select details, such as interesting collars or pockets, for use on your own garments. You may have nothing planned immediately that they would suit, but keep a record and you will then have details to refer back to in the future. History of fashion books can be extremely inspirational. If you are not happy making sketches, trace over anything you feel you might use in some way. Made up garments, whether old or new, can also be made use of extensively. They will not only inspire you but (unless being worn by a stranger in the street) satisfy your curiosity, as you will be able to examine closely how a particular point of interest has been cut and constructed. Apart from this obvious advantage, if a garment has a perfect fit in any area, it will have an extremely practical purpose too. Any paper patterns you have used succesfully may have similar practical advantages, although an unusual cut may well lead you to consider further design possibilities.

For every garment you make, the original inspiration will probably have come from a different starting point. In one instance, you may want to adapt a favourite day dress into a full-length evening dress by using a different fabric and adding beading and ruffles to a lowered neckline. You may fall in love with an exotic print which you later decide to make into a huge, gathered skirt, as you already have a silk shirt and wide suede belt in perfect matching colours. Perhaps you have seen an attractive blouse in a drama on television and are inspired to make

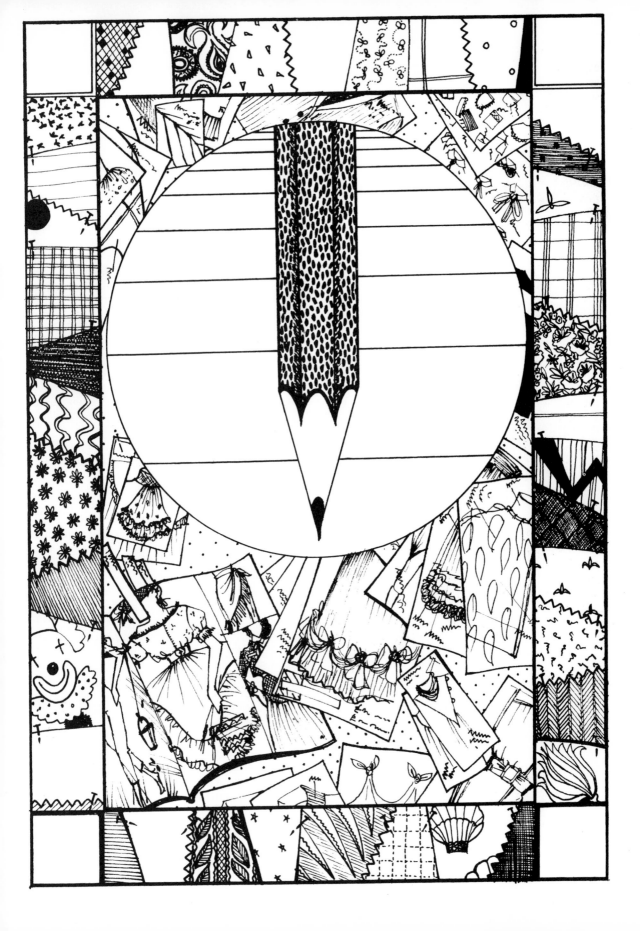

your own version, or you realise a marvellous way to make up an original idea for a collar and need to think of the best garment on which to put it.

The main emphasis in this book is on the practical and technical side of dressmaking. Without this, any number of ideas will come to nothing. Anything you can learn from the technical information given here should go a long way to help you recognise and modify your more impractical ideas.

Before you begin to cut your design, you should be as certain of as many of the final details of the garment as possible. Original ideas may need to be modified if you discover problems with the fabric, or if you already have part of a pattern or garment upon which to build the rest of the design. You will also need to know every detail of how the garment will be constructed. Experiment at the machine to understand the best ways to handle the fabric and, with practice, you will develop a professional approach to design.

The best way to work is from a sketch or diagram with a written description and list of every relevant detail. You should have notes to remind yourself of the results of any experimenting you might have done. From this, you can list the name of every cut piece necessary, including interfacings, and also a step-by-step order of construction. This will help you to sew with a clear and practical approach, and you can keep the instructions for future use and interest. These areas are covered more fully in the relevant parts of the book.

POINTS TO CONSIDER

There are many practical considerations to be taken into account before finalising the points of any design you intend to make up. Breaking these points down in the following way will hopefully encourage a clear and logical approach which will increase the chances of success of the finished garment. To begin with, you must have in your mind the kind of garment you wish to make, when and where the fabric you are to use both falls and handles under the machine.

Silhouette

The silhouette of a design refers to the basic outline shape that results from the 'mass' of the garment and contributes greatly to its character. It is basically formed and affected by the size and shape of the cut fabric pieces which determine how full or otherwise the garment is to be and, to an even greater extent, by the character of the fabric itself. The way in which any fullness is controlled will also alter the silhouette

considerably. You will have chosen your fabric with an awareness of its effect on the silhouette and, if it has the right qualities, you can cut to give the look you require. A soft, bias-cut satin will cling to the body and fall in gentle, liquid folds, whereas you can gather stiff net to interline tafetta to increase the amount it will stick out. These are extreme instances, but illustrate well the spectrum of effects that it is possible to engineer. Any type of interfacing alters the qualities of a fabric, so consider where you may use it to help you achieve a particular silhouette.

Silhouette is as much altered by fashion as any other factor that changes with the seasons. Before you surge ahead, however, stop to think of how flattering to your own figure type the silhouette might be. Figure type is a logical area from which to begin as it already has a silhouette of its own. You will be well aware of those aspects you prefer to hide and those that are worth emphasis. The silhouette of the clothes you wear on top can therefore disguise and flatter those areas and you should always try and imagine how a design will particularly suit and flatter you. Having read this, you may feel you are extremely limited for suitable choice, but by thinking about the proportions of the design, you will realise there are many things that can alter the visual effect.

Stand before a full-length mirror and simply think honestly about what you feel you can wear successfully and what you should avoid. Proportion has no hidden mysteries. The reason many people dislike something without realising why is usually because what they are looking at is disproportionate. Try on various clothes and question why you particularly like or dislike the way your shape looks to the eye. Where you are unhappy, see if you can find a slight alteration that would improve the whole image. Often, it is only small and subtle changes that are necessary to make the design succeed. Minor alterations, such as raising or lowering the hemline, will change the proportions of the garment, which may then have a much more pleasing look to the eye. You must also be aware of how much the colour and fabric adds to the visual impact of a garment and so play an important part where proportion is concerned. Light, dark, dull or bright colours will all give a different look to the same dress as will a bold or delicate print, a stripe or check and the ways the light is absorbed or reflected by the surface texture of the fabric.

Remember that you are working with three dimensions and the way the garment looks from the back and sides are equally important. As the viewpoint changes, so does the silhouette. Much of what you choose will be without conscious thought; you will be concerned with seaming and style lines which will give the garment its structure and automatically form the silhouette to a certain extent. You can then make a positive decision about how much fullness to add and what to do with the 'mass' of fabric to form a silhouette that is exactly as you wish. There is no correct order or plan to follow when designing. Your thoughts should overlap at every stage; you will consider the final silhouette when you have your first idea, when you choose the fabric, as you decide on the final details of the design, as you find the best way to cut the garment and also in the ways you find to make the garment up.

Styling

The styling of a garment is concerned with the practical considerations necessary to achieve the silhouette. This means determining the position of the seams. You will decide what the main fabric pieces are to be and any peculiarities they might have, how you will achieve the fit and fall you intend and how to solve practical problems such as getting the garment on and off the body. Wearability should be at the front of your mind, with comfort and ease being priorities. Nobody enjoys wearing ill-fitting or uncomfortable clothing, nor is it acceptable constantly to have to adjust and reposition any part of a garment as you wear it.

As so much of what you are concerned with at this stage is to do with the structure of the garment, try and find the simplest methods of construction that will give you the results you want. Unnecessary seaming detracts from the impact of a design, apart from the fact that it is a pointless waste of time. There should always be a good reason for where the seams of a garment are positioned. Make certain they will not lie in an unflattering line on the body. Pay attention to the proportions and balance they create as the seams divide up the mass of the garment into areas of differing shapes and sizes which must look good in relation to one another.

Seaming is always necessary to control such fullness as gathers, which are held in position in a seam and so suppressed. There are other methods of suppression that are stitched down on to the fabric, such as tucks, which are not held in a seam. As suppression is such an important part of the garment, it should be decided upon at an early stage and, whichever method you use, it will be a feature of the design. Another equally important point that may or may not be a prominent feature of the design is the opening and the method used to fasten it. This is necessary in every case where a garment is other than a large sack with a wide neck or where elastic is used.

The fact that this is such a necessity should not mean that it is overlooked as a potential design feature. Too often a centre back zip or a plain row of buttons indicate lack of thought. The design possibilities available are plentiful, but should not include a fussy or over-stated finish. The actual details of the method of fastening must appear well thought out, and so, too, should the position on the garment. The other features of the design will suggest the best position.

Other basic style lines may need to be added that make no difference to the silhouette of the garment. They may, however, be necessary where insertion or contrast fabrics are cut to form a design feature, for example. The basic garment shape remains the same, but is sub-divided into different areas.

Once the design has all its style lines, you will be able to plan how the pattern should be cut and see what the most important measurements to be decided are. You can also be virtually certain of the order of consruction and be in a position to make any alterations that may simplify the work ahead.

Detailing

The details are just as important a part of any design as the more obvious points and they can have more thought and actual 'design' applied than any other area. Some details are functional, such as pockets or cuffs, and others are purely decorative. Again, careful positioning is vital to give good proportion and balance to the design, and consideration of scale is also important. Try not to let your imagination run away too far so that the detailing is kept in context with the rest of the design. This is where you must be careful not to overcrowd the design and destroy the visual impact originally intended.

If you are aware of the infinite variety of possibilities, you will realise that you can work with one basic shirt shape, for instance, that fits well and suits you. This can serve as a base for countless shirt designs. Use a different type fabric and alter the collar and pockets. Add feminine ruffles and lace or a corded contrast piping. Concentrate on the detailing and you will be able to use the same base pattern repeatedly, with little or no modification. This is ideal work for experimenting at the machine as you only need small bits and pieces of leftover fabrics. It is only by experimenting that you will be able to find the best and most suitable methods to achieve the results you want. You can also practise, so that you are confident when you come to work on the actual garment. As so much depends on the kind of detailing and the styling of the garment to be worked on, each individual case will have its own needs.

CHAPTER TWO

fabrics

Finding a suitable fabric for an intended design commonly leads to frustration and mistakes, and one of the disadvantages of working with commercial patterns is that you are encouraged to buy the pattern first. There are so many points to consider when trying to find a possible fabric that it is far easier to meet some of these by designing around the many problems that may arise if you are in any way adventurous in the fabric shop. By appreciating the immensely varied and exciting qualities of fabric, you will be encouraged to use a wider range of types. Understanding the requirements of these different types will add to your skills in handling and you will not be restricted in choice by a fear of what have been termed 'difficult' fabrics.

You will probably have some idea of the kind of fabric you are looking for – the colour, print or plain, whether it needs to be warm or cool, whether it is for casual holiday wear or a spectacular evening dress, and roughly how much you are prepared to spend. It is obviously far easier if you are not too restricted financially. As with many things, you usually get what you pay for in terms of quality, and settling for a cheaper fabric often proves in the long run to be a false economy. Your first impression of the fabric on the roll is visual and this is one of the first and most important points to be checked for suitability. Whether it will add to or destroy the image you wish to convey will be an almost subconscious decision. Once you are satisfied with the visual qualities of the fabric you must turn to the many practicalities. Reading through every detail in this way may make finding the right fabric seem as likely as hitting the jackpot. In reality, you will find you can weigh up the advantages against the disadvantages. The main thing is to be aware of any problems you may be up against so that you are in a position to work around them.

POINTS TO CONSIDER

Character of the fabric

The fibre content directly affects much of the character of a fabric. Different fibres have different advantages and a little knowledge of the qualities of various fibres is extremely useful. The surface texture and feel of the fabric on the skin will vary with the fibre content, as will the wash and wearing qualities. You should think of the amount of wear you expect the fabric to give and how much time you are prepared to spend washing and ironing. The handling of a fabric is also dependent on the fibre content. The amount a fabric creases or drapes varies as does the ease with which it can be cut, pressed and machined.

Fabrics are constructed from long threads which are spun or otherwise formed either from pure, natural fibres from plants and animals, or from man-made fibres which consist of natural materials that have been chemically treated, or from synthetic fibres which come from wholly chemical sources. Each of these 'families' has particular advantages but often the most successful fabrics consist of various blends and mixtures, where the best features of the fibres used over-ride the disadvantages. The balance of fibres is shown as a percentage and such are the developments and variety of modern textiles that the listing of fibre details of every fabric now becomes impossible.

Check the labelled fibre content for, with such variety, even fabric experts find it difficult to detect fibre content by feel alone. This will tell you more about the positive points of the fabric than any other detail and you will, among other things, be in a better position to judge what value you are getting for your money. You should confirm that the fabric is suited to the kind of wear you expect the garment to give and to its comfort, especially as the warmth or coolness are determined by the fibres.

How a fabric handles when being cut, machined and pressed and the way it falls when worn are both important. They are affected by the weight, the way the fabric is constructed, the surface texture, any special finish the fabric has and, as previously mentioned, the fibre content. Unroll a sufficient length of fabric to see how it really hangs and whether it falls in a way that pleases you. Screw up tightly a small area in one hand to see if it creases readily, or whether there is plenty of 'spring' and resistance to creasing. See how much light the fabric allows through so that you can decide whether a lining may be needed and, if it is, you may prefer to make an alternative choice.

The fabric weight and construction will determine the way it can be most successfully and most easily sewn. The most suitable methods of controlling the fabric with the hands and the different ways the machine should be used must be found, to ensure that secure and correctly tensioned seams result. Bear in mind the bulk of the fabric when deciding upon the most suitable type of seams. The way a fabric is constructed directly affects the surface texture: a knitted fabric that stretches will demand different handling from a fabric with a firmly woven twill weave, and a sheer, slippery fabric, such as satin, may cause problems when cutting and require special attention when seaming.

The construction of the fabric, together with its tension, also affects the amount it is likely to fray. A looser weave of one type will fray much more readily than a more solid kind of weave that has a tighter tension. So, too, will silky and lustrous fibres that are smooth, as they do not cling together as much as more hairy fibres. There are many ways to cope with a badly fraying fabric and you may want to allow a little extra length when deciding how much to buy. You also need to know whether the fabric is 'one-way', as fabrics that require each garment piece to be cut in the same diretion may also need extra length allowed. When using fabrics where there is a large pattern repeat, this problem is exaggerated and even more careful thinking is needed. More fabric wastage is likely with a large pattern repeat, though greater fabric width may compensate.

It is important to check the less obvious points of the quality, as the most expensive fabrics can occasionally contain flaws. Make sure the dyes are of good quality and will not run or seep when the fabric is washed. You should also question whether a fabric has been pre-shrunk and if any special finishes have been applied, such as crease- or flame-resistance. Check that there are no distortions in the weave and that the grain is truly straight. Do not buy a fabric if you detect the slightest twist in its structure. Printing faults may not be immediately obvious, so be on your guard and check for these and any other flaw, slub, dirt or fade marks as the fabric is measured out before you. Insist that you have the chance to check the full fabric length to your own satisfaction.

Fabric widths

Fabric is woven in various different finished widths, the most common being discussed here. For reasons of economy of cut or specifications of design, you may find one fabric width far more suitable than another, and bearing the width in mind at the designing stage will both save wastage and help avoid problems when cutting out the garment. The following suggestions can be used as a rough guide either when choosing a fabric for a particular design or when designing to make the most of a fabric length that you already have.

Narrow fabric measures 90 cm (36 in.) wide. When folded in half lengthwise, an average front, back and sleeve will fit in a row along the fabric length. Therefore, the length of each piece, plus any extra pieces, will give you the total amount of fabric required. More unusual styles may need piecing – i.e. cutting in sections and seaming together – and larger pattern pieces or those with an unusual shape are generally uneconomical when cut in this width. It is well worth struggling until the most economical way is found. Folding the fabric widthwise, especially where the pattern pieces are asymmetrical may help. The difficulties of a one-way fabric may be greatly exaggerated on a narrow width.

112-115 cm (45 in.) is generally a much more accommodating width with which to work. There are many possible ways to arrange the fabric and you will find the most economical to suit each design you cut. Fold it lengthwise, parallel to the selvedge, and most pattern pieces will fit. One skirt length, plus extra for waistband and pockets, will be sufficient for a skirt with a hemline of no more than 100 cm (40 in.). Folding the fabric with a widthwise fold will give a fabric area suitable for larger pattern pieces: where a sleeve and bodice have been cut in one, for example. This width is undoubtedly more economical for most patterns than a narrower fabric and it is an easy width to work with, often allowing alternative placing of pattern pieces.

The widest fabrics are 150 cm (60 in.) wide and, when using them, try to exploit the opportunities offered: they are very useful when working with circular and bias-cut garments as the maximum effect of the fall of the fabric can be achieved without breaking the line of the garment with seams; very full styles can be cut in few pieces, preventing the need for seaming multiple pieces together; continuous pleating is easiest to make up when plenty of fabric width is available. One single garment length is sufficient for the average style, with a sleeve placed alongside the main pieces, but it seems a pity not to make the most of such a fabric for more exciting ideas which would cause great difficulties with a narrower fabric.

Metreage

There are different ways of approaching the problem of how much fabric you should buy. The points that have already been mentioned only concern individual problems that may have some bearing on your final decision. To say that experience is the best possible answer to this question is neither helpful nor informative, but it is nevertheless true; individual figure types will give extreme variations in the final length required. If you have the finished design clear in your mind or, at least, some idea of the type of garment you wish to make and its silhouette, you can work out accurately how much fabric you will need before you go out. List every cut piece included in the garment and decide on the fabric area. For this, you must work from your body measurements and make decisions on the widths that are necessary to achieve the look of the design. You can forget about the detailed shape of each piece for these purposes. Instead, consider their greatest length and width and, allowing for the direction of the straight grain, 'block' up the area of fabric each will cover, not forgetting any repeats of a piece. It is then easy to draw a small diagram, interlocking the pieces in the tightest way rather like a jig-saw, with each block representing the position of each garment piece. This will also show you which fabric width will be the most economical. As you gain experience, you will be able to judge whether you can risk buying a little less than your original estimate.

Many people, however, prefer to buy material for future use with no specific design in mind. The impulse buyer should bear in mind measurements that relate to body length, including your back bodice length at the longest point – from the neck edge of the shoulder seam to the waist – the average skirt length – measured from the waist at the centre front – and the outside length of your arm, from the shoulder to the wrist. You must always allow extra so there is room to move, allowance for blousing, plenty of adjustment for hem positions and, of course, seam turnings. You should also allow for a degree of 'swing' on the cut pieces as, depending on the direction of the straight grain, more fabric length may be taken up simply because of the shape of the piece and how it lies on the fabric. 20–30 cm (8–12 in.) will generally be enough extra length to allow, but you will know how generous you have been with other allowances and you might feel that there is already enough to cover this. Garments cut with large amounts of flare may well require more than 30 cm (12 in.) extra fabric length, however.

Working from the fabric width, you can then reach a decision. For a skirt, ask yourself whether the total hem width, not forgetting to allow for seam turnings, will fit across one fabric width. The waistband may fit lengthwise, too, so you will need to buy your skirt length measurement plus the allowance for hem alteration. If the waistband will not fit, cut it across the fabric, adding its depth plus seam turnings to the skirt length. For a narrow fabric or a very full skirt, you will need to allow twice or four times the skirt length plus the same considerations for the waistband as before and adding any extra that the design may need.

Think of a dress in a similar way. Allowing for seam turnings should become instinctive, as it is the cutting lines you must be aware of. Consider the width of fabric you wish the dress to include and, if the fabric width accommodates this measurement, one bodice plus one skirt length will suffice. If the width is not adequate, twice that length will be needed. Sleeves must have their width calculated and you should be aware of the minimum width at the underarm that is comfortable for you. You know the length for a long sleeve, so add this to the amount already required for the front and back, where relevant. With a wider fabric, the front and back lengths together (dress length ×2) may be sufficient, as excess fabric is left alongside that will accommodate sleeves. An extra 50 cm (20 in.) will usually allow for simple collars, cuffs, plackets and pockets, but your individual dress style may demand more or less fabric.

Write down what particular thoughts resulted in you buying, for instance, 2.8 m (3 yd) of 112 cm (45 in.) wide fabric, and then see how well you cope when cutting it. Whether you have to compromise because the fabric is tight or whether there are 50 cm (20 in.) left over, you can identify the reason and adjust your thought process the next time round. If you can design your garment exactly to the fabric length, you will find that you repeatedly utilise almost every fabric thread. Think carefully about how much fabric any detailing may use, as it is often far more than you might immediately think. Allow extra fabric from a designing point of view, especially if you are intending to make something a little special or unusual.

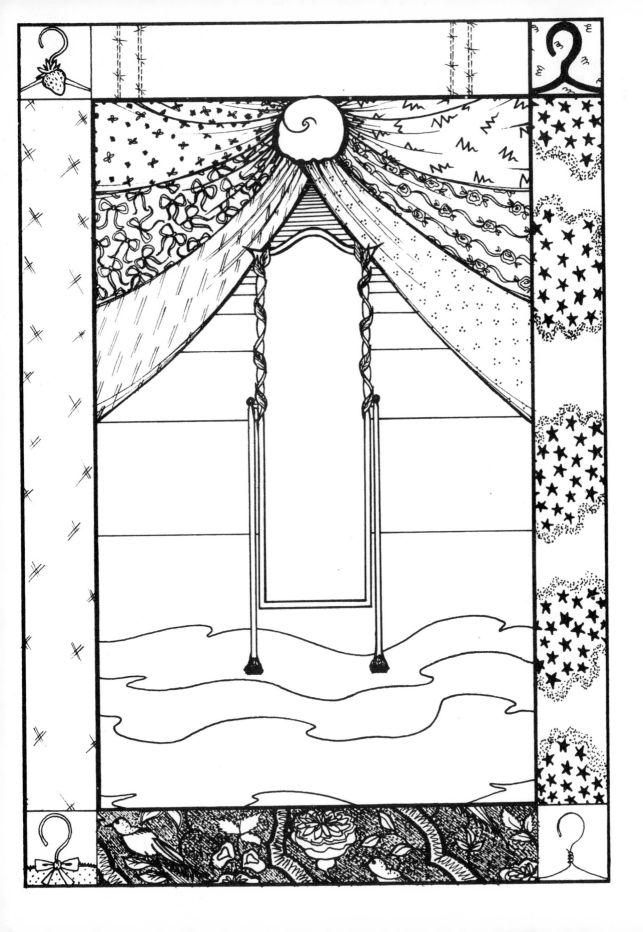

This point is important for impulse buyers to bear in mind. Many people who prefer to buy their material before they have decided on a design find that the fabric inspires a particular garment type. Trusting to instinct as to metreage is not bad advice if you know what you are doing and, if you do not, well, you soon will. While you may find you constantly buy more fabric than if you were more cool and calculating, you will, no doubt, make full advantage of every centimetre of fabric.

While you may not think of yourself as an impulse buyer it is quite possible that you will one day find yourself attracted by a particular piece of fabric with no specific design in mind. If you already make your own clothes you will have some experience to work from; if you do not, apply some logical thinking and be brave enough to jump in at the deep end and gain some experience. Use commercial pattern books for rough guidance on metreage if you feel completely lost, but do try to make friends with a tape measure and familiarise yourself with various measurements so that they mean something in terms of size and quantity that you can relate to a fabric length. It is only thinking through problems for yourself, rather than following a bought pattern without really understanding or questioning it, that you will begin to make sense of cutting your own designs from fabric.

FABRIC CONSTRUCTION

Woven fabrics
Most fabrics are of a woven construction where lengthwise, warp threads are interlaced at right angles with crosswise, weft threads. The weights of the yarn, the tightness of the weave and the pattern of weaving can all vary considerably, allowing infinite possibilities in textile design, and explaining the wide variety of woven fabrics available.

The warp threads are the strongest, as they bear the most strain during the weaving process. They are, therefore, extremely firm and unlikely to give, which is why their direction – the straight grain – is of so much importance to the cut of a garment. The weft threads are generally less firm and will give slightly when stress is placed upon them. The lengthwise edges of the fabric have a narrow, tightly woven finish which does not fray, called the selvedge. This is to hold the fabric and take much of the tension that occurs in the various processes it undergoes during its construction.

Plain weave
This is the simplest possible weave where the weft thread runs over and then under each single warp thread and in the same direction but alternating position in every row. This construction can pass over double threads in a similar way, resulting in a softer and looser fabric. Variations in yarn thicknesses or differences in positioning can give other effects such as a ribbed fabric.

Twill weave
The pattern of weaving gives a diagonal ridge across the fabric which can be emphasised by the nature of the yarns used. There can be slight differences in the weave used to give this effect. The herringbone weave is a variation of a twill weave, where the diagonal line changes direction at regular intervals to form a definite zigzag in the weave.

Satin weave
Any satin weave gives a smooth, lustrous surface on the right side. The warp threads are positioned much closer together than the weft threads which do not show on the right side. The weft threads pass over the warp threads to catch them down in as few places as possible, resulting in a secure fabric. Again, there are many variations in the weave that will give a fabric of this general type.

More complicated weaves give endless decorative effects and variations to the finished character of the fabric.

Knitted fabrics
Knitted fabrics are easily recognised by their characteristic plain and purl surfaces. Industrial knitting machines produce a flat or tubular fabric. The vertical rows of a knit are called 'wales' and the horizontal rows, 'courses'. These should cross at a 90-degree angle, as do the threads of a woven fabric. Because of the loopy interlocking that forms a knitted fabric, there is not as much stability as in a woven fabric, and a knitted fabric is liable to stretch in all directions. There is also the danger of a caught thread laddering the fabric. Jersey fabrics have undergone many developments and the variety of fibres, patterns and basic construction methods is enormous. The use of different weights and surface textures adds to the excitement and originality now found in knitted fabrics.

Pile fabrics
Pile fabrics have a surface interest caused by the fabric threads. Towelling has a loop pile, where the threads are uncut, whereas velvets have a cut pile. The fabric is basically woven and a variety of complicated methods and machinery results in the

end fabric. The construction may be compared to that used in carpet manufacture.

Lace and net-type fabrics
These are now made on sophisticated machines which are capable of producing an ever-widening variety. The traditional open, light and decorative qualities of lace still remain in the better quality sheer and delicate fabrics that are available.

Felted fabrics
Here, fibres are matted together by the action of heat, moisture and pressure. Wool fibres are especially liable to 'felt' and because of this, are often used in felt fabrics. The nature of felt means it has no grain and does not fray when cut. Felt tends to stretch out of shape, does not drape and wears badly.

Various weights are available, but because of its disadvantages, is rarely used in garment manufacture.

Bonded fabrics
These are similar in structure to felt, but are made from varying fibres that are literally 'bonded' together with an adhesive, such as synthetic rubber. There are different ways to achieve this which vary from a method that is similar to paper-making to passing a web of fibres through sticky rollers. The most common use for such fabric is interlining. Fabrics that are bonded are also used for 'backing' fabrics that require added strength and stability, such as knitted fabrics. The two are fused together, giving a firmer finished fabric. Mock leathers and vinyls are also backed in a similar way.

CHAPTER THREE

Equipment

THE SEWING MACHINE

Almost all the methods of construction covered avoid the time-consuming and tedious use of pins and tacking thread, and an electric sewing machine allows both hands free to control your work. If an old hand machine is all that is available, it would be advisable to pin at very regular intervals and to tack any particularly complicated areas to avoid the frustrating task of unpicking. If the thought of pinning and tacking is unbearable, you could try and find someone else to turn the handle for you, but watch your fingers.

All modern sewing machines are very simple to thread. Follow the handbook instructions and read it through so that you are fully aware of all the machine's capabilities. Get used to inserting the bobbin without looking. Always be generous with the top and bottom threads when starting to sew, to save the tugging and chopping of knots caused by the machine chewing up mean ends; holding them at the back of the work under a finger of the left hand for the first few stitches is a good habit to form because, if they are going to disappear down the hole, you have the chance to stop them. Starting to sew with the needle on the downward half of the stitch will help prevent this annoying problem, and strain the motor less. To make threading the needle easier, trim the thread end at a sharp, diagonal angle, so giving the thread a 'point'.

Stitch length

Using the stitch length dial, try the longest and shortest setting at which the machine will comfortably sew. Set at O, the needle will obviously bounce up and down on the spot. A setting of 2.5 is the average length used for ordinary straight stitching. Note the difference in the fabric passing over the feeder. Always allow it to pass through the machine otherwise the feeder mechanism could possibly be damaged and the needle will almost certainly bend or break. The greater the stitch length, the more danger there is of this happening.

Stitch width

Most domestic machines are swing needle machines, where the needle will move from side to side to form a zigzag stitch. Again, try adjusting the dial to alter the width as well as the stitch length to familiarise yourself with its use and appearance at various settings. The handbook will indicate what its other uses are, if any, on your particular machine.

Tension

By now, if there is something drastically wrong with the tension of the stitch, you will have noticed. The strongest seams and the most attractive stitches are achieved by establishing the correct tension for the particular setting and fabric in use. The correct tension on the two threads as the machine forms the stitch is that which results in the threads locking in the centre of the thickness of the fabric being stitched. This is why it is generally inadvisable to machine through a single thickness of fabric only. For the correct tension to occur, the tension on both threads must be equal. If the top thread is too tight, it will pull up the bottom thread through the fabric, where it will show as little bumpy loops lying across the tight top thread and will look like the map symbol for a railway line. If the top thread is too loose the stitches will be loopy and will pull out very easily. Adjust the tension dial until the stitches look identical on the top and the underneath and it is no longer possible to pull the seam apart (within the reasonable amount of strain you would expect the seam of a garment to bear, of course). If you use a different colour thread in the bobbin, it is easy to see if one thread is showing where it should not. For a loose top thread, tighten the tension and for a tight top thread, loosen the tension.

If altering the tension dial does not give a satisfactory result, check that the machine is threaded properly. Also, if the needle is blunt or fractionally bent, change it and this will improve the stitch, if not solve the problem altogether. Any fluff or thread caught in the discs through which the top thread passes behind the tension dial, or around the bobbin casing or bobbin may also be the cause of a bad tension.

The bottom thread passes through the bobbin casing and the tension is usually altered by turning a very small screw. This is extremely difficult to adjust correctly, as the slightest alteration affects it greatly, and it is normally best left alone. However, if all the above suggestions do not help with correcting the tension, you will be close to giving up or telephoning the dealer anyway, so not that much can be lost – other than patience – by trying. Place a wound bobbin in its casing and hold it up by the thread. If the bobbin casing tension is roughly correct, the casing will drop very gradually as the thread runs through it. If it will not drop at all, even with the help of a slight jerk on the thread, the tension is far too tight. If it drops instantly, and at speed, then it is far too loose, though you should check to see that the casing has remained threaded properly. Tighten or loosen the screw as appropriate, but with minimal adjustments; test each time. Alternatively, buy a new casing.

The foot
The standard machine foot for straight or zigzag stitching is used most of the time. Apart from the fact that it must be attached securely and in the correct position, the pressure on the thick spring that forces it down when released should be set correctly to suit the particular fabric and process being worked at the time. This may appear unimportant, but when tacking thread has been abandoned, correct pressure upon the foot enables you to handle the fabric correctly.

This is more important with thicker fabrics because, if the pressure from the foot is too much, the top layer will be squeezed forward and will be gradually but increasingly pushed out of place. On a very fine fabric, if there is not enough pressure to hold the pieces together in the correct position beneath the foot, the work may slip and slide and be very difficult to control. Therefore, the thicker the fabric, the less the pressure required. For pile fabrics like velvet, too much pressure will crush the pile, leaving unsightly marks alongside every seam. For finer or slippery fabrics, or where multiple layers are being sewn together, greater pressure is required.

The other most commonly used foot is the zip foot. This is, in effect, one half of the normal foot, designed so that stitching can be placed very close to the metal teeth of a zip. It can also be used when it is helpful to see a greater area of the work and is useful when accuracy of placement is of special importance. If you regard it not as a zip foot but as a 'visibility' foot you may choose to use it far more often to great advantage.

Many machines have various other attachments and gadgetry, some of which are no more than gimmicks.

Needles
Keep a stock of spares. Sewing machine needles have the same nasty streak as light bulbs. One may last for weeks and weeks and never wear out and then, when it suddenly breaks at closing time on a Saturday evening, the last three in the box will all break within an hour of each other.

Familiarise yourself with changing the needle before you begin so that you will see how easy it is, and make the effort, for the sake of the quality of your work, to change it whenever necessary. Different fabrics require a different size and sometimes shape of needle and a guide for suitable use is usually given on the back of the packet.

When it is necessary to stop sewing mid-seam, remember never to leave the needle out of the fabric. If the needle is down, the work cannot slip out of position and a bump in the stitching line will be avoided.

Bobbin-winding
A bobbin which holds 50 m (50 yd) of thread is ideal as, when fully wound, there will be an equal length of top and bottom thread when winding from the average 100 m or yard reel. Again, follow the specific instructions given for your machine for threading and winding. Make sure the thread end is neatly tucked in on the bobbin to prevent it catching or jamming and snapping the top thread mid-seam. As you wind, the thread should pass evenly from one side of the bobbin to the other, forming a slight bulge in the centre. It should not wind unevenly with more thread to one side. Do not force the bobbin into its casing. If this appears likely to be necessary, it has been overwound. Unwind the thread until the bobbin will drop easily into the casing.

Feeder
There will be a button or knob on your machine that will lower the feeder teeth below the plate and therefore render it functionally useless. This is

necessary when sewing the bar tacks at the ends of a buttonhole, sewing buttons on by machine and for various other embroidery or darning uses that the machine may be capable of.

Low gear

The low gear is useful for when it is necessary to machine at a very slow speed, giving great ease of control. In most instances, speedy machining gives an even and more accurate finish, with practice, of course. However, there are some circumstances in construction when slow, controlled machining is necessary and the use of the low gear will then save the motor of the machine from excess strain. If your machine has an electronic pedal control you may very rarely need to use the low gear.

Special stitches

Many machines have a large variety of functional and decorative speciality stitches. Decoration is a complete subject in itself and the variety of functional stitches, gadgets and attachments will all be explained in your handbook. Familiarise yourself with all of them and you will find those which are obviously going to be most useful to you. However, by at least being aware of all your machine is capable of, you will be able to solve some of the problems in garment construction. A modern machine is a versatile tool; for quick, clever, inventive sewing that is also neat, accurate and strong, exploit all it has to offer as often as you can.

Maintenance

It is important to keep the machine clean and well oiled, not to over-strain the motor and to remove dust and dirt as often as possible. Fluff, dust, fibres, thread ends and pins can collect in the most awkward places and constant cleaning out is necessary. Always keep the bobbin area beneath the feeder free of muck. Wipe up any oil spills carefully so that precious fabric is not stained. Some modern machines do not require oiling at all, but you should still oil the feeder generously and run unthreaded at full speed for a few seconds. Then run a scrap of fabric through until all the surplus oil has been absorbed. If the machine is left for some time repeat this again immediately prior to use.

Keeping the machine covered when not in use will minimise the amount of extra dust that always accumulates around those areas that are most difficult to clean. Take notice of any special instructions in the handbook with regard to maintenance.

OTHER EQUIPMENT

Scissors

Use a good quality pair of scissors and take great care of them. All you need is an excellent pair of shears and a small, light-weight pair of pointed needlework scissors. Try not to drop them and lock them away so they may never be used on paper, or even more disastrous, cardboard.

For the shears, use a pair that are comfortable and not too heavy: plastic-handled shears are lighter for obvious reasons. The sharper the blades the better and this especially includes the last 5 mm ($\frac{1}{4}$ in.) or so. This is very important as little nips for marking balance notches, cutting into corners and other awkward shapes all require a high level of accuracy.

Always have your needlework scissors with you at the machine. The points should be extremely sharp and they should cut cleanly to the very tips of the blades. Use them higher up the blades to cut thread ends to save the tips for more important jobs.

Look after your scissors and they will be of great service to you. The quality of cutting, trimming and clipping is just as important to the successful outcome of your work as is the stitching, fitting or even pressing.

Iron

When dressmaking, keep an ironing board set up as closely to the machine as is reasonably possible. Use a steam iron or, if you only have a dry iron, use a houseplant mister to dampen the fabric when necessary. Use the highest temperature the fabric can take and never apply any more pressure than is absolutely necessary. Remember that fabric is made up of tiny little soft fibres. Crushing them flat with the base of an iron will leave you with a limp, characterless fabric. Heat, steam and the careful use of the toe and side edges of the iron will leave the fabric 'unstressed' when the work is finished.

No special pressing equipment is needed for dressmaking. Use exactly what you use for the household ironing. Never press a new fabric without having first tested a small area to see how it reacts. The smoother the surface on to which you press, the better, so that at times when pressure does need to be applied – such as when fusing interfacing - indentations do not appear on the right side of the fabric. If the ironing board cover has a slightly textured surface, often caused by the padding beneath it, lay a smooth fabric over it.

Tape-measures

You will probably use your tape-measure more than any other single item and, unless you can get into the habit of wearing it around your neck, buy two or even three and keep one in each area where you work. Centimetres are very easy to work with, but if you really feel more at home with inches, use them. Ideally, you should feel equally comfortable with both metric and imperial measurements and a tape-measure that shows both is the most useful. If you are struggling to 'convert' from inches, write down and try to remember metric equivalents of those measurements you most commonly use, such as seam turning widths, fabric widths and body measurements, to make sense of new figures and give them some identification and scale in your mind. You should be concerned with accuracy to the nearest millimetre and the tape-measure will, therefore, be your constant companion. Make sure that the markings are clear and sharp. Clumsy, thickly printed lines are unhelpful. Avoid tape-measures that have long, rigid ends, as you will want to measure accurately around curves with the tape-measure standing up on edge. The plastic strips are usually quite thick, making even straight measuring difficult. Tape-measures are liable to wear out and not only do they become difficult to read, but they weaken and stretch. Replace an old tape-measure before it gets too badly worn.

Pins and needles

Keep a generous quantity of fine, stainless-steel dressmaker's pins; their length can be left to personal preference. Glass-headed pins, although expensive, are easier to pick up and less likely to be accidently left in the fabric. Avoid thick pins and ruthlessly weed out any that show the slightest signs of rust. Throw away immediately any that are bent, or those with damaged points; leave them in the tin and they will be the ones you pick out at the most inconvenient moments. Personally, I prefer to avoid magnets where pins are concerned, but the behaviour of magnetised pins may not be quite such a point of annoyance to everybody. Using a large, fat, old-fashioned pincushion is one way of preventing the need to scrabble around on the floor after accidents with pin tins.

Make sure that you have a good variety of sewing needles so that you have the right kind available for the fabric and job in hand. Throw worn or bent needles away. Whilst the emphasis in this book is to minimise hand-sewing as much as possible, there are times when circumstances call for a hand finish. Do not overlook the importance of hand-sewing.

Dress stands

Unless you are fortunate enough to come across a second-hand, professional stand with a reasonable shape, don't feel you need to rush out and buy one. Professional stands are extremely expensive and are used solely for design purposes. Dressmaking stands are an unnecessary expense and are a good example of the gimmickry and superfluous gadgetry manufactured and marketed to exploit the dressmaking public. Designing on a dressmaker's stand is, in fact, difficult, if not impossible, as pins cannot be easily and securely stuck in to hold fabric in place. So far as fitting is concerned, their importance is negligible, as a stand does not breathe, move, or in many cases even have arms. Your own body and a full length mirror gives a much more realistic and useful image of the progress of the work and serious mistakes can usually be felt as much as seen by the eye when the garment is tried on. Many fitting problems that occur can be solved at the cutting stage and this is obviously preferable to cutting out and partly making up the garment, only to begin unpicking and devising alterations halfway through. If you learn to work using your body measurements from the outset, relating the garment to the body will be automatic, leaving the dressmaker's stand with little more use than a three-dimensional clothes hanger.

HABERDASHERY

Keeping your own stock of various bits and pieces is always a good idea as lack of a small item is a frustrating way to delay progress. You can also avoid this by checking that you have everything you need before beginning. Spend some time in a good haberdashery department simply looking through the wide variety of little extras that are available so that you are aware of what you can incorporate in the construction methods you choose. Design problems can also be solved if you know about the existence of a particular type of elastic or stud fastening, for example. Choose specific haberdashery once you know the fabric type as there is, as always, suitable and unsuitable.

Sewing thread

With the development of fabrics, there have been the necessary changes in sewing threads and, to avoid complication, the basic rule is to match the fibres, or at least the fibre family, of the thread to the fabric. Use mercerised cotton for natural fibres and synthetic threads for man-made or synthetic fibres. Thread is graded in thickness where the higher the number, the finer the thread. The most commonly used thickness for machining is 50s, which is suitable for most types of fabric. 40s is slightly thicker and is equally suitable for machining; use in preference to 50s for top-stitching as it gives bolder stitches. Special top-stitching thread of greater thickness can be bought for use on heavier weight fabrics where ordinary thread would be lost; when using this you will need to change the machine needle to one with a large eye.

Polyester threads are equivalent to 50s thread. Previously, these have been liable to twist and knot, particularly when hand-sewing, but they are now greatly improved. They are suitable for fabrics in all man-made and synthetic fibres and, as they have reasonable stretching qualities, are ideal for jersey and other stretch fabrics. Their strength makes them useful for machine-gathering as they are less likely to snap when the fabric is drawn up.

If in doubt about the best match for colour, choose a shade darker. With prints, match up the most predominant, or background colour or, if neither of these are suitable, choose a more neutral colour that easily blends in. If this is still difficult, squint at the fabric and this will give you an overall effect of the colours and help you make your choice.

An average, reasonably simple garment will usually only take one reel of 100 m (100 yd) if there are not too many seams and you avoid too much unpicking. If there are long seams to be neatened by machine and a lot of work in the construction, or you are unsure, buy two reels.

Other threads for more specialised use are available, such as silk sewing thread for use with fine wool or silk fabrics. Strong, thick buttonhole thread is best for working hand-made buttonholes. Embroidery threads and metallic threads have been developed for decorative work that are especially suitable for machine use.

Zips
Zips are available in various lengths, colours and weights to suit every possible fabric and the type of opening it is intended to close. The colour of the tape should not be too important as the tape of a well set-in zip will not show, but make as close a match as possible. The tapes can be of different fibres, cotton or nylon being the most common, but this is more to alter the weight of the zip and it is not necessary to worry about matching the fibre content of the fabric into which the zip is to be set. You will be more concerned with matching the weight of the zip to the weight of the fabric. The most usual, medium-weight zip with cotton tapes and metal teeth is quite suitable for most average weight fabrics.

More chunky, heavier-weight zips with large metal teeth set on heavier canvas tapes can be used on denims, canvas and any tough fabrics that will be heavily worn. Chunky zips with large, brightly coloured plastic teeth are meant to be included as a design feature and are set in so that the teeth show. Open-ended zips for setting into jacket fronts are usually of a heavier weight.

Dainty, nylon zips with tiny nylon teeth are ideal for delicate, light-weight fabrics. The tapes are narrow, light and flexible so these zips are also preferable for soft fabrics with good draping qualities. This type of zip is also a better choice for fabrics that snag easily, where metal teeth might cause obvious problems.

The nature of the opening will suggest the correct length of zip to use. The zip length is measured along the teeth from the zip stop at the base to the zip stop at the top, not along the length of the tape. The length of the opening will depend on where it is and on the amount of space in the garment. More fitted areas need longer openings. The garment should be easy to put on and take off, with no strain placed on any seam or area of fabric, or around the opening.

Buttons
The buttons you choose will either be meant to enhance the design and add interest or to be discreet and concealed. In either case, make sure that their size and thickness are suitable, so that they look as though they were specially made for the garment. As with zips, compare the weight of button to the weight of fabric for suitability.

In order to attach them, buttons will have two or four holes, or a shank of some sort on the back, or a channel that runs through the underneath of the button. They can be made from a seemingly endless variety of materials including glass, wood, plastic, bone, leather, ceramic, fabric or knotted yarns. An alternative is to buy buttons specially made to be covered with fabric. These are not difficult to make up and often solve the problem of finding a button that is just right. Scraps of the garment material, or a contrasting colour can be used and the buttons are usually re-usable.

Consider the washing of the garment and whether you are prepared to remove the buttons, if necessary, at every wash or dry clean. Also beware of the red buttons you put on a white blouse if you have not first checked whether the dye in the buttons is fast. High temperature washing and ironing can sometimes mean disaster.

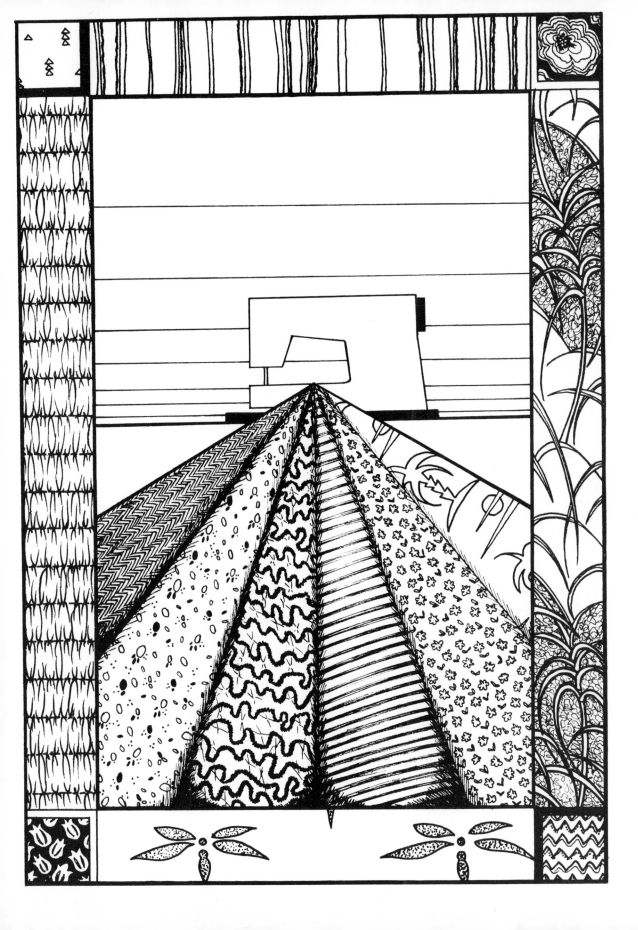

Other fastening aids

If you use zips as centre back fastenings, you will need a hook and eye to hold the fabric edges together to prevent the zip from slipping down a little during wear. A hook and eye may also be used instead of a button to fasten a waistband; otherwise, the occasion when it is the best answer to a fastening problem is rare. Where you do decide to use one, choose a suitable size and strength as well as the most inoffensive colour available. Very large, covered hooks and eyes for coats or cloaks can be successful, but often a more rigid, decorative toggle and loop or frog fastening is better.

Press studs, again, are rarely the ideal solution to fastening problems but, at times, there may be little alternative. Indiscriminate use of press studs can give work a distinctly home-made and un-professional look. The same sort of considerations as for hooks and eyes should be given to their choice. Shirt-type stud fastenings are meant for use in place of buttons and if properly attached, are strong and hard-wearing.

Velcro is not often suitable for use on garments and can also give a home-made finish to work. There are times when you may find it ideal, however, such as on children's clothes, aprons and overalls, or very casual beach and leisure wear. It is certainly useful and versatile in many household sewing jobs.

Elastic

Elastic comes in many different weights and widths and is either flat, or round like cord. It has limitless uses on virtually any fabric type. The end use will determine your choice as will whether it is to be applied directly or threaded through a casing. Do not use an elastic that is any wider or stiffer than necessary. Some have greater stretching qualities than others so feel the 'pull' and watch how readily it returns to its original state, to check its suitability. If it is to lie against the skin, a soft elastic with a brushed surface on one side might be the best choice.

Round elastic has excellent stretching qualities and is light-weight and more dainty, so it is a good choice for inserting in very narrow casings on soft, delicate fabrics. It does not twist inside the casing as often happens with very narrow, flat elastic.

Shirring elastic can be used on the machine, where it is wound with tension on to the bobbin and sits on the wrong side of the fabric. Some machines have special stitches where the elastic can show on the right side. Metallic shirring elastic is also available.

Tapes and bindings

A variety of tapes and bindings are available. Cotton tapes are useful for skirt hangers, and also for 'staying' fabric where it is likely to stretch or distort. Wider tapes may also be applied to the wrong side as casings. Seam bindings can be used much as cotton tape and give a smarter finish which may be important if visible. Bias bindings and seam bindings are available in a much wider range of colours than ordinary tape. Bought bias bindings are really only suitable for use on the wrong side of a garment as the fabric used is of poor quality and colour matching is often difficult. It is easier to work with than crossway strips cut from fabric scraps. For decorative effects, it is better to cut your own strips from self or contrast fabric but if a large quantity is needed, bought binding may be an advantage.

Cotton piping cords of different widths may be used with your own crossway-cut strips. It is a good idea to soak cotton cord to shrink it before using. Gimp is a very stiff, wiry, narrow cord for strengthening and improving the appearance of machine-made or hand-worked buttonholes, or satin-stitching (achieved on the machine by setting a very short zigzag stitch).

Petersham

Thick, non-woven and non-fusible interlining, perhaps folded double, or petersham is used for stiffening waistbands. It can be bought in various widths, usually in black or white only and is available curved as well as straight. A bonded petersham can be bought from a roll in varying widths, but it does not wear as well as a stiff petersham and the firmness is soon lost with repeated washing.

For other stiffening, necessary in collar points or strapless bodices for instance, stiff but reasonably flexible, narrow plastic is available and replaces the old-fashioned whalebone.

Shoulder pads

These can be bought with either a triangular or a rounded shape and are made of foam or wadding. Foam pads are extremely light-weight and can not only be trimmed to a suitable shape, but 'shaved' to alter the thickness, if and where necessary. If more unusual padding is required, it is better to make up your own properly sculptured pads with layers of wadding, flannelette or lint, as required.

DECORATIVE AIDS

Braids, ribbons and lace are made in an endless variety to suit every taste. Check the fibre content and washing instructions and make sure that any dyes are colourfast. Some trimmings may have a functional as well as a decorative use: lace can be inserted or applied and, if it has suitable holes, these may be threaded so that it acts as a casing; fringing can finish off a raw edge and disguise seams; straps, belts and drawstrings can all be made from or decorated with trimmings; beading and sequins can be applied in strings or as ready made-up motifs; novelty yarns can be couched on to fabric by machine with a zigzag or embroidery stitch; top-stitching and metallic threads have already been mentioned.

Decoration is a subject which needs covering in considerable detail, but as it is not fundamental to the cut and construction of clothing it has only been introduced here briefly.

Part II:

Cutting a design

Introduction

Cutting into a length of beautiful, new fabric without feeling nervous requires a good deal of confidence. This section includes a variety of methods of cutting the correct shapes, without necessarily using a pattern, to make up into the design you have chosen.

Anybody who has done some dressmaking is likely to have used commercial paper patterns. These have many disadvantages and are best used merely as a stepping stone in cases where a particular point may be of help in cutting an original design of your own. How to gain the most from already existing information is an important area to appreciate, as much struggling, frustration and disappointment can so easily be avoided.

In the following pages, the emphasis is placed on working from relevant measurements taken from the body and transferring these directly to the fabric. A little understanding about the basic theory of flat pattern shapings and various allowances is useful when arriving at the final decisions that will give the finished shape of each piece. To begin with, methods of direct measurement are discussed as this is the most simple and basic way to cut a garment. To solve the majority of fitting problems, you need only build up a selection of the most basic garment shapes that are right for you, and use these as a foundation for all your work. Simplification is the key to success. However ambitious and complicated your ideas, by beginning simply and cautiously, you will learn to solve the problems in a straightforward way. Simplicity does not mean dullness: the most exquisite detail can enhance any basic garment. Detailing is an area of design with infinite possibilities and the few suggestions included here are to be used as a springboard for your own ideas.

The practical suggestions included later in this section may or may not be of some help to you. Your individual circumstances and working conditions will vary as much as your experience and you will find your own solutions where the marking up and the cutting of fabric is concerned. Every design you come to cut will have its own unique complications and problems to be overcome. Do not begin until the practicalities discussed in the design section have all been considered especially where the quality of the fabric is concerned. Starting without thinking through carefully every aspect of the cut will either lead to mistakes and compromise or disaster; cutting lines cannot be rubbed out.

CHAPTER FOUR

Basics of pattern cutting

All cutting starts from a basic set of measurements and an understanding of a few fundamental rules. The finished 'mass' of the garment is considered from the beginning and, once a very simplified outline is decided, the individual style lines are added. Each separate section of the garment is then altered in whatever way is necessary to give the final shape that meets all the requirements of the design. Finally, any extra detailing is added and any additional pieces needed for detailing are completed.

The body areas are divided up into bodice front, bodice back, skirt front, skirt back, and sleeve. All patterns are originally worked from the centre lines of the body, whether the pieces of the garment are symmetrical or not. Often the front and back areas are symmetrical about their respective centre lines and, where this is the case, the right side of the body only is worked on. The pattern is then cut on a foldline of the fabric which forms the centre line, or two 'opposites' of an identical shape are cut if they are to be joined or fastened down the centre line.

Getting used to which side is which and where the right and wrong sides of the fabric should lie should be a priority. Frequently, irreversible mistakes are made: for instance, when two left fronts are found to have been cut. To help keep this clear, remember that the right side of the fabric is shown as RS and the wrong side of the fabric, WS. The right side of the body or garment is shown as RHS (right-hand side) and the left side, LHS (left-hand side).

Where either the right sides or the wrong sides of double fabric are together, two opposites will be cut to give a left-hand side and a right-hand side. If both wrong sides, or both right sides, of double fabric are uppermost, then two identical pieces will result.

If you can imagine the body areas in sections and think of what is necessary to cover those areas, you will be less likely to become confused. Imagine 'wearing' the fabric and the WS will then be automatically against your body and the LHS and RHS will not be so easily muddled or forgotten. Left front and right front, left back and right back and left sleeve and right sleeve are enough for these purposes. It may help to devise your own personal numbering system to use as a checklist, or touching each body area and speaking out loud may suffice. Talking to yourself is an excellent way to maintain concentration. Much of this soon becomes instinctive; you may have the sort of mind that easily sees such things clearly, and are wondering what all the fuss is about but, when faced with a fabric that has a right and wrong side that are not immediately distinguishable, a logical, more straightforward approach is often necessary.

MEASUREMENTS

Allowing for ease
Taking your vital statistics will give you a list of absolute minimum measurements for those areas of the body and if you cut directly from them, you will obviously finish up with something in fit similar to a frogman's wet suit. Design apart, clothing must be comfortable and easy to wear, allowing for adequate movement in stretching and reaching, walking, climbing stairs and sitting; breathing, especially, should not be restricted. For this reason, extra width allowance is always made on garments that are not excessively full, especially on the bust and hip measurements. This extra amount is known as 'ease' or 'tolerance'. A minimum total amount of 5cm (2 in.) added to the body measurements will give a closely fitting garment. Waist seams are cut with ease allowed but are set on to waistbands of exactly body measurement. A more bulky fabric may demand that an even greater amount of ease be allowed.

The particular design and styling will dictate what specific body measurements are the most important in each case, and these will vary considerably. Length is always important: bodice and sleeve lengths may need an additional amount for blousing on top of what you would add on to the body measurement for ease of movement. Measure your outer arm from shoulder to wrist with the arm straight and then bend it sharply at the elbow. This will demonstrate how much extra allowance for movement is necessary in a full length sleeve. Finished garment hem lengths should always be cut generously with an extra 10–20 cm (4–8 in.) added to the length you might think is right, as the fall of the made-up garment and alterations to improve proportions may vary the final length by this much.

Taking measurements from existing garments

You will get used to measuring any relevant area of your body and will learn to judge what a suitable allowance might be. Achieving the effect of your design in the particular fabric you have used will depend on reaching the correct decisions on the measurements you cut. The best way to gain some confidence and acquire a basis from which you can gauge your decisions is to turn to your own clothes. You are familiar with the fit and feel of the clothes you wear. From the corresponding body measurements, you can see how much the actual garment measurement differs and, if the fit is satisfactory, make a note of the comparative measurements from which to work. If you do not wear a certain shirt because it gapes open at the bust when you move, do the same check. You will learn as much from badly fitting clothes as you can from those that fit perfectly. A blouse that untucks itself has too short a centre back length and you can be sure that you will never make a similar mistake. To measure garments accurately, lay them on a non-slippery surface and make sure the area you are to measure is completely flat and is not distorted in any way. If you are not certain where the bust points come, for instance, try on the garment and mark the positions with pins. You will then measure the correct area when the garment is lying flat before you. Not only will this information remove an element of trial and error from your work, but you will quickly become familiar with your own body measurements.

Drawing up a measurement diagram

You may find it helpful to work from a diagram that shows clearly the measurements you will most often use both for width and length, rather than trusting to memory or re-measuring yourself every time. If you use what you consider to be a suitable garment of average fit (a waisted dress would be useful) from which to measure, you can then judge all future deviations from the fit of that garment.

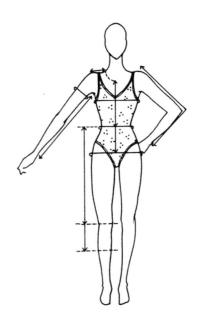

I *Figure showing important body measurements*

Draw a straight line that represents the centre front, labelled as CF. The top of the line represents the level a plain, closely fitting, round neckline would fit comfortably at the centre front. To divide this line you need to mark the measurement from here to the level exactly opposite the bust point, from the bust point to your natural waist, from your waist to the level where the hip measurement is taken – the widest part around the buttocks – and from there to where you consider to be an average hem length. This will give you four separate measurements. Total them, and the result will be a basic CF dress length. For the centre back dress length a little extra is added to make up for the higher position of the neckline. On an average size 12-14, this is about 5 cm (2 in.). The waist–hip–hem will give you a basic CF skirt length. The top three measurements from top–hip can be used as a shirt or blouse length and the top two, when you need a measurement for a bodice or a placement line at the waist.

Rather than simply labelling a rough sketch, divide each body measurement accurately by four. Use these measurements to make up your diagram and this will give you a correctly proportioned diagram which is one-quarter scale of your actual measurements. This should fit on A4 or foolscap paper but, if you prefer a slightly smaller diagram, divide all actual measurements by five, which will then result in a one-fifth scale diagram.

As the diagram represents only one quarter of

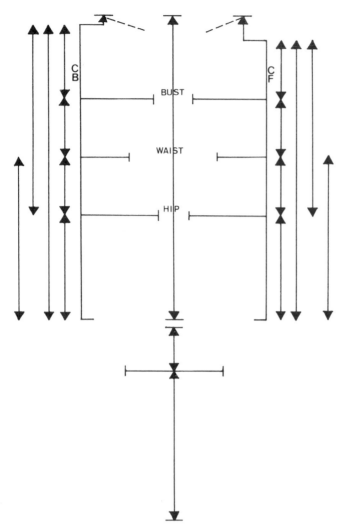

2 *Width and length measurements for back, front and sleeve*

A very simple diagram will show the most basic measurements required for a sleeve. If you have a pattern for a plain, standard, set-in sleeve that fits well or have an old, well-fitting garment with a full-length sleeve and a sleeve-head seam that sits on the shoulder from which you can measure, so much the better. The two main measurements you will need are the length of the centre line of the sleeve and the width around the arm at the underarm, adding about 3 cm (1⅛ in.) for ease of movement. Measure how far down the centre line from the shoulder this measurement comes and this will give you the depth of the sleeve-head. This line must be marked exactly at right angles, with its centre point crossing the vertical line. Again, draw this accurately to scale, as for the body measurements.

Drawing simple diagrams such as these to either one-quarter or one-fifth scale will help you see things in their correct proportion. You will become used to seeing your scale body measurements before you on flat paper and familiarity will enable you to make correct judgements where balance and proportions of styling and cut are concerned. As well as your eye becoming accustomed to these proportions, the set of figures that result from these body measurements will have some meaning in your mind's eye, as you relate each one to the relevant area of the body and compare them with each other. Once these measurements begin to mean something in this way, you will begin to make judgements of distance easily and correctly, not only where cutting itself is concerned, but where decisions must be made about how much fabric is required.

Considering the 'balance' of the garment

Already, the importance of right angles has been mentioned and the main points you have drawn could all be marked on graph paper as a grid-type layout. By measuring out from the centre line, the most important points of any design can be marked in position at the correct width. This will result in a series of points which then require joining up, similar to dot-to-dot, although, as the joining lines are not always straight, it is a little more complicated. The main 'mass' of the pattern piece is, however, already correctly marked. The majority of garments consist of many pieces and, although each individual piece can begin to take shape in the way described, you must be aware of each piece in relation to the others, each one being part of a three-dimensional jigsaw. The construction of the garment must, therefore, be in the forefront of your mind as every piece has to fit in place with the others. Without getting too involved with complications at this stage,

your body circumference, divide your bust, waist and hip measurements by four. Mark each in position at right angles to the same scale used for the first set of measurements. Label each with both the total body measurement and the measurement represented to scale on the diagram. The other measurement to be included on a diagram such as this is the extra amount of length from the neck level to the shoulder, so that you are aware of the greatest total length required when cutting. The neck edge of the shoulder is the highest point, as the shoulder slopes away. Measure across from the neck, and from that level take the measurement up to the shoulder at the appropriate point. This will add about 7.5 cm (3 in.) to the total length.

you will become aware of the 'balance' of the cut of the garment necessary to give the intended finished three-dimensional shape with the correct fit.

In this section, only the most basic of garment shapes are included. By starting at the very beginning of a subject that is otherwise so easily complicated and confused, it can be explained in a simple and straightforward way. There is no reason why these basic shapes cannot be used to make successful clothing; what can be done to alter and add to these first stages is covered in further sections.

BASIC PROCEDURES

To begin, you should be concerned with no more than the correct position of your dots. You will either mark up directly on to the fabric or work on paper first. Whichever method you prefer, the suggestions included under 'Practical cutting' (p. 90) may be of help. Your garment will have a CF and a CB line and you will work with the RHS of the garment only. You will need to refer to your diagrams of body measurements. Depending on the particular garment shape required, you will select the crucial points by thinking in an 'up and along' way, as though working on a grid. At this stage all that is intended is to reach a basic pattern shape, symmetrical about the centre lines. *Note that seam turnings are not included.* The following steps indicated for each main garment group are virtually always followed at the beginning of even the most complicated designs but, with experience, this becomes a mental, rather than a practical process.

Skirts (*Fig. 3*)

Work from the CF and CB lines in the same way. The amount of fullness in a skirt determines its character to a large extent. You are working on one-quarter of the skirt only, so keep this in mind and divide all total width measurements by four.

1 The length is marked first on the centre line. This will not be possible to decide upon exactly unless you already have a skirt of the same style with a satisfactory length. Both the fabric and the styling will play a part in your decision as to the final garment length, and this is finalised in the last stages of the construction, when the garment can be tried on and scrutinised before a mirror. You will, however, know what approximate length is required and will include an allowance for possible adjustment.

2 The total skirt width at the hem is an important measurement to achieve the desired silhouette of the design. You may well bear the fabric width in mind and reach a final decision accordingly. Divide this by four and mark in position at right angles on the approximate hem level that has already been marked.

3 From your hip measurement decide how much extra fullness the style requires around the hips. Mark your hip level as on your diagram and then add the extra width required. On some skirts, the measurement at hip level is marked at exactly the same point as at the hem. This means that the side seams from the hip level down are parallel to the centre line and will, therefore, fall on the straight grain of the fabric. It is better to avoid this occurrence and to throw this seam slightly off-grain, as a

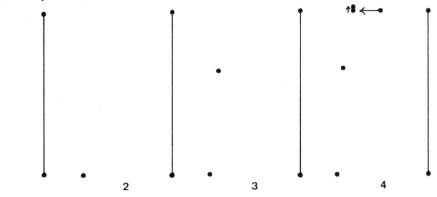

3 *Example of a skirt grid*

seam that joins two fabric pieces cut exactly on grain does not hang so well and is liable to pucker. This is particularly noticeable on skirt or dress seams that hang, and will often be worse on medium- and light-weight fabrics. Allowing as little as 1 cm (⅜ in.) less at the hip measurement (or 1 cm (⅜ in.) more at hem level) is sufficient to give an off-grain seam. Exceptions might be where stripes, a check or any other obvious feature of the fabric would cause a particularly ugly or obvious distortion.

4 The waist measurement should first be marked in exactly as on your diagram of body measurements. The styling of the skirt will then depend on how much extra fabric width is to be allowed. The width at the hip, which has already been decided, will act as a guide: the waist will never be cut any wider (unless a particular 'peg top' silhouette is specifically required). Base your decision roughly around the difference between your actual waist and hip measurements, so a reasonably gradual shape will be cut at the side seam.

The final width at the waist will be marked on an extension of the waist measurement line. This point should then be raised about 1.5 cm (⅝ in.) at right angles (remember the grid), so the position of the waist at the side seam is then that much higher than its position at the centre lines. This allows extra length at the side seam which is necessary for the skirt to sit well over the hip curve and prevents an unsightly bulge in the centre front and back areas of the skirt just beneath the waistband. If you have a very pronounced waist you may need to allow a little extra additional height. If there is not too much difference between your hip and waist measurements, then possibly allow a little less.

5 All skirts must have a strong, hard-wearing finish at the waist and the most usual method is to attach a waistband. The waistband is cut at exactly the waist measurement with no ease allowed. Extra length is then added to allow for a wrap-over of suitable size to fasten the waistband. Generally, waistbands are cut in one, as a straight strip, with a foldline which forms the top edge of the band and results in double thickness fabric which encloses whatever kind of stiffening is used. Once the finished depth of the waistband is to be greater than 8–10 cm (3–4 in.), some form of shaping should be incorporated in the cut of the waistband, both to make it comfortable to wear and to prevent it from rucking up and turning over. In other cases, a circular waistband may be used.

The most important measurements to mark up on a straight waistband to be attached to a skirt with a side fastening are as follows. (Side skirt fastenings are always on the LHS of the body.)

A Mark a straight line exactly the length of the waist measurement.

B Divide this exactly in half and mark the position of the RH side seam.

C Divide each section in half again, so that the whole length has been equally divided into four sections. These quarter marks show the positions of the CF and CB.

D The wrap-over must be added to the side back of the waistband: 2.5 cm (1 in.) is generally adequate. The total length of the waistband is thus the waist measurement plus wrap-over.

Bodices (Fig. 4)
Work the front from the CF line.

1 Mark the hip line as shown on your body measurements diagram. The waist line can also be marked, although this is not so important unless the waist features as a main part of the design. The position of the level of the waist can be marked at the CF line, in any case. To determine the correct length, you will need to consider possible extra allowance to give any blousing effects the design might have. For any garment that is to be worn belted or tucked in, or held around the body in any other way, a certain amount of blousing is always needed to allow for movement, and anybody knows how annoying it is if a garment is not long enough to remain tucked in. If the hip line is used as a guide for the positioning of the hem of a blouse, anything up to 5 cm (2 in.) above the hip line should be sufficient to prevent these problems arising. Extra width will obviously be necessary at or around the hip level for ease of fit, but the details of these amounts will depend on the styling of the garment.

2 Mark in the bust line at the correct level and, again, the extra width that is more than likely needed is determined by the styling and silhouette required. This simple cut works best with loose-fitting bodices, as complications involving bust fitting are not included at this stage. The width of the garment around the bust will also be related to the armhole and type of sleeve, and there should, obviously, be enough room to move comfortably when wearing the garment, and a final decision should not be reached without consideration of these points. The bust level will fall across the bust point (as bust measurements are taken at the greatest width around the bust), and if it is relevant or useful in any way, mark the exact position of the bust point. This can be measured

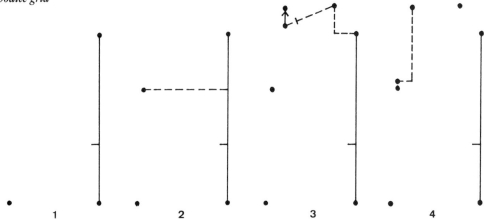

1   2   3   4

from the CF line. Even on very loosely cut garments, the garment measurement at bust level is rarely larger than the width at the hip, unless a sleeve is cut in one with the bodice.

3 The shoulder and neck positions can be marked in as shown on your body measurements diagram, either to use as they are, or to serve as a base from which the positions can be altered to meet design requirements. If you are to have a 'dropped' shoulder – i.e. where the shoulder seam is extended beyond the shoulder to come some way down the arm – it should be possible to mark the length of the shoulder seam by measuring from the neck edge to the position down the arm that the armhole seam will lie. In these cases, the slope on the shoulder should not be so great, so raise the original shoulder point from 1–3 cm ($\frac{3}{8}$–$1\frac{1}{8}$ in.), depending on how long the extension is to be. If a very casual, baggy look is desired, there is no reason why the shoulder seam cannot be placed at an angle that would cross the centre line at a right angle, resulting in a very simple, square cut. The neck can be cut as a fitting, round neck as a more unusual neck-line can be marked correctly at a later stage. The way the garment sits on the shoulders may well affect final decisions on the width, depth and shape of the neck edge.

4 There are three possible alternatives where the armhole is concerned: the sleeve, whether long or short, may be cut separately and seamed in place around an armhole seam; it may be cut all in one with the bodice; or the garment may be sleeveless. The cut of a more standard, fitting sleeve-head requires a little knowledge of the draft of the cut of such a sleeve and its corresponding armhole. In every case, the position of the depth of the armhole can be marked. It is a basic rule that, as the armhole becomes deeper, so must the bodice become wider.

This avoids distortion of the main body of the garment when moving the arms – i.e. allowing enough room to move. The under-arm position of a fitted sleeve at the side seam comes at about 5 cm (2 in.) above the level of the bust point on an average-sized figure. For these more simply cut shapes it is advisable to cut the depth of the armhole at or below the level of the bust point. The line of the armhole seam where a sleeve is set in will fall better if the width of the garment at the level of the under-arm point is 2.5 cm (1 in.) or more greater than the width from the end of the shoulder seam across to the CF line. On very large garments with enormous kimono sleeves and a very wide bodice area, this seam can be cut straight, with the two above-mentioned widths equal. The level of the under-arm point in these instances is not very much higher than 10–15 cm (4–6 in.) above the waist level.

For the moment, this is enough to form an adequate set of 'grid' positions for the main bodice area. It is obvious that further information is needed about sleeves and armholes and this is discussed at the next stage.

The back of the bodice should be constructed in the same way as the front, with all the same measurements. The RH back and RH front must each represent exactly one quarter the total measurements of the garment at this level of cutting. The only difference will be that the CB line is longer, as the back neck is not cut away as much as the front neck. The level of the back will be approximately 1.5 cm ($\frac{5}{8}$ in.) below the level of the back shoulder at the neck edge. If the shoulder points are marked exactly as the front first, it is then a simple matter to extend the centre line up and mark in the back neck at the correct level.

Dresses

If what is included in the sections on skirts and bodices has been absorbed, there is not very much detail that needs to be added for the marking of a simple dress grid. A dress can either be cut as a single straight length from shoulder to hem, or cut with a separate bodice and skirt which are seamed either above, below or at the waist, depending on styling. A dress that is cut in one length can be intended to be worn with a belt, or a more permanent method of controlling some fullness may be added, such as a casing to carry an elastic.

Dresses to be cut in one length

Mark up the grid as for the bodice, with the waist level in position. Be careful to allow sufficient width at the waist and especially at the hips. The extension of the side seam down to the approximate hem level, which is marked measuring from the waist at the CF and CB, will follow the same points discussed for skirts. If the dress is to be worn belted, allow enough extra length for blousing; the same applies if the dress is to be elasticated or held in on a drawstring. The silhouette of the design may call for an excessive amount of extra length to achieve the correct amount of blousing.

Dresses to be cut with separate bodice and skirt

In these instances, the skirt may be cut with much more fullness than the bodice, or vice versa. Again, the same basic procedures for each section should be followed and, when the garment reaches the construction stage, both the top and bottom of the dress will be made up so that they are equal in width and can be joined with a seam of the correct fit.

Whether this seam comes around the ribs, waist or hips or at any position in between, it must have an amount of ease added to the actual body measurement that is taken at the level this seam is to lie. More ease is required at hip level as this area has a great deal of movement. Imagine trying to sit down wearing a dress with a tightly fitting seam around the hips: there would be an inevitable split. A little less, but still sufficient, ease is vital in a seam that is to come around the rib cage, to avoid a discomforting restriction in movement.

While the waistband of a skirt is cut to exact waist measurement, a fitted dress waist seam should have some ease allowed for movement. In all these instances it does not follow that such seams around the body will necessarily require a fitted look. The silhouette and design of the garment may well include an overall cut and line that is more generous where a seam joining top and bottom might occur.

Trousers (*Figs 5 and 6*)

To achieve a satisfactory fit to a fitted pair of trousers requires more knowledge about the construction of their cut than is to be covered here. Trousers are the most complicated garments to fit with excellence, not because they are at all difficult to understand, but because the nature of the particular fitting requirements necessary to cut trousers varies so considerably from individual to individual. The best way to acquire a pattern for fitted trousers is to take one from a pair you already have. Ideally, chop up a worn-out pair along the seams.

A simple grid can be marked up for cutting more casual, fully cut or more unusual trouser designs. These basic instructions are still similar for the cut of any trousers so, even though you may never use them, they serve to illustrate the principles which might increase your understanding.

Work the front leg first. The differences between the front and back are indicated as they arise.

1   Mark the CF line and the widths required at the hip and waist levels, exactly as for the skirt grid (*Fig. 5*). There need be no restriction on the amount of width, if excessive width is a feature of the design.

2   Now mark in the crotch level (*Fig. 6, measurement A*). One way to do this is to tie a tape or ribbon around the top of the thigh at a reasonably comfortable height, imagining this to be the level of the crotch. Make certain it is level and then measure down from the waist to the tape. This gives you the minimum measurement for the crotch level and, depending on the styling, can be lowered as far as the knees or beyond, so long as there is adequate width allowed in other areas so that walking and sitting is possible and comfortable.

3   Once the crotch level has been decided, the extra width needed to fit under the crotch and around the leg must be added to the centre line. Problems will occur if the length of the total crotch seam is too short. If the fit is too tight under the crotch, the trousers will not sit properly at the waist, but are pulled and distorted at the CF and CB. The discomfort can be left to the imagination. So, again, determine a minimum measurement. Pass a tape measure down the CF from the waist, under the crotch and up the CB, ensuring you reach the correct waist level. If in doubt, tie a tape around your waist or clearly mark your natural waist level. When taking this measurement do not pull on the tape measure too tightly. Remember to allow enough extra length so that sitting is comfortable. This length will be your minimum total crotch measurement (*measurement C*). When marking up a style

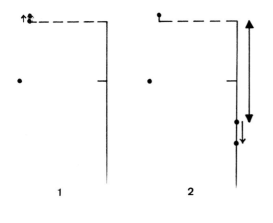
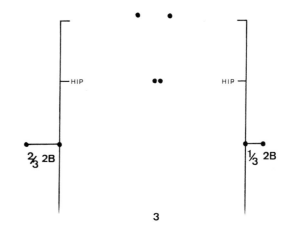

1   2

$\frac{2}{3}$ 2B $\frac{1}{3}$ 2B

3

5 *Example of a trouser grid showing minimum crotch level lowered at stage 2*

6 *Body measurements necessary for cutting trousers: (A) minimum crotch level measurement; (B) amount crotch level is lowered, (C) minimum total crotch measurement; (D) total crotch measurement required; D = 2B + C*

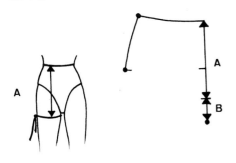

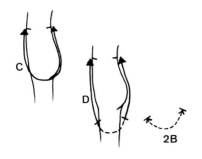

2B

where the crotch level has been lowered (*amount lowered = measurement B*), add twice measurement B to the minimum total crotch measurement just taken (*measurement C*).

On very loosely cut trousers it is possible to divide this measurement equally between the front and back leg. Otherwise a greater amount is added to the back leg than the front leg, for the simple reason that people have a larger area to cover behind than in front. The crotch width is added to the other side of the centre line at crotch level. The difference between the total crotch measurement and twice the original crotch level measurement (ignoring any extra length added to lower the crotch level) is the amount of length to be divided between the front and back. Aim to divide this amount roughly one-third to the front leg and two-thirds to the back leg.

The length of the legs and the shape of both the inner and outer leg seams are cut as the silhouette of the trouser leg demands. Although the inner and outer leg seams may differ in shaping, the corresponding front and back leg always match where shaping is concerned. Usually the quarter line falls down the centre of the leg. The total cut width of the back leg may, however, still be slightly wider than the front leg if styling makes this necessary.

Waistbands are cut exactly as for skirts, more usually with a CF opening. The measurement is divided up in exactly the same way, but the half-way mark represents the CB and each quarter mark, the respective side seams. The wrap is added to the LHS of the waistband at the CF.

JOINING UP MEASUREMENT GRIDS

With the key positions of the pattern for the garment marked up, the next step is to join them together correctly. These lines give the stitching or seamlines to be followed when making up the garment, and the construction of the garment now needs consideration. We are still concerned, at this stage, with reasonably basic garment shapes, with no styling or detailing incorporated to confuse matters as yet.

Where two points are joined together in a straight line, the resulting seamline is straight and has no shaping. Shoulder seams are almost always straight. Some seamlines have a section that is straight and usually a grid point will be marked in to indicate the end of the straight section. The side seam of a skirt may be shaped from the waist down to the hip, but from the hip to the hem, it will be straight.

There will be many instances where the grid shows two points which are to be joined with a curve, such as a round neckline or arm-hole. Drawing smooth, accurate curves freehand is not easy, even for those with a well-practised eye. Lay a thread down in the position of the curve and mark a series of dots to indicate its position. These can then be joined more easily and accurately. Always remember that you are marking half or less of a continuous curve. Your ideas of what looks correct may surprise you when the shape is joined up, so be careful. Stand back to check the line of a curve before you cut. Look for areas that form a definite bulge that disturbs the smoothness of the line, or for any areas that might need filling in a little.

Many of the main seams of any garment will require shaping, which often takes the form of a very gradual curve. Sometimes this may be for a particular section of seamline, the remainder being either completely straight or extremely curved. Shaping is necessary to allow the garment to fit around and hang from the body well, as the body is of a cylindrical nature with a set of quite complicated contours. There are different ways to mark up the line a shaped seam is to follow, depending on the reason for the shaping. Similar rules apply as given for curved seamlines although, as these shapings are far more gradual, it can be more difficult to identify immediately a scoop or bulge that should not be there. Care must be taken when running a gradual curve into a straight section of seamline, as it is very easy to be a little clumsy and form an angular bump. You will find that, with a little practice, forming a gradual curve in one fell swoop is preferable to struggling painstakingly section by section. This may be easier to achieve with the sweeping blades of the scissors, although judge carefully the level of risk that is involved; marking every 10–15 cm (4–6 in.) should be sufficient.

This is where you must begin to consider the construction of the garment as a whole. For every seamline that you fix in place, you must be aware of the corresponding seamline to which it is to be joined: the front shoulder joins to the back shoulder, the front side seam joins to the back side seam, and so on.

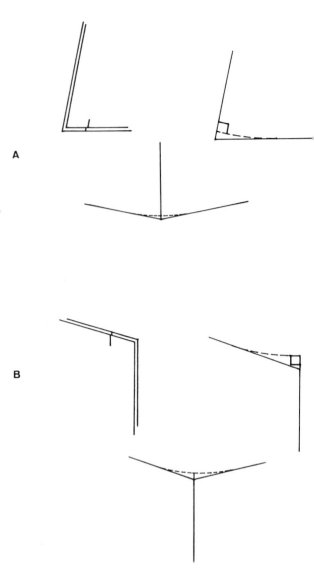

7   *Correct shaping cut at seam ends*

The direction a seamline follows, especially in relation to the adjacent seamline, is extremely important. This means that all the positions on the grid that represent the end of any seamline, which will be at every corner where two seamlines meet, must be carefully angled so that the garment will be made up correctly.

When two corresponding seamlines have been stitched up to the end of the fabric and are opened out and laid flat, there will now be a resulting raw edge that will either form a further seamline, or is to be hemmed or neatened in some way. The shape of this raw edge is just as important to the garment as the seam was and, while this may appear obvious, if the angle of cut of both seamlines is not correct, the resulting raw edge will be distorted. *Whether the subsequent seamline is completely straight or curved, at the point where the first seam meets the raw edge, the two angles must, between them, add up to 180°, this being a straight line.* If the total angle is greater than 180°, the resultant raw edge will have an outwardly pointed shape (*Fig. 7A*); if it is less than 180° the raw edge will have a nick (*Fig. 7B*). If either of these shapes is ever specifically intended, then mark up the correct angles to give whatever shape is required.

Usually the two angles will be cut exactly alike, at 90°. The same principle applies when cutting from a foldline – at the hem or neckline for instance. The cutting line must be exactly at right angles to the foldline so that a smooth line results when the fabric is unfolded. If it is not, the same distorted point, either up or down, will result.

Even the very simple, basic shapings that have been included in the grid instructions need to have this rule applied. For instance, where the side seam of the skirt grid has been lengthened by raising the width mark at the waist, shaping must be added to the waist and side seams to incorporate the necessary right angles. If the two marks were joined in a straight line, not only would an outward point appear at the side seam, but an inward point would be cut at the CF. Instead, the seamline at the waist runs into the CF line at 90° and to the side seam at 90°, shaped as a gradual curve. Fig. 7 shows suggested seamlines for the particular grid examples chosen, with the places where right angles occur clearly marked.

Only the very basic structure of the cut of the main body areas has so far been discussed, but it has, hopefully, been presented in such a way as to make the relationship between body measurements and the actual garment measurements of any design more easily understood. 'Up and down' measurements to determine required length, left to right 'across' measurements to determine required width, and a brief introduction to the necessity of seam shaping and the importance of angles are a start.

CHAPTER FIVE

Direct measurement

The instructions and diagrams for pattern shapes in this chapter are simple enough to be directly cut without the use of a paper pattern. Many of the garments cut from these principles are relatively loosely fitting, as complications such as shaping and suppression are not included, simplicity being emphasised throughout. Possibilities of style lines are covered in a further section, to avoid confusing the examples chosen. The diagrams serve only to illustrate a principle and are widely open to alteration or adaptation to meet individual preferences.

While the construction of these garments should be considered as the cut of your pattern develops, this should not worry even a totally inexperienced dressmaker. The most important point that has to be made before any attempts are started by the novice is the vital necessity of the inclusion of balance marks. When you are faced with a pile of various cut pieces to be joined together, a certain amount of information is needed at each stage of the making-up to aid identification – matching seams, widths of seams, widths of seam turnings, placement, distribution of fullness, and so on. The making-up of the garment will be easier, faster and – even more to the point – more accurate. The positions on a garment where balance marks are always relied upon during construction are almost standard and the reasons for their positions generally need little or no explanation. The exact position of a balance mark is placed with extremely careful use of a tape-measure and should really be marked in as the seamlines are decided upon and the pattern progresses. This is easier and quicker to do while all the measurements you are working with, together with every aspect of the construction of the garment, are in the forefront of your mind.

In the diagrams, the positions of any balance marks are clearly shown, where they look like a small spike stuck in the seamline, because seam turnings are not included. In reality, they are marked by a small nip, cut in the fabric in the seam turning at the correct point opposite the seamline so that, if you imagine the cut extended right through the turning to the seamline, it would meet at the exact position indicated by the 'spike'. Where it is necessary to identify an area of any cut piece that is part of the back of the garment, two nips are made approximately 1 cm ($\frac{3}{8}$ in.) apart, forming a double balance mark.

Note
No garment can ever be cut without the addition of seam turnings. In all these diagrams, it is only the shape of the finished garment pieces that are shown, as the outside lines are stitching lines, not cutting lines. Seam turnings are discussed in detail later (*p. 115*). Their omission at this stage also allows for clearer, uncluttered diagrams, which would not otherwise be the case.

SKIRTS

The skirt is the most uncomplicated, simple garment possible. One shape of any size and proportion hangs freely from the body, secured in position by a strip fastened around the waist. The design possibilities are numerous and this very simplicity makes them even more so. The basic possibilities for the cut of a skirt include the following areas.

Circular-cut skirts
This is an attractive cut, revealing the full qualities of a fabric that must not be excessively bulky, nor have too great a tendency to stretch or lose its shape. The amount of fullness can be adjusted dramatically to suit the particular fabric to be used as well as to achieve the right silhouette. If you are not aware of the way a circular cut falls, cut a piece of scrap fabric, about 15–20 cm (6–8 in.) square. Draw a circle roughly to fill the square and then a much smaller circle in the centre. Cut out the large circle, fold it in

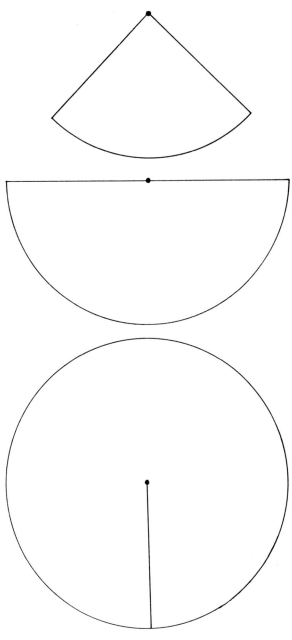

8　*Quarter-, half- and full-circle hem shapings*

as the length of the skirt increases, so will the size of the circle and its circumference, so increasing the amount of fullness. To reduce the fullness and the amount of 'kick' in the skirt, a half-circle skirt can be cut, and to reduce these features even further, a quarter-circle skirt can be cut. These names describe the shape of the cut of the skirt all round at the hemline and are the most usual divisions. Any fraction of a total circle can be cut to give the exact hang required, although any cut less than a quarter circle will not hang very well and defeats the object of choosing this particular method in the first place.

The other important line is the cut of the waist seam which plays a dramatic part in the amount of movement in the skirt and its silhouette. The waist seam, again cut circular, automatically follows the same fraction of a circle as the hemline. The shape on the curve will, therefore, vary greatly as one constant waist measurement forms either a full, half- or quarter-circle and, as the intensity of the curve lessens, so does the effect of the amount of 'kick' or swing in the skirt when that curve is pulled into a straight line (*Fig. 9*).

The waist curve is marked in on the fabric first with care and accuracy, measuring from the corner point, which represents the centre of the circle, in every case. The distance required to do this is the full waist measurement in the case of the quarter-circle skirt, half the waist measurement in the case of the half-circle skirt and quarter the waist measurement in the case of the full-circle skirt. Once the correct waist curve is marked in position, the length of the skirt is measured from the waist down and, as an equal skirt length is usually required, this length is marked in by following the waist curve and so

9　*Waist seam shapings for (A) full circle; (B) half circle; (C) quarter circle*

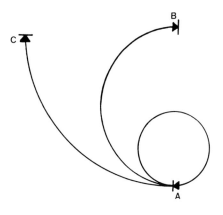

half and pull the centre semi-circle into a straight line, as though it were attached to a straight strip. The way the fabric falls will demonstrate the nature of a full circular-cut skirt.

The measurement of the hemline, which is the circumference of the circle, determines the amount of fullness in the skirt (*Fig. 8*). A fully circular skirt is as described, where the hemline forms a full circle:

marking in the curve of the hem. Mark regularly enough to make joining up with either chalk, pencil or scissors easy.

As you may imagine, large areas of fabric will be required in all but quarter-circle skirts, which present no problem. But there is no reason why a number of seams cannot join up the skirt, allowing it to be cut in a number of pieces. Do not forget to allow fabric for the waistband, especially if the full fabric width has been taken by the skirt pieces.

When marking up directly on to the fabric, you must remember to allow room for the seam turnings. This is one instance where this point is specifically mentioned, as it is so easy to measure up the fabric completely. Make sure the original 'centre' point of the circle, from which the waist curve is measured, is set into the fabric, allowing enough room for seam turnings down alongside the selvedge and across from the cut edge of the fabric, where necessary. Every circular skirt must have at least one seam to incorporate an opening, so that it is possible to put on the garment.

Straight-cut skirts
Skirts in their simplest form consist of straight-cut strips of fabric joined together, and the excess width, which can be considerable, held in place on the waistband by gathers, tucks, pleats (stitched or unstitched), elastic or drawstrings. The design possibilities are numerous, before even additional styling is considered. The more loose-fitting the skirt, the less waist and hip shaping matter. Length and width are all that are important, so choose measurements to suit the fabric and give the proportions you want. The fabric width will dictate how many seams will be necessary to make up the total width required. Always use fabrics with good draping qualities that fall in folds without the need for encouragement.

Working to your waist measurement acts as a rough guide when making decisions about width; remember that all the fabric must be joined on to the waistband without looking a mess. You may feel that your figure requires filling out and the volume of the skirt needs exaggerating, or that much less fabric is needed to give the illusion of a huge, full skirt. The amount of body the fabric has will affect the silhouette, but so, too, will the way that the fullness is distributed around the waist. Unless following the shaping described on the basic skirt grid, it is not recommended that the areas over the position of the side seams are left as plain, ungathered areas but, with this exception, it can be distributed as you wish. Make sure adequate balance marks are included to indicate clearly how much skirt should be stitched on

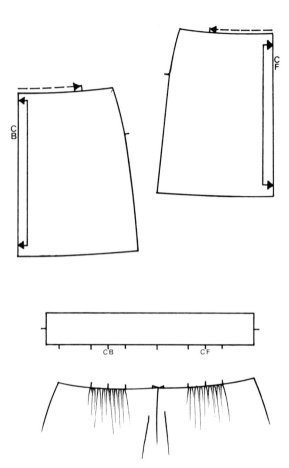

10 *Skirt showing extra width added at the centre lines and balance marks to indicate distribution of gathers at waist*

to how much of the correct section of the waistband (*Fig. 10*).

Remember that straight seams that lie exactly on-grain, may be better thrown fractionally off-grain when cut, as discussed when preparing the skirt grid (*see p.35*)

Flared skirts
Flare can be added at the seams of a skirt either to give it a specific A-line silhouette or to add extra swing and movement to the garment. These skirts are often cut in panels where the seams can each have an amount of flare added. Four, six, eight or more sections can be cut and the positions of the seamlines will depend on the styling of the design (*Fig. 11*). The same amount of flare that is added to the sections that make up the front of the skirt should be added to those making up the back of the skirt, so

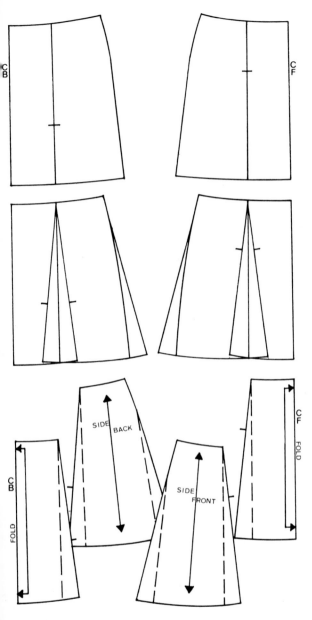

Often, the flare begins to be added at or around the hip level – especially on skirts where above the hip is fitted – giving a classic A-line silhouette. Flare is often incorporated together with other types of cut where an A-line look is undesirable but extra width is needed at the hem to increase fullness and add more swing to a skirt. Here, the flare can begin from any height above the hip or, if a full-length skirt with a fish-tail silhouette is to be cut, the flare will begin to be added somewhere below hip level. The flare should always be run into the seam to which it is being added with a very smooth line (*Fig. 12*). Sharpness in the change of angle, so that the exact point where the flare begins is obvious, should be avoided, as it is ugly and the hang of the skirt will tend to collapse to one side.

There are limits to the amount of extra width that can be added to each seam. The longer the length of the seam, the greater the amount of extra width may be. The decision is based on cutting the correct proportions, so that the base of the triangle of extra fabric does not become too wide in relation to its height. The bulkiness of the fabric is also important: more firmly woven fabrics that tend to stick out will require less flare than more softly draping fabrics that will fall well with larger amounts.

However large or small the amount of flare, the shape of the extra area of hemline must be correct. Measure from the exact point on the original seam where the flare begins, to the hem. A wider area will need a further guide to give the correct hem level so, pivoting from the same point, mark in the seam measurement as many times as are necessary, when

11 *Six-panel skirt with flare added at panel and side seams*

that the garment hangs evenly and the side seams fall exactly where they should. The other general rule is that two seamlines which are to be stitched together should have equal amounts of flare, so that the seam lies centrally through the added fullness. Flare is better added little and often, so that the total amount of added fullness may be more evenly distributed around the garment.

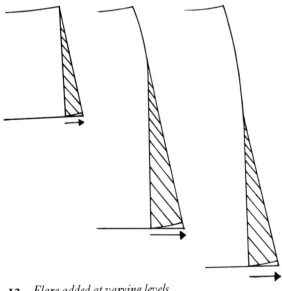

12 *Flare added at varying levels*

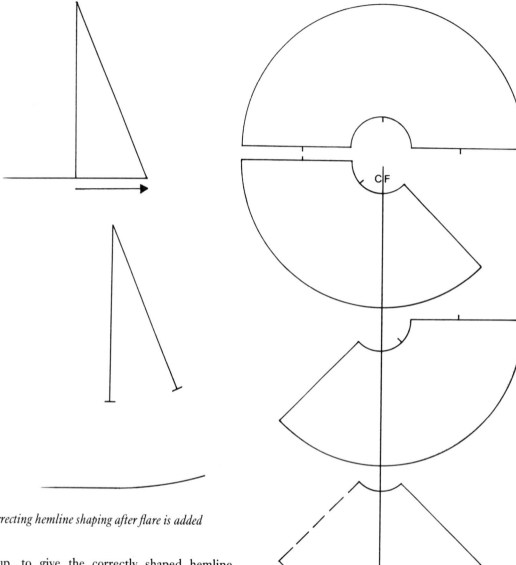

13 *Correcting hemline shaping after flare is added*

joined up, to give the correctly shaped hemline (*Fig. 13*).

Apart from ensuring that the total front and the total back of the skirt balance, there is no rule that says that an equal amount of flare has to be added to every seam. Common sense and remembering to cut symmetrically about the CF and CB lines is all that is needed to cut the silhouette you require.

Wrap-over skirts

A wrap-over skirt can be of any kind of cut, with any styling imaginable. The reason that such an enormous variety of skirts should be grouped together is that they all have in common the fact that they are not seamed up into a cylindrical form and fastened, but are simply wrapped around the hips and held

14 *Full-circle wrap-over skirt showing area of wrap*

together at the waist only. So that decency is maintained when you move, walk or sit in this type of skirt, an area of fabric continues beneath the top flap which is revealed as the loose edge moves about. This means that there is always an area of double fabric. The width of this varies and will depend on the bulk of the fabric, the amount of general fullness in the style, and personal preference – i.e. how much leg you might be prepared to show on a windy day.

In all cases it is better to cut the wrap on the generous side as a tight-fitting skirt will give problems when sitting down. Bulk can be reduced by cutting the fabric that lies beneath without fullness; as it does not often show, the more simply the under-wrap can be cut, the better.

The wrap itself can be positioned anywhere around the skirt. You will decide on a position which will indicate the centre line of the area that is to form the wrap, and the total wrap is often symmetrical about this line, so that the area of double fabric is symmetrically positioned to give some feeling of balance, although not necessarily. To use a simple example: the CF line of the skirt has been chosen; to this is added the wrap, so that when both the LHS and RHS of the skirt front are cut, the RHS will include the top wrap and the LHS, the under-wrap – the CF lines will lie together as the skirt is worn (*Fig. 14*).

As well as practical considerations when choosing the width of the wrap, the edge of the top wrap automatically forms a conspicuous feature of any design. In some cases this is disguised; in others it is made into a design feature. When the wrap is placed around the CF or CB line, the edge will lie on the LHS of the garment, towards the side seam, but, as previously mentioned, this is not a hard and fast rule, and many designs give balance to asymmetrically positioned wraps.

The CF line is used again to show an example where the RHS and LHS are not cut alike, specifically to reduce bulk (*Fig. 15*): the lines where the edge of the under-wrap lies when the garment is made up is the same distance from the centre line as the edge of the top wrap (*Fig. 16*). This excludes the gathers from the area of wrap that is to lie underneath and not show.

The finish of the edge of the wrap is important. If the line of the cut edge is off-grain, it is necessary to prevent any possibility of it stretching and losing shape. The WS of the top wrap must be finished with special attention to neatness as it is likely that the flap will lift at times and reveal the inside finish. The under-wrap need not be finished with such meticulous attention as the WS will never show when the garment is worn. The top wrap will often be finished with a facing. Bear in mind the fabric being used when deciding these points. Another possibility is to choose two suitable fabrics and make up two identical skirts. Then place RSs together and join down one wrap edge, around the hem and up the remaining wrap edge. Turn through to the RS, and

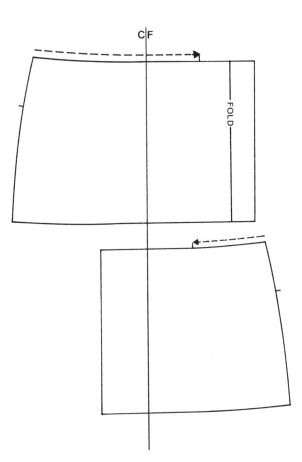

15 *Wrap-over skirt with gathers at waist where fronts are not cut alike*

16 *Skirt shown in Fig. 15 made up*

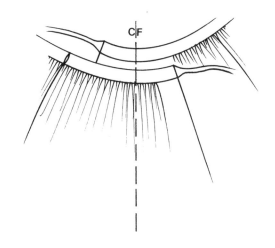

45

attach a waistband, to give either a fully lined skirt, or a skirt that is reversible.

The waistband can fasten in several ways or be cut with extensions that can be tied together. Whatever the particular method chosen, care must be taken to indicate sufficient balance marks to align centre lines and wrap edges correctly on the waistband.

TOPS AND DRESSES

It is surprising that such a large variety of garments can be cut in such very basic ways. Most of the fitting problems of bodices are caused by the bust and armhole areas. Bust problems can be avoided by simplicity of cut alone; armhole and sleeve problems require careful attention to particular measurements, and the necessary time to stop and think before cutting. Neck, cuff, fastening and other details are not included in this section.

The top can be thought of in three main sections for both front and back (*Fig. 17*): above bust level to the shoulder; below bust level; and the sleeve. The sleeve is not considered a separate piece for the moment. Work from your diagram of body measurements. Ignore any shaping on the shoulder, but mark straight from the centre line at right angles through the shoulder level as indicated at the neck edge. This line represents the shoulder seam and the centre line of the sleeve, so add sleeve-line measurement (*A*) to the shoulder measurement (*B*) to give the total length of this line from the neck-edge position at the shoulder. Now extend the bust-level line to the same length keeping the position of the actual bust measurement and bust point clearly marked. Join the end points of these two lines to give a line (*C*) that represents the sleeve hem which will be parallel to the CF line. Now draw a further parallel line (*D*) to

run through the position of the end of the shoulder. The last step is to decide on the width of the lower section in order to place the line (*E*). As this automatically determines the length of the underarm of the sleeve, bear both points in mind. If the armhole is to remain at this depth (which is the shoulder to bust-level measurement), about 7–10 cm (2¾–4 in.) can be added to the actual bust measurement as the position for the side seam. If you are skinny, 7 cm (2¾ in.) will be about the right amount. If you are more fleshy around the arm and have a larger bust, 10 cm (4 in.) or more will need to be added. Although the under-arm measurement has been mentioned as being important, do not expect the resulting under-arm seam length to be equal to that indicated by your sleeve-measurement diagram (the length of the centre line below the arm-width line). It will be shorter because the depth of the armhole is greater than that of a standard fitting armhole and is not meant to reach up so far. The extra width of the garment also compensates for this.

Extend the side-seam line down to the hip-level line which represents the hemline. For an average figure shape the seam will meet the hip level at a point that is wider than the actual hip measurement. If you are heavier on the hips and this is not the case, simply remember to increase the hemline width in some other way, such as by adding enough flare to the side seams.

This gives three blocks of proportions that have been dictated by your body measurements. These can now be altered slightly in various ways to give a slightly more sophisticated pattern shape.

Extra width to bodice

You may wish to give greater width to the bodice sections, especially where the hemline is extended down to be cut as a dress and the particular style fails to give extra width automatically. Firstly, flare can be added to the side seams, although the amount should not be excessive. Remember that the addition of 2.5 cm (1 in.) to each side seam will give a total of 10 cm (4 in.) extra width in all, which may be plenty to add on at hip level. It need not be added right from the under-arm point, but should begin a little higher than half-way between bust and waist level. Exactly the same amount and exactly the same shape of seamline should be cut on the back bodice side seam.

If further width is required, draw a line from the shoulder to the hem, passing through the bust point (*Fig. 18*). Cut up this line. Keep the CF line straight and swing out the side section, keeping the two sections touching at the shoulder. As the amount of

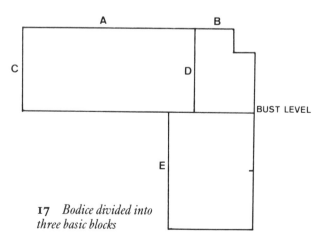

17 *Bodice divided into three basic blocks*

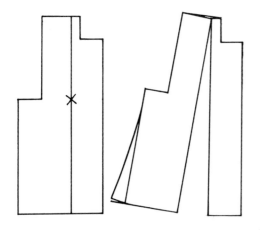

18 *Extra width given to bodice; flare is also added to the side seam*

width at the hem increases, so does the width at bust point. Do not over-exaggerate this swing, otherwise the area of garment above bust level will become too large. It is better to add a little here and combine it with additional flare at the side seams so that the full benefit of the extra fullness is felt at the waist and hip levels. All that remains is to join each end of the shoulder seam to form a straight line and to shape the hemline. As this flare has been added to the main area of fabric and not to a seamline, it need not be added to the back bodice. Remember that the back will already look slightly fuller than the front as there is not so much body area for the fabric to cover. This prevents the garment being thrown out of balance and, unless an alternative silhouette is required, no special provision for the back is necessary.

19 *Under-arm wrist to waist measurement (AB) showing difference between close and looser fitting garment with corresponding points on block diagram*

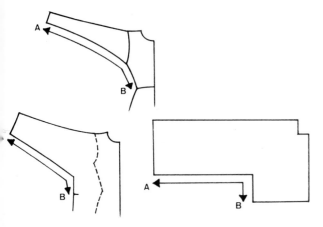

Armhole depth position

When marking up the bodice grid, certain points were mentioned concerning the level of the under-arm point in relation to the position of the armhole seam and the width of the garment (*see p. 35*). You may want to alter the position of the under-arm point from bust level (*Fig. 19*). Whenever this is done the most important thing to remember is the total wrist to waist measurement (AB) and the need for allowance to be made in the cut for the arm to be able to move. This is more crucial on garments that are to be closely fitted or held at the waist and that have a fitted cuff on the sleeve. The more fitted the garment, the longer is the distance necessary to raise the arm to shoulder level without distorting the garment at the waist or hemline. The looser the sleeve and the wider the bodice, the more fabric there is to allow room to move the arm in the same way; it still should not distort the rest of the garment but it will have a total under-arm and side seam length much less than the actual body measurement from wrist to waist. Whatever the styling demands, always think carefully before you cut, to make certain that the combination of under-arm and side-seam length, together with the amount of room in the garment, is enough to raise the arm comfortably at least to shoulder height when the garment is held in at the waist. If the sleeve is to be cut separately there are further shapings that can be added to increase this length.

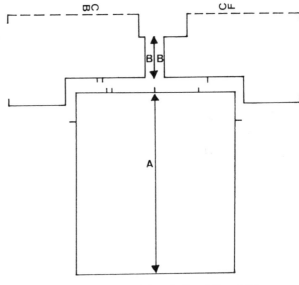

20 *Sleeve section separated from bodice: (A) and (B) correspond to Fig. 17*

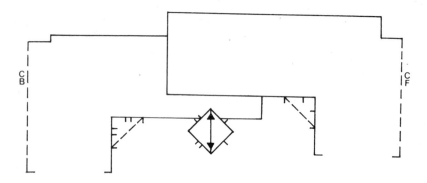

Separation of sleeve

If the sleeve area is removed, a square armhole is left with a seamline which will sit on the end of the shoulder (*Fig. 20*). The top edge represents the centre line of the sleeve about which it is, so far, symmetrical. If the sleeve is to be cut in one – i.e. without a seam running down the centre line – the centre line position is marked on the sleeve head with a balance mark, together with another to mark the position where the under-arm seam ends and the side seam meets the sleeve. If the cut of the armhole and sleeve head are to remain as simple as this, the only reasons to cut a separate sleeve may be that the fabric is not wide enough, or that a particular fabric effect is required – such as an alternative direction of stripes – or that the seam is necessary for an insertion that is included in the design. Otherwise, the garment may just as well be cut with the sleeve and bodice in one.

The armhole may vary in shape for styling reasons, as may the sleeve head, for instance, where gathers or pleats are to be included. Whatever the specific details, when the sleeve is separated, the armhole shaping and the sleeve-head shaping must be worked out together.

Gussets

In many cases, a gusset can be cut of any size to be inserted at the under-arm. A huge gusset cut in a contrasting fabric can make a stunning design feature. More practically, the addition of a gusset can increase the comfort of the garment and prevent any 'pull' lines that may otherwise come from an armhole that is too tight or insufficiently shaped. For instance, if the armhole seam forms a dropped shoulder, this may well be cut in a straight line which runs into the side seamline with a sleeve that sticks out like a signpost. In this case, firstly all the seams will meet at one point which will cause bulk, a possible weak point and discomfort in wear and, secondly, the armhole will be cut with no shaping at all; a gusset here is vital. The inclusion of a gusset also increases

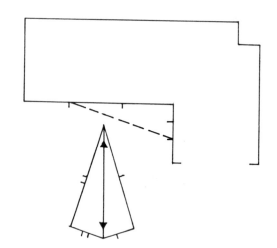

slightly the under-arm length from the sleeve hem to the waist of the garment, as well as allowing extra room for movement.

Gussets can vary in size considerably (*Fig. 21*). The top half is inserted into the under-arm seam of the sleeve and the bottom half into the side seam. A variety of proportions are possible, as a gusset need not be equal in length for each seam, although front and back must, obviously, balance. Mark in balance marks carefully on the bodice seams to show how far down each seam the gusset comes. On larger gussets, mark in a half-way balance mark on each section, as the cut edges of the gusset are bias, or cross cut, and will easily stretch if not handled with care.

Armhole and sleeve shaping

Fig. 22 shows a basic example of a loose, rounded armhole with a set-in sleeve, with the shaping that is necessary for more closely fitting under-arms. Extra width is added to the sleeve seam where it is set in under the arm. Extra length is also added to the seam to increase allowance for movement. With this type of cut, the armhole and bodice can fit to the body as intended, right up to the highest under-arm point that is possible, while remaining comfortable.

On more fitted sleeves, the front and back are cut differently but, in this case, the garment is loose enough for each side to be cut the same. To cut the armhole, shape a curve gradually as shown, from the under-arm point up to the shoulder seam. Notice that the shoulder seam is marked in with its slope, taken from the bodice grid (see p.35), so that the armhole seam must meet the shoulder seam at right angles. This line forms the stitching line of the armhole. The sleeve head follows this line down from the shoulder until a level of about 10 cm (4 in.) above the level of the under-arm point is reached. Mark across the line to indicate the position for a balance mark and, from here, the sharpest area of the curve is shaped. The sleeve can now be cut away, following the armhole seamline. Instead of leaving

the area below the balance mark as a convex curve, it is reshaped as shown. This is where the extra length comes from and this can be adjusted without distorting the new shape of the sleeve-head too much. This section must not alter in length as it has to fit into the same length of armhole seam as it did before it was separated. A mirror image of the curve about the dotted line in Fig. 22 gives a suitable curve. As can be seen, the width of the sleeve is also automatically increased.

Shaping sleeve seams

Shaping can be cut on the under-arm seam to alter the way the sleeve falls around the arm and achieve the desired silhouette. On a short sleeve, if the under-arm seams are cut straight, the sleeve will be loosely fitting with a lowered under-arm point (Fig. 23). It will also stick out away from the arm down the centre line, unless gathered in on to a band. Loose sleeves that fall straight when worn do, in fact, need to be shaped away at the under-arm seam so that the poking out effect does not occur. If extra fullness is required lower down the sleeve, flare can be added in the same way as it is to a skirt side seam, with equal amounts on each side, of course. Where shaping is included on the sleeve-head, and extra sleeve width has been the automatic result, this might be a reason for shaping being necessary lower down, to reduce the sleeve width by this amount, or

22 *Curved armhole showing separation of sleeve and re-shaped sleeve-head*

23 *Short sleeve cut with under-arm seam shaping*

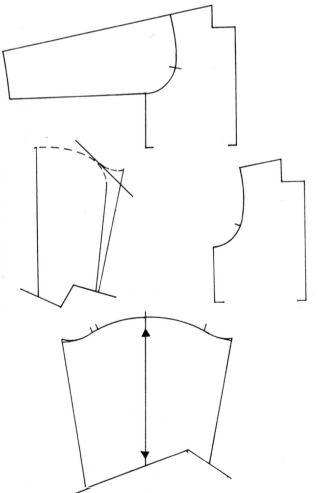

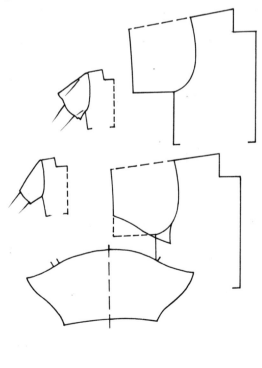

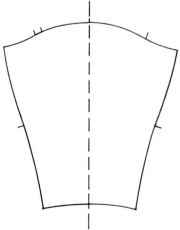

24 *Sleeve in Fig. 21 with under-arm seam shaping to reduce width at wrist*

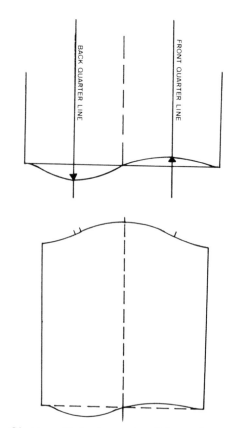

BACK QUARTER LINE

FRONT QUARTER LINE

25 *Shaping added to lower edge of sleeve where cuff is to be attached*

more (*Fig. 24*). Add any kind of shaping gradually into the original seamline and run into the sleeve-head seam and lower edge of the sleeve at right angles.

With the sleeve laid flat, it is, so far, symmetrical about the centre line. To the left of the centre line is the back of the sleeve and to the right, the front. Any sleeve to be attached to a cuff will benefit from a little shaping on the lower cut edge to allow for the difference in length that the outer and inner lines of the arm require (*Fig. 25*). The line of the outer edge will follow the quarter line to the back of the sleeve and the line of the inner edge, the quarter line to the front. The centre line can be measured from the shoulder edge to the wrist bone, with the arm hanging loosely in its natural position. If the sleeve is to be gathered on to a cuff, you will want to add extra length for blousing. From the level of the final length, the rest of the shaping can be added. The actual amount of shaping will depend on the width of the sleeve. A wide cut sleeve will need much less shaping than one that is more narrowly cut. The following is an average example. To the back quarter line add 2 cm (¾ in.) below the centre-line level and to the front quarter line mark 1 cm (⅜ in.) above the centre-line level. The shaping will run as shown from the under-arm seam (which is the same level as the centre line) through each point marked. This gives a relatively gradual shaping. By adding the same measurements to a narrower sleeve, a sharper curve will automatically result. If you alter these measurements, always add more to the back in length than you remove from the front, taking care not to over-exaggerate the shape of the resulting

curve. At the quarter lines, it should be possible to 'flatten' the shaping slightly, so that a small area is cut parallel to the original straight line.

'All-in-one' cut sleeves
The cut of a bodice and sleeve together usually has a front and a back that are seamed in a continuous line from the neck down the shoulder and on down the centre line of the sleeve. This seam and the seam that combines the under-arm and side seam are usually cut exactly the same for the front as for the back. The same principles apply concerning adequate allowances for movement, and the position of the under-arm point, through which the seam will be stitched, is marked in place with the same degree of importance as for the cut of a garment with a set-in sleeve. The particular styling and silhouette of the sleeve are largely achieved by the shaping that can be included on both seams (*Fig. 26*). Whatever this might be, shaping on the top seam should be reasonably gradual. The under-arm seam may incorporate more pronounced shapings if required, but

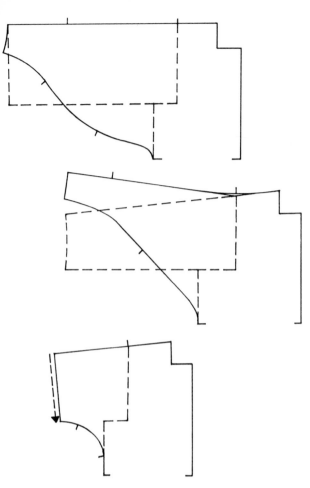

26 *Examples of all-in-one cut sleeves showing variations in shaping possible on top and under-arm seams*

mark in the area that will form the side seams first so that you can be certain there is enough width in the bodice. The section of top seam that forms the shoulder seam may need shaping to fit the slope of the shoulder. The seamline may then alter direction beyond the end of the shoulder and swing upwards to give the line of the sleeve. This may be further exaggerated to allow for increased arm movement on a sleeve that is tightly fitting at the lower arm.

Sleeveless bodices

If the sleeve section is completely removed, the bodice is left with a square armhole that is cut away to the level of the bust point. To leave such a hole in the side of a garment that is to be worn without another garment underneath is clearly unsuitable. On such an unfitted bodice, a snugly fitting, round armhole will necessitate raising the under-arm point to roughly 5 cm (2 in.) higher than bust level and reducing the width of the bodice at the new level to one that is more closely fitting (*Fig. 27*). The curve of the front armhole will need a greater area scooped away than the back armhole so that the armhole edge does not rub the skin as the arm moves. If the side seamline were extended straight up to the shoulder (cut square with no slope) and the side seam raised a little higher to a raised under-arm point, which can be determined both by height for decency and depth for comfort, the effect of a small cap sleeve would result. The bodice must have sufficient width to prevent unsightly pulling and those with less 'busty' figures will wear such a simple cut more successfully. To achieve a better fit and a more successful cap sleeve which is a little larger, extend the armhole edge and shape the under-arm. If the shoulder is cut with a slope, the cap can then be shaped to meet the shoulder seam at a right angle, as indicated (*Fig. 28*). The point where it meets can be decided by measuring how wide you wish the cap to extend beyond the end of the shoulder.

27 *Armhole shape for sleeveless bodice*

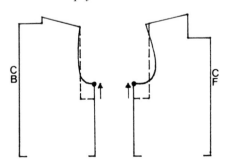

28 *Armhole adaptation for cap sleeve*

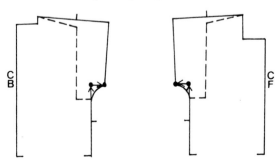

Summer and evening (low-cut) bodices

The two bodice sections are needed for reference to the measurements they indicate (*Fig. 29*). It is also necessary to measure around your chest, so that the tape measure sits comfortably under the arms and at a level of about 5 cm (2 in.) above the bust-level line. Cut the front longer then the back at the centre front to prevent problems arising with fitting because of the bust, and cut a loosely fitting style, again to avoid complications of fitting arising. The fullness in the style must be secured in some way and is usually controlled by attaching a band around the top edge or a casing that can carry an elastic.

Cut any further shaping required with careful consideration of the bust level, under-arm point and differences between front and back, not forgetting the kind of opening, if this is necessary. As a general rule, straps can be positioned half-way between the centre line and side seam.

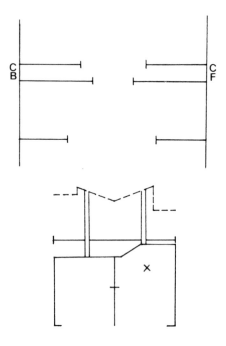

29 *Bodices without shoulder seams*

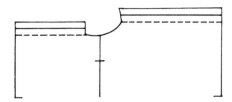

flat pattern cutting

The cut of a design has been introduced in an extremely simplified form, to arrive at a basic garment shape with no complications of styling yet included. The introduction of styling will need a little knowledge of the methods that are used to draft flat paper patterns so that the styling methods can be presented without the need for lengthy and involved explanations. Further understanding will also be necessary to cut more fitted or more complicated garments. The following chapters on styling and detailing should not be any more difficult to understand than the previous chapter. A selection of pattern drafts are included to illustrate general methods used to meet the specific requirements of a design, and may be useful as points of reference if indecision is a problem.

It must be emphasised that this is not in any way meant to provide instructions for how to cut flat paper patterns. For the purposes of this book, this has been omitted. The whole basis of flat pattern drafting tends to be rather technical and is unlikely to inspire confidence in anybody wishing to cut designs for themselves. Learning a trade is also unnecessary for the purposes of most people who enjoy making their own clothes. Intense involvement in paper alone makes it difficult to keep the relationship of paper to fabric in the front of your mind and it is all too easy to lose sight of the fact that the shapes that result are actually to be cut and made up in fabric.

PRINCIPLES

Patterns are developed from a set of cardboard 'blocks' which fit either an individual body shape or a standard commercial size. To achieve a three-dimensional shape, darts are included. These darts suppress the exact amount of fullness that is necessary to give the correct body shape to flat fabric. A certain amount of tolerance is included around the bust, waist and hips and also around the sleeve head,

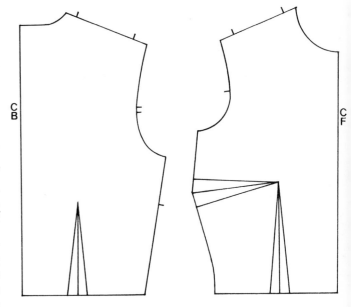

30 *Typical bodice blocks*

again so that the made-up shape of the blocks will give a correct basic fit.

Every pattern piece begins from the relevant block. Back and front are worked simultaneously. Whatever the particular block adaptation used, the pattern is worked by altering the block in a logical order until the final shape has been reached.

Bodice blocks

The bodice block is shaped to give a standard-fitting, rounded neck edge and a standard armhole for an ordinary set-in sleeve (*Fig. 30*). The centre lines are, of course, straight, and generally indicate the direction of the straight grain of the fabric. The front bodice has darts which suppress the amount of fullness needed to give the correct bust shaping.

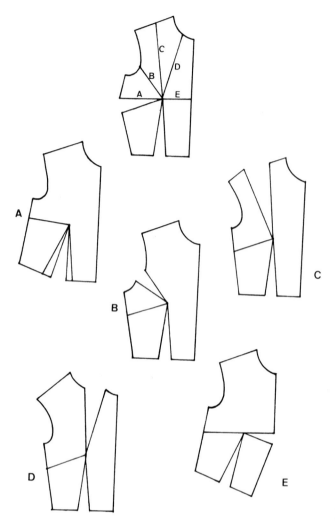

31 *Bodice front suppression is divided on block between under-arm and waist dart. Alternative positions are shown as follows: (A) total suppression into waist dart; (B) suppression divided between waist and armhole darts; (C) suppression divided between waist and shoulder dart; (D) suppression divided between waist and neck dart; (E) suppression divided between waist and CF dart*

This amount is spread over two darts on the block: a basic bust dart, which runs into the waist seam, and an under-arm dart. To illustrate the effect of suppression, cut a paper circle which need not be larger than 20 cm (8 in.) in diameter. Now cut a straight line from the circumference into the centre point of the circle. By overlapping the paper at the cut edge, a three-dimensional cone is formed and the greater the amount of overlap, the more shaped

the flat paper circle becomes. Imagine the centre point of the circle to be the bust point on the bodice block. A set amount of fullness must be folded away to give the correct bust shaping. If you take this to be 2 cm ($\frac{3}{4}$ in.), for instance, you can imagine that whatever position the cut line takes on the circle, wherever 2 cm ($\frac{3}{4}$ in.) is overlapped, exactly the same shaping will be formed. In fabric, the cut lines are actually foldlines to give the same effect. It can be seen that suppression may be placed in any position around the block (*Fig. 31*). By keeping the same total amount as the two block darts, the correct block shape and fit will automatically result if the position of the darts is altered. The bust point is that used when pivoting the block to alter the position of the suppression. The actual darts themselves stop some way short of the bust point; if the dart were stitched right up to the bust point it would only accentuate the bust and look extremely ugly.

The back bodice includes a dart to fold away excess fullness to give the correct waist measurement and a snug fit to the bodice below the armhole. The side seam will be exactly the same length as the front side seam, after the under-arm dart has been folded away. The back shoulder seam is always cut longer than the front. This results in excess fabric in the back shoulder which is either eased away or incorporated into a dart which is placed at the centre of the shoulder. This is to give extra width across the shoulders at the back to ensure a good fit.

On a well-fitting bodice block, the actual position of the shoulder seam lies not half-way around the armhole from the side seam as you might expect, but 1–2 cm ($\frac{3}{8}$–$\frac{3}{4}$ in.) towards the front. This means that, when the blocks are placed together at the side seam, the back shoulder will appear higher than the front.

Skirt blocks

The front and back skirt blocks each have one dart to give the correct fit around the skirt from the hip to the waist (*Fig. 32*). The side seam in this area also includes shaping. From the hip level down to the hem, the block may either be cut exactly straight, parallel to the centre lines, or have a standard amount of flare already added. A fitted skirt that is cut exactly straight will give the illusion of being slightly tapered when worn, and the small amount of flare that may be included on the block is there to compensate for this. The parallel line is marked up on the block so that the amount of flare added is immediately obvious. The hip level is also clearly marked at right angles to the centre lines.

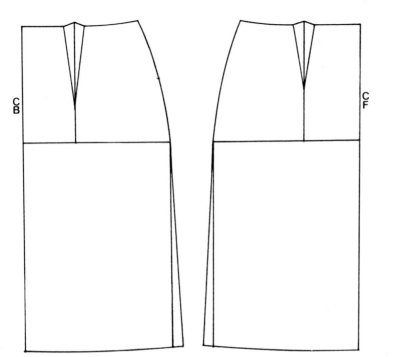

32 *Typical skirt blocks*

Sleeve blocks

The sleeve block gives a standard fitting sleeve-head which includes an average amount of ease (*Fig. 33*). Ease is necessary around a fitted sleeve-head so that the sleeve fits comfortably around the arm and allows for movement. The actual measurement of the sleeve-head seamline is, therefore, longer than the total armhole measurement. 3–4 cm (1⅛–1½ in.) may be considered as an average amount of extra length. (Ease is discussed further in the construction section, *see p. 181*.)

The sleeve is divided up with a centre line and two quarter lines. A balance mark will show clearly the position on the sleeve-head where the shoulder seam meets, which is usually 1–2 cm (⅜–¾ in.) towards the front of the sleeve, indicating that the bodice is cut with a forward shoulder-seam position. A straight-sleeve block will run parallel to the centre and quarter lines. A fitted-sleeve block will incorporate a small dart at the elbow to give shape to the back area of the sleeve. When the arm hangs naturally, it will fall to the front of the body from the elbow down. This dart gives a similar hang to the sleeve.

Procedure

The relevant block sections are chosen and positioned as necessary to begin the pattern adaptation. The blocks are then positioned on paper and drawn around. The style lines are drawn in place, carefully noting the proportions they give in relation to the

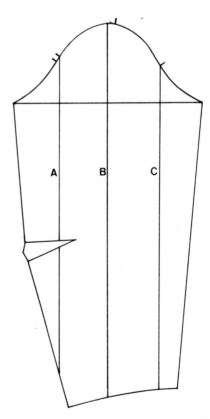

33 *Typical sleeve block (A) back quarter line; (B) centre line; (C) front quarter line*

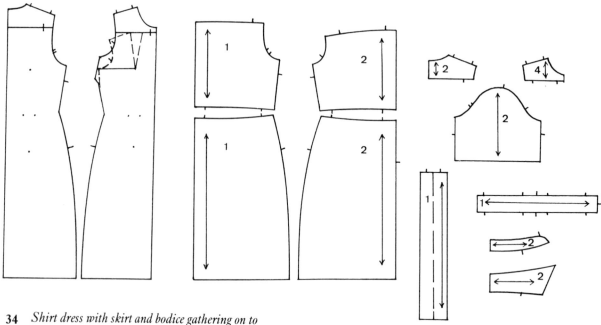

34 *Shirt dress with skirt and bodice gathering on to waistband and yoke, CF placket and shirt collar*

35 *Blouse showing extended sleeve with flare and CF box placket, stand collar and patch pocket*

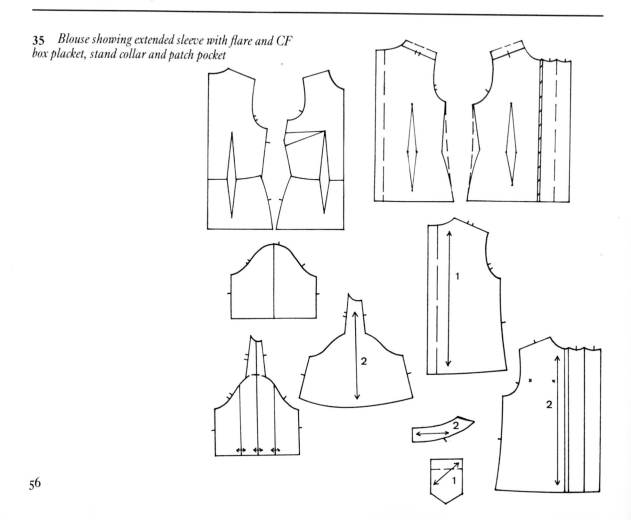

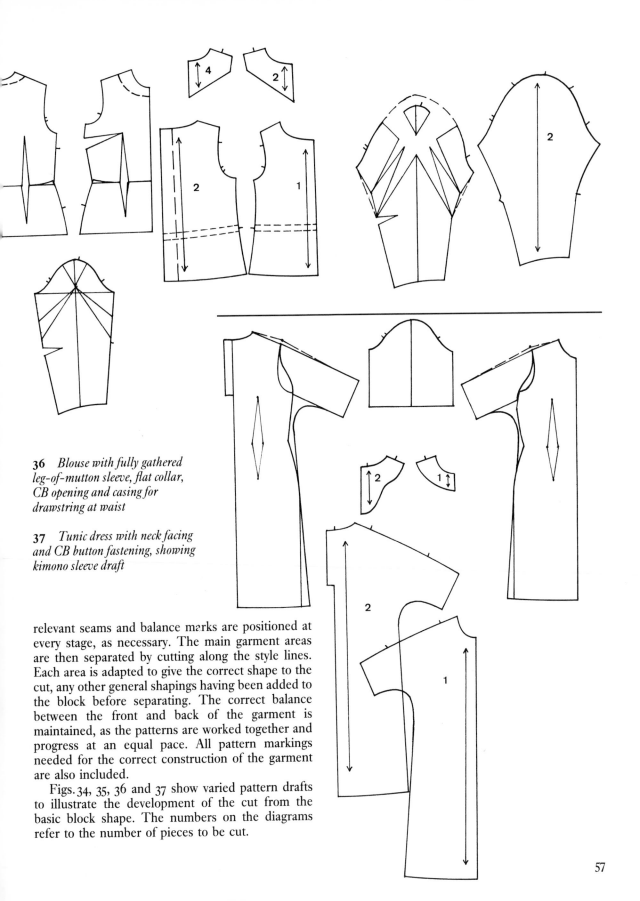

36 *Blouse with fully gathered leg-of-mutton sleeve, flat collar, CB opening and casing for drawstring at waist*

37 *Tunic dress with neck facing and CB button fastening, showing kimono sleeve draft*

relevant seams and balance marks are positioned at every stage, as necessary. The main garment areas are then separated by cutting along the style lines. Each area is adapted to give the correct shape to the cut, any other general shapings having been added to the block before separating. The correct balance between the front and back of the garment is maintained, as the patterns are worked together and progress at an equal pace. All pattern markings needed for the correct construction of the garment are also included.

Figs. 34, 35, 36 and 37 show varied pattern drafts to illustrate the development of the cut from the basic block shape. The numbers on the diagrams refer to the number of pieces to be cut.

CHAPTER SEVEN

Styling

You have so far reached basic front, back and sleeve shapes by working directly from your body measurements. Each section can be divided into further areas which may be individually altered by increasing or reducing fullness, adding shaping and introducing further seamlines, to state the most usual developments. This is what is termed styling.

One single set of basic shapes may be developed in such an enormous variety of ways that it would be impossible to include them all. As more detail is included, it becomes even harder to generalise, so greater emphasis must be placed on the point that the particular examples used (*Fig. 38*) serve only to illustrate the principle being discussed.

The more that is included in the cut of a garment, the closer the attention to its construction must be; the importance of fitting together the jigsaw becomes more critical as complications are introduced.

SKIRTS

Whatever the basic cut of the skirt, in order that it will fit to the waist, suppression of some kind usually needs to be included. An exception is the circular-cut waist seam which gives enough shaping for the skirt to sit snugly. This is cut to waist measurement or with a minimal amount of extra length that is eased away on to the waistband. 2 cm ($\frac{3}{4}$ in.) ease is plenty for front and back, giving 4 cm ($1\frac{1}{2}$ in.) in total. Skirts with hip yokes, or panelled or gored skirts with flare on each seam, will also give a curved waist seam that can be stitched to the waistband with no suppression necessary.

Darts
Darts are positioned in the area half-way between the centre line and side seam. The front dart is usually shorter than the back dart. The total amount of fullness can be divided up to give multiple darts which can be grouped around the skirt according to

design. For example, a dart that folds away 3 cm ($1\frac{1}{8}$ in.) of fullness at the waist seam can be split into three much narrower darts of 1 cm ($\frac{3}{8}$ in.) each. These remain the same length as the original dart.

The seam into which the dart runs (in the example shown [*Fig. 39*] this is the waist seam) will almost always require shaping of some kind, so that, when the dart is pressed to one side, the folded edges lie exactly against the cut edge of the seam. The easiest way to achieve the correct shaping is to mark up, in paper, the area of garment that includes the dart, fold away the dart so that it lies in the right direction on the WS, and cut the seamline, ignoring the dart (*Fig. 40*). The correct shaping will then automatically appear when the dart is unfolded, and can be transferred to the fabric. The stitching line of the dart is shown by balance marks. As a general rule, all darts which lie vertically are pressed towards the centre of the garment and those which lie horizontally are pressed towards the hem. Skirt darts are, therefore, folded towards the CF and CB.

Gathers
It has already been mentioned that gathers may be distributed in groups, rather than evenly, around the waist. The quantity of fabric that can be gathered up depends on the nature of the fabric that is used. Far less actual width is needed to give a full effect with a fabric that has some 'spring' and body that will disappear into gathers readily. Bear this in mind when you consider gathers. Three times the finished seam length will give very full gathers, twice the finished seam length will give average gathers with a pleasant effect, and one-and-a-half times the finished seam length will give rather sparse gathers. If you work on the assumption that cutting twice the fabric width will give an attractive appearance, then you are better able to judge the final width you wish to cut.

Gathers can be included in any cut of skirt. Original pattern shapes are altered to incorporate the

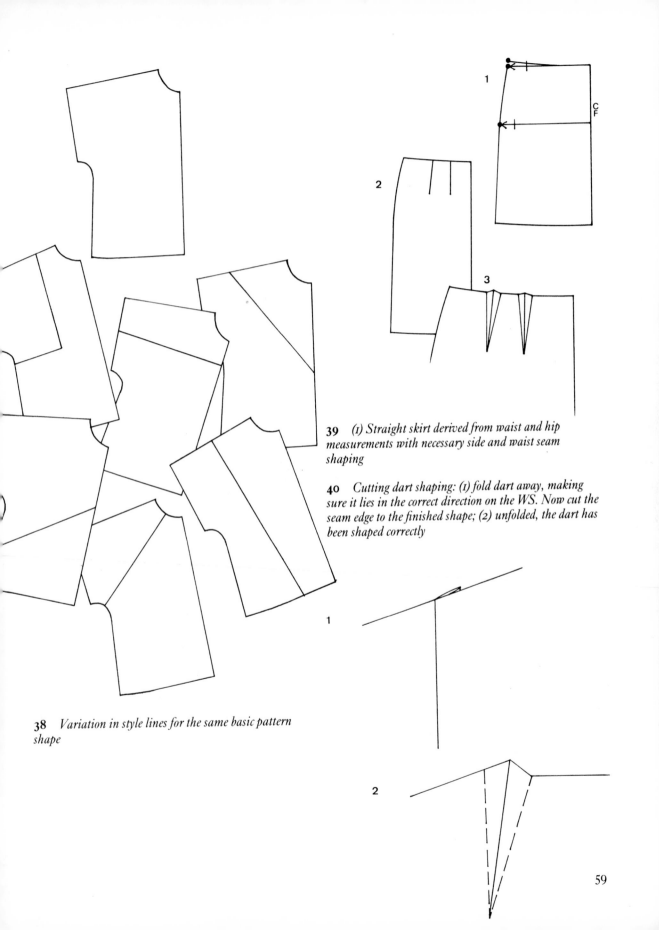

39 *(1) Straight skirt derived from waist and hip measurements with necessary side and waist seam shaping*

40 *Cutting dart shaping: (1) fold dart away, making sure it lies in the correct direction on the WS. Now cut the seam edge to the finished shape; (2) unfolded, the dart has been shaped correctly*

38 *Variation in style lines for the same basic pattern shape*

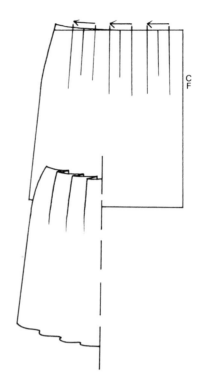

42 *Unpressed pleats: arrows show direction to fold*

41 *Skirt cut with additional width added to centre line showing examples of distribution of gathers*

extra width in the fabric. A simple strip can be added to give the total amount of extra fabric required (*Fig. 41*). Incorporating gathers in more complicated shapes is described on page 68.

Unpressed pleats

This is an alternative method of disposing of large amounts of fullness into a much shorter seam length, where the fabric is folded away as opposed to being gathered away (*Fig. 42*). This always gives a flatter, less bulky appearance to the skirt around the waist and hips. The size of each fold or pleat can vary enormously from tiny 1 cm (⅜ in.) pleats placed all

around the waist to larger 3 cm (1⅛ in.) pleats, carefully positioned according to styling. The size of each pleat, as stated, refers to the finished width – the length of the seamline that results. Each pleat will, in all, require three times the width of its finished size, so the 1 cm (⅜ in.) pleat will take 3 cm (1⅛ in.) of fabric width, to result in 1 cm distance of seamline. Similarly, the 3 cm (1⅛ in.) pleat will take 9 cm (3⅜ in.) of fabric width. If the pleats are to be placed so that they are touching all around the waist seam, the seam – the width to be cut – will be three times the waist measurement, whatever the finished size of each individual pleat.

Smaller pleats can be folded in the same direction all around the skirt. Otherwise they are placed either all facing away from or all facing towards the centre lines. Pleats that are folded away from the centre line fall flatter and with a smoother line than those that lie towards the centre lines; the latter give more 'body' to the appearance of the skirt. The pleats may also alternate in direction to give interesting effects.

The two positions that are to be placed together when stitching the folds in place must be accurately marked with balance marks. If the resulting seamline has shaping, every pleat must be cut with the correct shaping so that, when every pleat lies in its finished

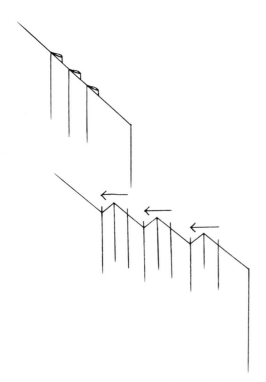

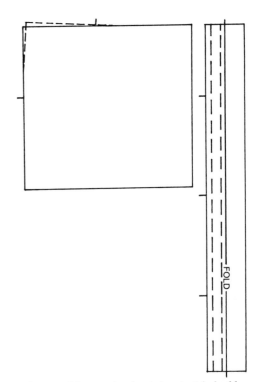

43 *Importance of correct shaping at the top of pleats*

44 *Skirt front and front casing/waistband with double channels for elastic*

position, the cut edge will form the right seamline shape. You must make certain of the direction in which the pleat is to lie, as the area of pleat shaping will differ (*Fig. 43*). The best way to do this is to fold away the fabric or pattern with every pleat in position and then cut along the shape of the seamline in the same way the shaping was cut across the top of a dart (*see p. 59*). The correct shaping on each pleat will then automatically result. The example (*Fig. 43*) shows the shaping on a seam to be pleated up and stitched to a diagonal yoke seam, and the difference to the shaping if the pleats lie in exactly the same position, but in the opposite direction. The same principle must be applied to a waist seam cut with shaping, even as minimal as that first shown on the skirt grid (*see p. 33*). The effects of the shaping will, of course, be far less dramatic, but just as important.

Elastic/drawstring at waist

This is one of the easiest ways to control fullness at the waist of a skirt and, as no other fastening is required, it is a very simple finish. However, the simple method – folding over a hem to form a casing – does not give a satisfactory fit to a skirt. A straight casing should be cut separately with the same waist and side-seam shaping as a skirt which is to be

gathered, and joined to the skirt. The waist shaping over such widths becomes so gradual it is almost imperceptible. The width of the skirt will be roughly twice the waist measurement or more. The casing is cut to the same measurement.

Where an elastic is simply to be enclosed in the casing, consider the possibilities of stitching multiple channels to take narrow elastic, rather than one very wide elastic which may be stiff and uncomfortable (*Fig. 44*). You are then free to decide the exact finished depth of the waistband, rather than being dependent on cutting to the widths of available elastic.

If a drawstring is to be inserted, mark the positions for the two openings equal distances from the CF. Occasionally, one single opening is sufficient, positioned exactly on the CF, unless the design calls for an alternative placement (*Fig. 45*). The drawstring itself may be cut straight to pass around the waist but each end may be shaped, depending on the type of bow you wish to tie. The skirt will sit far more comfortably around the waist and the gathers remain more evenly in position if the main part of the waist casing is threaded with an elastic and the ties stitched securely to each end of the elastic. Make sure that the ties are cut long enough and the elastic

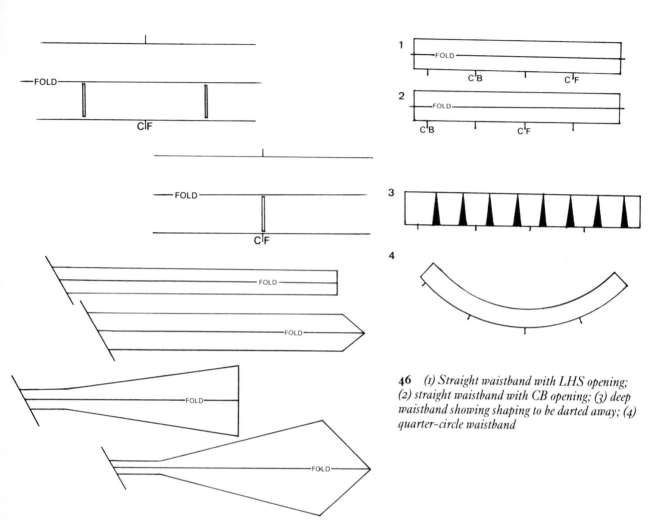

46 (1) Straight waistband with LHS opening; (2) straight waistband with CB opening; (3) deep waistband showing shaping to be darted away; (4) quarter-circle waistband

45 *Suggested positionings for opening(s) on casing and drawstring end shapings*

short enough so that, as the elastic is pulled, it still remains totally encased and will not peep out and show at the openings in the casing.

Waistbands

The majority of waistbands are cut as a straight strip of fabric of waist measurement exactly, plus a wrap allowance for fastening. A foldline runs along the top edge of the waistband where it is doubled over and finished either on the RS or WS. If the fabric is too bulky for this, then a narrow seam allowance will be added to the foldline so that a lighter-weight fabric can be used as a 'backing' for the inside of the

waistband. 5–6 cm (2–2¼ in.) finished depth is the most that can be worn in comfort. Where any styling may be incorporated into the waistband it will have a functional purpose as well as being a feature of the design. The waist level is always the place from which to begin. On a standard, straight waistband, the lower edge – i.e. the seamline at the top of the skirt – is the area that should sit exactly on the natural waist level. Where a deeper waistband is to be cut, which also sits with its lower edge on the waist, some shaping should be included, so that the band will remain in place when worn and will not roll down on itself. The top edge should have a longer measurement than the lower edge, which always remains at exactly waist measurement. One way to achieve this is to cut a straight strip at the larger measurement: measure around your body at the height to which the waistband will come; now divide up the difference in measurements and distribute this evenly in darts. A minimum of eight darts should be placed all around the waist, otherwise the resulting shape will be too angular. Stitch or fold the darts away, depending on whether you are using fabric or paper. The angles formed at each dart can then be smoothed out so that a respectable curve can be cut.

If a waistband is to lie partly above and partly below the waist level, shaping of a similar sort will be necessary. Two curved sections can be formed, as already described, and then joined with a horizontal dart or seam. This will result in a seamline around waist level, which may defeat the purpose of styling such a waistband. The alternative is to include vertical darts, evenly spaced around the waistband, the exact size depending on the difference required between the top edge, lower edge and waist measurements. You may well seek alternative methods of introducing the shaping necessary to each specific design.

Waistbands that sit below the waist – i.e. with their top edge intended at waist level – must also be cut on a curve. In some cases a circular cut can be used. All waistbands that are cut with shaping will need to have a seam running around the top edge and the inside of the waistband cut exactly the same size as the outside. There is no reason why, if a fabric strip is used to dart away the excess length to give the correct shaping, this itself cannot be used on the inside, as the darts will not show.

Hip yokes

The skirt styling may specifically include a fitted yoke at the top, with the main part of the skirt falling from the yoke seam instead of the waist seam. The yoke may be plain or shaped and differ from front to back. The level of the yoke and the type of skirt attached to it will give the garment its silhouette. These two points can each vary considerably, so be careful to decide on measurements of both depth and fabric width that will not be unflattering to wear and that have good proportions, so that a pleasing visual balance is created (*Fig. 47*). The yoke is almost always well-fitting, and this means ensuring that the shaping is correct at the waist and at the side seam, over the hip. Mark in the waist level, the lower level of the yoke and the corresponding body measurements perpendicular to the CF. Draw a line between the two, about half-way between the CF and the side seam. Divide the difference between the two measurements (*A*) in half and mark this amount either side of the half-way line at waist level. This gives the amount to be darted away to give the waist

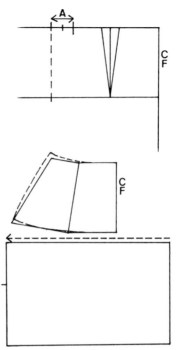

47 *Separating skirt to cut hip yoke*

shaping but, before you mark in the curve, raise the waist point at the side seam 1–1.5 cm ($\frac{3}{8}$–$\frac{5}{8}$ in.). Now mark in the waist shaping and hip shaping as shown. The sideseam will begin in a straight line as it comes from the lower edge of the yoke at right angles and curve gradually up to meet the raised waist point, again at right angles. The back waist and side-seam shaping should be cut to match. The skirt is cut according to style, and the important measurement to work from is the length of the seam at the lower edge of the yoke. Remember that where the seam is cut with shaping, such as when flare has been added to the side seams, or a circular-cut skirt is to be attached (an extreme example of a shaped seam), the hem length must remain equal at the CF, at every vertical seam and at every other point in between, so that a level hemline results when the garment is made up.

The yoke should be cut with a matching backing which may be of the same material or a contrast lining fabric. The total area of yoke is thus of double fabric, giving it added strength and stability. A waistband may, or may not, be added. Often skirts with yokes do not have a waistband attached, as the backing serves as a facing, leaving the top edge of the yoke sitting at waist level with a neat finish. The seam around the waist should always be held firmly in shape by the addition of a stay tape, hidden inside the seam.

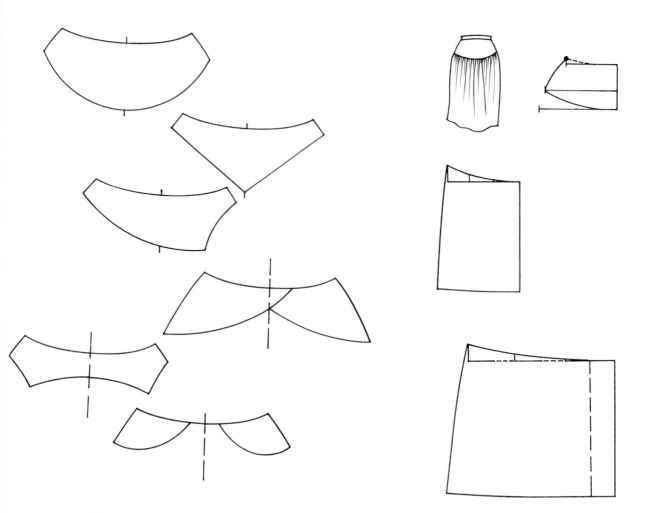

48 *Hip yokes: variations in design*

49 *Shaped hip yoke and gathered skirt*

The lower edge of the yoke may be shaped according to design and need not necessarily be cut symmetrically about the centre lines (*Fig. 48*). The waist and side seams will still require the shaping necessary for a good fit. Draw a straight line to indicate the lower level width from the depth of the yoke at the side seam, when cutting the correct shaping that the skirt must have. Follow the instructions given for spreading a gathered bodice on to a yoke (*see p. 68*), as the principles are exactly the same (*Fig. 49*). When you are cutting a shaped yoke, remember that, although the fabric is cut flat, it assumes three dimensions on the body. Concentrate on the central area of the body, from the CF to a little more than half-way to the side seam; from roughly half-way to the side seam, the shaping need not be quite so pronounced, as the yoke will curve away over the hip to the side seam.

Panel seams

Any basic skirt shape can be divided up into a series of panels, which are almost always evenly spaced around the skirt (*Fig. 50*). There is, however, no point in doing this unless there is a specific reason for introducing more vertical seamlines. Never place a seam in a garment without a very good reason for doing so. The reasons for cutting a panelled skirt are as follows:

To achieve a specific skirt silhouette

By adding flare in varying degrees, and shaping the seams so that the flare begins at particular levels, a wide variety of appearances can be achieved. These are known as 'gored' skirts. Basic rules concerning the addition of flare are covered in the direct measurement section on flared skirts (*see p. 43*).

For the insertion of further fabric

This may either be for decorative purposes or to give a particular silhouette, or both. Godets are an obvious example, where a circular-cut section of fabric is inserted into the seam at the hem area, to give an extremely flounced effect. The size of the godet can vary considerably and depends on the fabric being used and the desired silhouette. The seam is left open below a certain level and the godet inserted into the triangular space formed as the remainder of the seam is separated.

One of the main features of the design may be that each panel is to be cut from different fabric or a single contrast fabric introduced. If different fabrics are not used, then particular effects may be achieved by cutting each panel in a varying direction and combining straight-cut, crossway-cut and cross-grain-cut sections.

The only other excuses for introducing seams are where there is insufficient fabric width, or the lay is tight due to short fabric length.

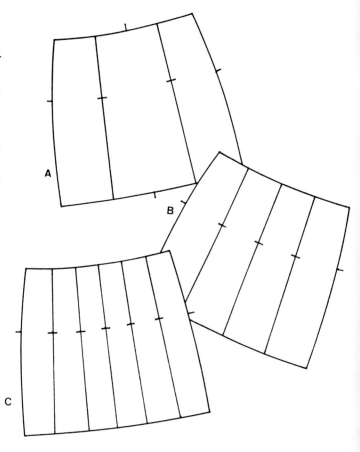

50   *Skirt front divided up for (A) six-panelled skirt; (B) eight-panelled skirt; (C) twelve-panelled skirt*

Tiers

Tiered skirts are divided up by horizontal seams and, while a basic skirt shape can be cut into sections for decorative reasons, a tiered skirt will often be chosen because of the possibilities the silhouette offers. A simply cut tiered skirt will consist of a top section gathered or pleated into the waistband, and subsequent sections, each gathered or pleated on to the lower edge of the previous section. The total number of sections into which the skirt length is divided, the individual measurements of the depth of each section and the amount of fullness to increase each section must all be chosen with careful attention to the proportions they will create (*Fig. 51*). Always check there is plenty of width on the lower edges – i.e. when deciding on the width of each section, consider the level on the body at which the lower seam will lie. This is especially important where

seams are to lie around the hip and thigh areas: any stress placed on a seam when walking or sitting will cause an unsightly bulge in the line of the silhouette as the section above puffs out. Proportions where each section increases in depth down to the eventual hemline are more pleasing to the eye, and it is worth remembering this, even when it may not be the visual intention. If equal depth tiers are intended in the design, still cut each section 1 cm (⅜ in.) deeper than the last and the appearance of the finished garment will look that much better for it.

Pleats

Skirts that are pleated all around must be cut with careful thought and attention. There is nothing difficult to understand about pleats but one or two may be easier to cope with at a time than 24. The most important thing is to chose a suitable fabric:

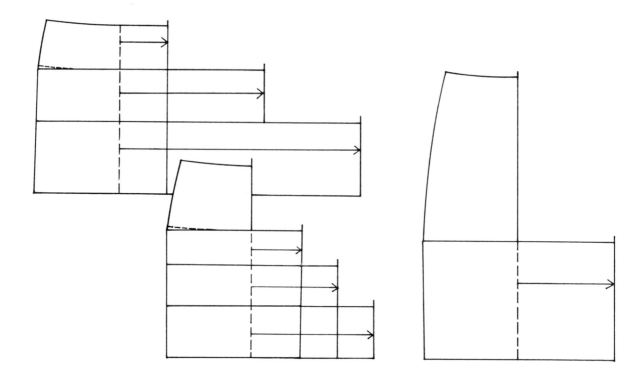

51 *Examples of tiered skirts*

52 *Pleats: (A) knife pleat; (B) inverted pleat; (C) box pleat*

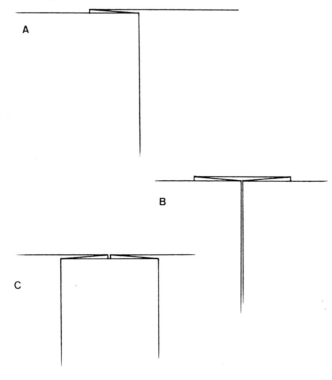

usually a medium-weight or medium/heavy-weight fabric with a reasonably firm weave is needed. While it must certainly not crumple easily, it must 'hold' a crease. This is not, by any means, the same thing. The crinkles and creases of everyday wear should readily drop out, but the application of heat and maybe a little steam should give a definite 'edge', though not necessarily a crisp edge, to the foldlines of each pleat. The fabric should remain as pressed throughout the wear of the skirt and ideally only require re-pressing occasionally.

The knife pleat (*Fig. 52A*), inverted pleat (*Fig. 52B*) and the box pleat (*Fig. 52C*) are the classic types of pleat. The two latter pleats consist of two knife pleats, the inverted pleat being formed by the knife pleats folded together so they touch edge to edge, and the box pleat, where they lie in opposite directions, but away from each other. The WS of an inverted pleat forms a box pleat, and vice versa.

The same basics concerning fabric width apply as given for unpressed pleats, which is that three times the finished width must be allowed for each pleat.

Mark in the waist level and the level to which the pleats are to be stitched at the appropriate width, although this is usually at about hip level (*Fig. 53*). Below this, lines can be marked up, with the side seam parallel to the CF, and the approximate hemline indicated. Now divide this area up with parallel lines indicating the position of the foldline of

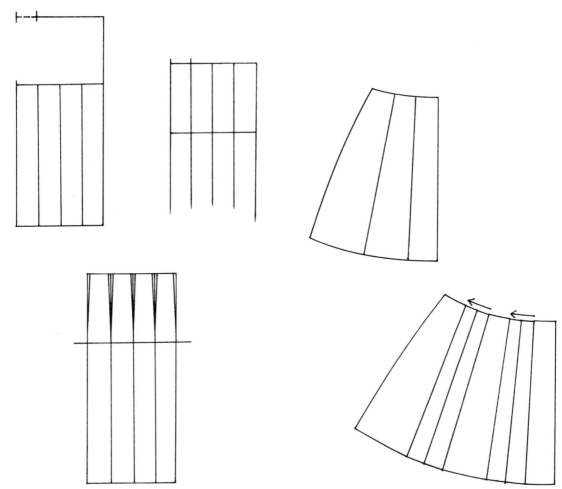

53 *Waist shaping included in cut of pleats*

54 *Example of flared pleats*

each pleat. Extend these lines up to waist level. Divide up the difference between the body measurement at the level up to which the pleats are to be stitched and the waist measurement, so that it can then be equally distributed at each pleat as shown. Here is one of the advantages of using metric measurements, as millimetres are easier to work with than tiny fractions of an inch. This will give a skirt with the hip shaping incorporated in the pleats. The pleat allowance can then be inserted at each pleat position marked in on the straight section of the skirt.

If a basic skirt pattern is not to have very many pleats, then the shaping that already exists in the cut of the skirt will suffice for the purposes of achieving the correct fit. The position of the foldlines of each pleat can then be marked exactly as intended on the finished garment. The allowance of extra fabric

width required for each pleat is then inserted. Pleats can just as easily be added to flared skirts, where the pleat allowance is also cut wider at the hem than at the waist. An example of this shows the importance of cutting good proportions (*Fig. 54*).

Bulk that is formed by the pleat allowances at the top area of the skirt can be cut away as much as is possible (*Fig. 55*). The pleat allowances must then be top-stitched to hold them in position, as they are no longer supported on the inside of the skirt by being caught into the waist seam.

It is advisable to work with a paper pattern. Always fold the paper down the foldlines of each pleat, so that you can check that the shape of the skirt is correct. Where seams are required to join in more fabric, position them so they lie along the fold edge of the WS of a pleat.

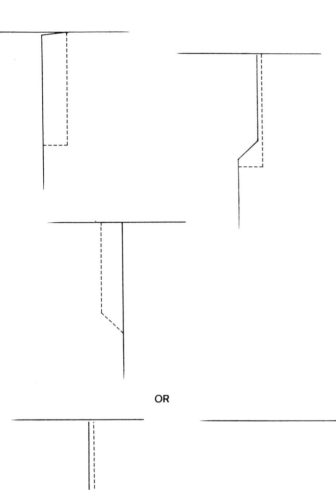

OR

55 *Cut-away pleat allowances with two methods of supporting the pleat: top-stitching or half-lining*

BODICES

Any basic bodice shape can be divided into further sections. The dividing lines that are marked in represent futher seamlines. Once the dividing lines have been marked in position, certain areas may already represent a finished pattern shape that is ready to be cut. Other sections will require further alteration before the finished shape that can be cut from the fabric is reached. Remember that there should always be a good reason for a seam.

Addition of fullness

The garment can be cut with extra width which is to be gathered away into a seam. The amount of fullness can be thought of as a simple measurement of width, but the seamlines are rarely cut without shaping of some kind. Where extra width is inserted, the cut edge must, therefore, be shaped so that, when the fabric is gathered up along that edge, it will follow the correct seamline.

As an example, the correct shaping is given to a seam that is to be gathered up on to a rounded yoke (*Fig. 56*). The shape of the curve of the yoke is the most important shape from which to work. Mark the area into which you wish the gathers to be stitched; in this example, the gathers are not required across the CF area. Now, working with the main garment piece and starting at the CF, mark the curve to match the yoke, until the first mark indicating where the gathers are to begin is reached. Note the height or level of this point, imagining a straight line running at right angles from the CF line. Return to the yoke and, with the same idea, imagine two lines, one through each mark. Measure the distance (parallel to the CF) between these two imaginary lines (*A*). This will give you a measurement that indicates the height of the rise. No matter how little or how much extra width is included in this area for gathers, this height must remain constant. As average gathers are required in this case, twice the length indicated on the yoke will give the amount of fabric to be added to the width. Go back to the point reached on the main garment piece and move up, parallel to the CF line, for the necessary rise, and then across, as if following a grid line, for the required width. From this point, the remainder of the curve is shaped to match the remainder of the yoke curve. A gradual curve, which indicates the gathering line, can then be cut, joining the two sections of seamline.

If a more complicated yoke, or any other shape, is to be cut work with several imaginary 'grid' lines placed at relevant positions and mark across and up,

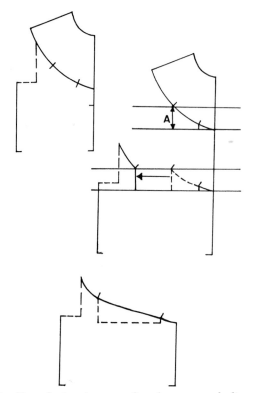

section by section, so that you will have several points through which the gathering line must pass to give the correct finished seamline shape (*Fig. 57*).

Reference to the sections on gathered skirts will provide some suggestions that may help you to decide the extra width to give the sort of gathers you want.

Extra fullness may also be pleated away into a seam, with due regard to the shaping. The same comments apply as for unpressed pleats on skirts (*see p. 60*). If there is no seam for the pleats to be stitched into, the excess fabric can be stitched away, forming tucks. The fullness is released at the level where the stitching ends, so this is, obviously, easily adjustable. To position the tucks, simply insert the width required where shown. Shaping at the seamline can be cut by folding away the tucks as they are to be finished. Be careful that the tucks lie parallel to each other and are spaced at the correct intervals. Imagine where they are to lie on the body. They may be placed at equal intervals across the garment or be positioned in groups, according to design. Mark the points that indicate the stitching line of each tuck accurately with balance marks. Always leave the width of at least one finished tuck between each tuck, or an overlap will occur on the WS, resulting in six layers of fabric at each area of overlap. This is why it

56 *Transferring the curve of a yoke seam to a bodice widened for gathering*

57 *More complicated seam shape illustrating the same principle shown in Fig. 56*

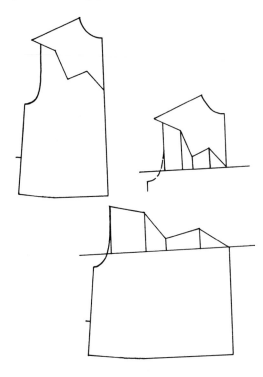

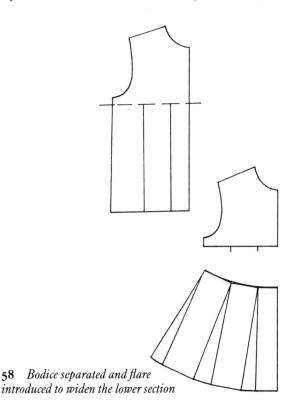

58 *Bodice separated and flare introduced to widen the lower section*

is so important to consider the construction in detail at every stage of the cut.

The shape of the garment, or part of it, may need altering to include more fullness, without necessarily introducing gathers or pleats. Here, flare may be added instead (*Fig. 58*). Mark vertical lines to indicate where the extra width is to be introduced. These lines are then cut along to separate the sections which are spaced out as required. A horizontal line or lines can also be marked in, perpendicular to the CF, so that, as the separated sections are 'spread' apart, the correct level of each section can be maintained. The new seamlines can then be marked accordingly.

Inclusion of suppression in a seam

Certain seams may be cut to give a simply cut garment some three-dimensional shape. Whilst a good seamline for a more fitted garment could not necessarily be achieved, a more sophisticated cut can be given to a simply shaped pattern. The illustrated examples (*Fig. 59*) show various divisions of a basic bodice shape and suggest the minor alterations necessary to improve the cut. All of these alterations are based on the inclusion of suppression in the seam and can be traced back to the theory of flat pattern cutting (*see p. 53*).

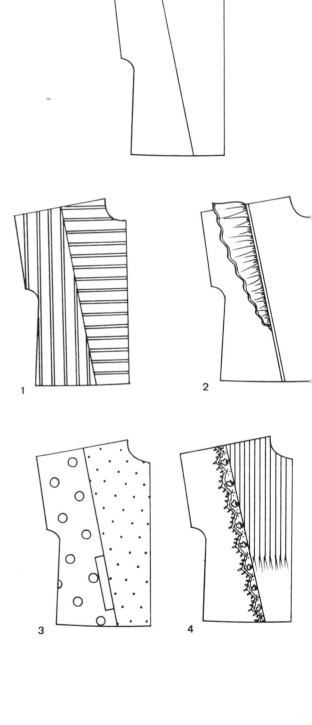

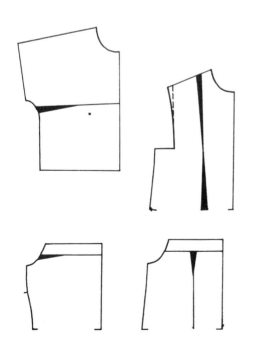

59 *Ways of improving cut by introducing a small amount of suppression into the seam*

60 *One example from Fig. 38 showing a variety of possible reasons for the positioning of a vertical style line*

Other reasons for style lines

Any other reasons for including separating seamlines will be for detailing and decoration (*Fig. 60*): contrast fabric may be used for one area, or a contrast effect achieved by altering the direction of the cut of the fabric; piping, binding, ruffles or lace may be inserted into a seam or, more practically, a pocket; top-stitching may be included as a specific design feature; sections of the garment may need quilting or tucking, both being decorative and possibly function-al as well. In cases where decorations are to be inserted into a straight seam, it may be possible to allow for a tuck in the fabric, rather than separate two sections completely. An advantage of this is that there will be no raw edges on the WS that require neatening, as a seam will have been avoided com-pletely and the raw edges of the insertion enclosed in the fold of the tuck. Also avoid extra seams where possible by considering means of application and 'binding on' (*see p. 134*).

In many cases, each seam that results in the dividing up of a basic garment shape will serve multiple purposes. It may incorporate unpressed pleats, a little bust suppression and have a gathered lace insert. Every design will have its own special requirements. Relate all the styling you include in the cut of the garment to the body at all times, remembering that the finished garment is three-dimensional.

Sleeve styling

The practical considerations of fit and sleeve shape have been covered in detail already (*see pp. 47–51*). Follow these principles carefully when you cut a sleeve and armhole shape without the help of a proven pattern. Fig. 61 shows a variety of possible sleeve/armhole seams. Whatever styling might be included (*Fig. 62*), always consider the front and back areas of the sleeve to ensure the balance is retained about the centre line. The best way to keep the balance of a sleeve correct is to work from the cross formed on the initial measurement grid. Keep the width line, which passes through the under-arm point and centre line at right angles, and the under-arm seam shaped so that both sides match and will not distort the width line 'off level' when the under-arm seam is stitched. Trying to cheat by keeping the width line level when the sleeve has been cut incorrectly is pointless as the sleeve itself will twist and be impossible to wear. The width line needs only to be out by a small amount to affect the hang of the sleeve adversely. If flare has been introduced into the shaping of the sleeve, great care must be taken to ensure that an equal amount is added to the front

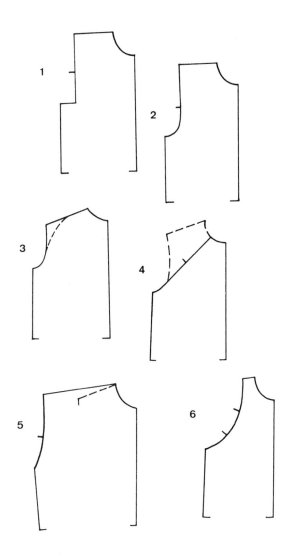

61 *Armhole shapings: (1) square, lowered armhole; (2) rounded, lowered armhole, (3) high raglan (square or rounded); (4) low raglan; (5) dropped shoulder; (6) cut-away armhole*

half and the back half, so that twisting is avoided.

When shaping sleeve-heads, remember that the back of the sleeve is usually more fully shaped than the front. At the under-arm area, the back is less cut away than the front. The quarter lines of the sleeve serve to divide the total width of the sleeve-head area and, when the sleeve is folded down its centre line, the difference in shaping between front and back becomes apparent.

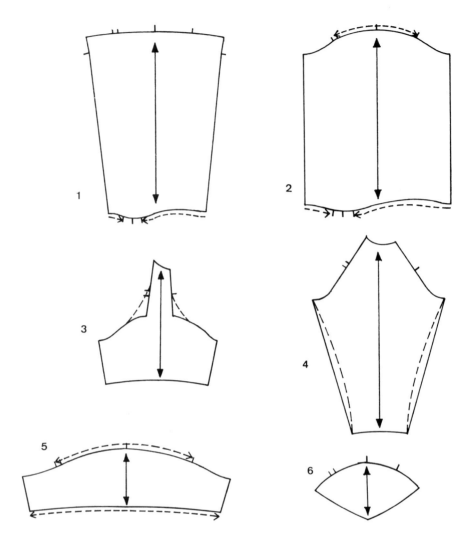

62 *Suggested sleeve stylings for the armholes in Fig. 61*

Extra fullness can be incorporated into the sleeve in several ways. If you are not sufficiently familiar with the shaping required by a sleeve-head to have the confidence to judge a cut so that it gives what is needed, then cut up the centre and quarter lines and separate the resultant sleeve sections to incorporate extra width as required. Join the new sleeve-head shaping with a smooth curve (*Fig. 63*). As well as the addition of extra width, an allowance in extra height (which is at its greatest at the shoulder or centre line) will increase the volume of fabric, and is vital if gathers are to be placed around the sleeve head for a puffed effect. The greater the extra height allowed, the more pronounced the silhouette of the sleeve will be.

If a raglan-type style line has been positioned, this may run into the neck edge or at some point along the shoulder seam. If the neck edge forms the top edge of the sleeve, the back shaping will vary considerably from the front. The addition of under-arm shaping as previously described should always be included in a raglan-sleeve seam as well as the corresponding under-arm shaping on the bodice. If the under-arm point on the basic garment shape is left square, mark in the raglan to the corner. Now add the same length to the side seam as to the under-arm seam and gradually shape the new seamline to run into the original.

So long as the most important rule of balancing the sleeve is observed, any methods of shaping can be applied to the sleeve in the same way as for other areas of a garment.

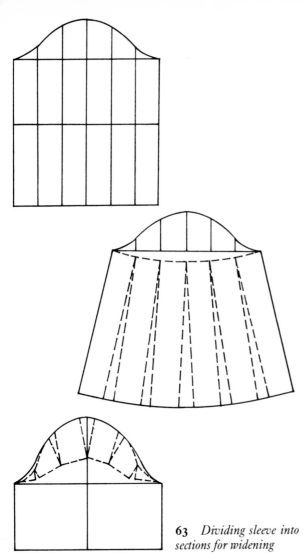

63 *Dividing sleeve into sections for widening*

FURTHER SUGGESTIONS

The three main body areas have been discussed and possibilities for styling suggested for skirts, bodices and sleeves. General hints for certain garment groups follow.

Skirts

Skirts may need to be lined if the fabric is loosely woven and allows daylight to show through. Lining can also be included for extra warmth, or to allow for comfort in a garment made from coarse fabric or one that might cling to the legs in an uncomfortable and unattractive way. It also prevents creasing and will help to keep a fitted skirt from 'seating' at the back. Lining helps to prolong the life of a skirt. It need not

be cut in the same way as the skirt so long as it meets all the requirements of fit. If necessary, and where possible, a simpler cut will be satisfactory for the lining. Splits can be left in the centre or side seams, so there is plenty of room to walk and sit in comfort. Avoid extra bulk around the waist using as few pleats and darts as possible.

The waistband will need stiffening with petersham or interlining of some sort, which is cut to the finished length of the waistband, wrap included. It is also useful to keep some narrow tape, so that hangers can be cut and positioned at the side seams.

Tops

The information on bodices should enable shirts, blouses and tops to be cut. Never forget to allow for necessary openings. This may sound absurdly obvious, but it is all too easy to become so involved with design ideas that the most obvious practical points can be forgotten. Interfacings may be necessary for certain areas of the garment discussed under 'Detailing' (*see p. 79*). Simplicity of cut, adequate width and allowance for length are the most important points to remember, as well as taking care with the armhole/sleeve-head area.

Dresses

If there is insufficient allowance for movement at the waist, a dress will be uncomfortable and movement will be restricted. A dress that hangs loosely will lift at the hem, especially at the side seams. Where a loose-fitting dress is cut with the intention of wearing it belted, it is advisable to add some method of controlling the fullness, such as an elastic stitched in at the correct waist position. The fullness will then be evenly distributed and the hemline and waist level (which will determine the amount of blousing in the bodice) remain in their correct positions. The belt itself will cover the stitching.

Summer dresses

Summer dresses will usually need careful attention to the top half of the bodice. Bands under the arms and around the chest should fit comfortably. Short sleeves and cap sleeves should be considered from the side view as the arm moves, with enough cover to avoid a free-for-all peep show but, at the same time, with a reasonably lowered armhole for comfort and coolness. Fine cotton linings are the most comfortable, where a light-weight fabric that is sheer enough to require lining is used. Design with simple construction as a priority, so that the finish on the inside of the garment will be neat and uncomplicated and the garment will stand repeated laundering.

Evening dresses

Evening clothes are often made of such stunning fabric that fussy design and complicated cut are best avoided. Proportion is important as much party time is spent standing. Comfort and ease does not mean boring or dreary clothing. Excellent fit should be top priority, so that you can feel relaxed and as unselfconscious as when wearing an informal dress.

Over-dresses (pinafore dresses)

These garments will ideally be designed and cut together with the garment that is to be worn underneath, whether this is a blouse or shirt, knitwear or a special under-dress. Work with an extra allowance added to the body measurements, so that a comfortable fit is achieved, especially around the bust and at the under-arms. Lower the under-arm point considerably so that deep-cut sleeves can be accommodated beneath, where required. The bodice may even be without side seams. If the garment can be cut without the need for an opening and fastening, so much the better, unless a specific feature is to be made of the fastening.

Maternity dresses

Disguise and comfort are the important points to consider when designing maternity dresses, not to try and conceal the fact of pregnancy, but to avoid the tummy being the focal point of attention. Cut with plenty of extra width, enough to accommodate triplets quite happily, as the average bump will then appear diminished. If you choose 'fluid' fabrics for wide-cut clothes, you will avoid an impression of vastness, so choose soft fabrics that gather away fullness beautifully. Avoid completely plain fabrics as you would those with enormous or busy prints. Cut comfortable sleeves so that you can lie down to rest during the day and be able to relax properly. If adequate garment width is cut, problems of a raised hemline at the centre front are avoided. If the style requires an allowance of extra length in the front of the dress, rather than cut a shaped and drooping hemline, incorporate the shaping in an upward curve at the top of the dress, where there is a horizontal seam to make this possible.

Nightwear

When cutting nightwear, allow for ease of movement. Sleeves must be loose enough to move, unrestricted, up the arm. Take care that the garment is not uncomfortable when lying down. Plenty of width will help prevent the garment riding up. Avoid using buttons for fastening wherever possible, but, if you must, use small, flat ones.

Jackets/coats

The suggestions given for bodices can be applied to the cut of jackets, coats, capes and other outer wear. Classic, tailored jackets and coats, however, need more specialist knowledge. Tailoring will not be covered in this book and is a subject not to be confused with dressmaking at any time. There still remains a wide variety of exciting and original design ideas that can be applied to outer-wear that range from the flamboyant to the extremely simple and straightforward. These garments may be cut unlined or the lining itself may enhance the garment design. Work from measurements taken over the kind of clothes you will wear underneath. Summer jackets should be loose and medium/light-weight and only require a relatively lowered armhole. The sleeves may be cut loosely and wide enough to be easily rolled up if you so wish. Medium-weight fabrics, again, need no special allowances other than the obvious considerations of fit. Heavy, winter-weight fabrics will need a much greater allowance, especially at the under-arm and sleeve width for comfort of wear. A fabric which might otherwise be difficult to wear can be improved greatly by the addition of a smooth lining, which is why satin linings are so often used in heavy wool coats. Joining very simple shapes to fall loosely from the shoulders, wrap around the body or anchor at the waist, for example, should be tried. Marvellous coat/cape combination garments can be made from the most basic of shapes that are far less complicated to construct than the average blouse.

Trousers

As it is the fit that causes most problems with trousers, follow the directions carefully and take accurate measurements. Waistbands should be cut with a stiffening as for skirt waistbands. Tapes for hangers may be required. Pockets are often included, so cut the bags in a light-weight fabric to avoid excess bulk, and avoid them in close fitting trousers. The greatest strain always occurs at the base of the opening, so be certain that there is enough length to allow for easy removal and putting on of the garment.

CHAPTER EIGHT

Detailing

The detailing of a design is most likely to individualise the garment and cause comment. It will rarely affect the main cut or styling of a garment. The design possibilities are enormous and functional details can also incorporate decoration. The suggestions given have been grouped into garment areas with no specific reference to any particular garment. You may have worked to achieve a blouse cut with a perfect fit and added simple styling to suit you. By using different fabrics you may cut several basic blouses in exactly the same way and, by altering the details, have a wide choice of garments (*Fig. 64*). I hope that the particular examples given will introduce ideas that you can develop. It is worth spending some time experimenting, and this should not present problems as such small areas of fabric are usually involved. Use construction methods to suit the fabric, find the best way to make up the desired effect easily. Try adding your own detailing to garments where you already have a pattern, maybe taken from an existing garment, or cutting the main garment pieces from a successful commercial pattern.

CROSSWAY-CUT FABRIC

At certain times it will be necessary to know how to cut fabric correctly on the cross and, in other cases, you will choose to use crossway-cut fabric either for its draping qualities or for the pattern effect.

In any woven fabric the warp (lengthwise) threads and the weft (widthwise) threads cross at right angles to each other, unless this has been distorted and the fabric is faulty. The warp threads are always the strongest and most rigid and the weft threads vary in the amount of 'give' they have, depending on the yarn, fibre and type of weave. The true cross runs at a 45° angle to the warp and weft (*Fig. 65*), and this line of the fabric will have considerably more stretch. Whether you intend to cut strips of fabric for using as binding or piping, or a complete pattern piece such as a collar on the cross, it is important that the angle of cut across the weave is accurate. If this is ignored, the fabric will be difficult to control when making up and, no matter how much care is taken, it will pucker, twist and wrinkle. It is well worth persevering; the more fabric you cut on the cross, the easier it becomes to cut with perfection.

Your eye will also become accustomed to following the line of the woven threads. Measure down the warp and then follow the weft across at right angles for an equal distance. The first and last point, when joined, should then indicate the true cross (*Fig. 66*). It may be convenient to fold back a corner of fabric at the correct angle. Here, the warp threads will run in exactly the same direction as the weft threads lying beneath, as do the weft threads that lie above the warp threads beneath. If you press a crease along this foldline to mark the line of cross, always run the iron in the direction of either the warp or weft. Do not pass the iron over the fabric in the direction of the cross as it is extremely easy to stretch and distort the fabric. In certain fabrics, the cross is far less manageable than in others, but, whenever you cut a fabric in this way, it is important to handle it carefully. Fabric may be accurately cut on the cross but, if it is stretched or distorted in any way, the shape of pattern piece or width of binding will be altered. Avoid this by always checking the position of the warp and weft threads immediately before and as you cut the fabric. Smooth the fabric out in these directions only and, if it is slightly distorted, correct this by pulling gently on the fabric in warp or weft directions only. You may find it easier and more effective to do this with your fingernails (facing down towards the fabric so that you do not 'claw' at it) as your fingertips may cling a little and pull the fabric too far in some areas. Alternatively, you may prefer gently to run the edge of a clean, plastic ruler in each direction. Treat the fabric delicately and watch the

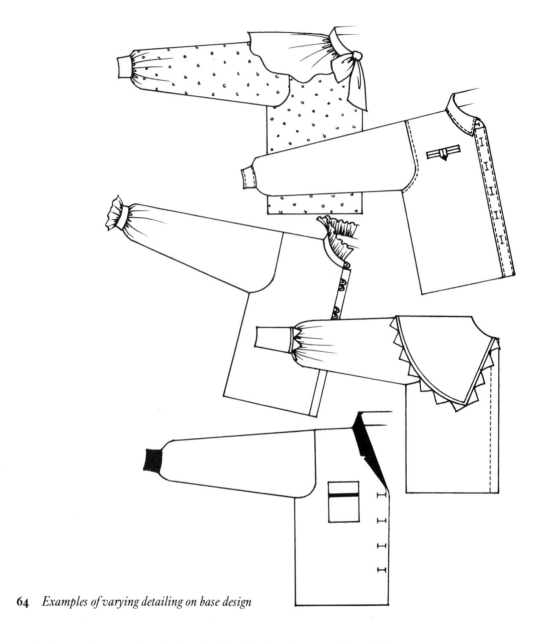

64 *Examples of varying detailing on base design*

angle between warp and weft threads. The blades of your shears should be as sharp as possible so that you can cut smoothly and effortlessly to avoid distortion. Cut exactly straight ahead so that the blades do not pull the fabric out of position. Fine, floaty fabrics that refuse to stay put may be placed on or between tissue paper and cut through together with the paper. The pushing pressure of the blades as they begin to cut is then absorbed by the paper and does not distort the fabric.

Cutting on the cross can use up surprisingly large quantities of fabric, so always take this into account. If pattern pieces have been cut on the cross for purposes of appearance only, then cut any backing on the straight grain so that the top piece can be supported and held firmly in position by the under piece. Cut and join a separate piece rather than cut any crossway piece with a foldline. Where a large amount of crossway strips are to be cut for binding, cut as long a length as the fabric will allow. If this is uneconomical, join wide crossway strips first, before cutting up into narrower strips, so that one seam

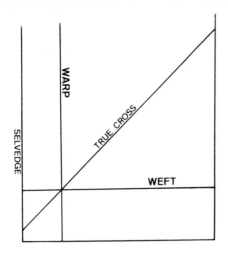

65 *Construction of a plain weave fabric*

66 *Marking fabric to cut crossway strips*

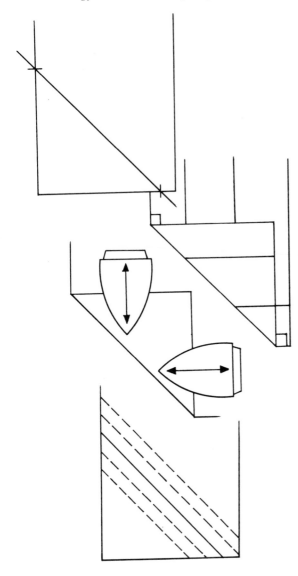

does the work of several little seams. Instructions for joining crossway are given on p. 132.

OPENINGS

All but the simplest and loosest garments require openings. The neck must allow the head to pass through, the cuff must open enough for the hand, and so on. These openings almost always include some method of fastening. The type of fastening to be used will determine the way the opening is to be cut and must be decided in detail before cutting. An opening may be incorporated in the seam of a garment, or be cut into the fabric as a straight slit, where the raw edges must then be finished off in some way. Alternatively, the garment opens out completely, leaving raw edges to be finished off and often the need for extra width to form a wrap-over. Where garments do not open out completely, correct length of opening is important so that the garment can be taken off with ease. Unreasonable strain should not be placed on the base of the opening and the finished length should never be much more than necessary, unless some kind of decoration is included or the design requires a particular visual effect.

Where a zip is to be inserted into a seam, a normal 1.3 cm ($\frac{5}{8}$ in.) seam allowance is required. Mark to indicate the position of the base of the zip stop with a nip. If a slit is cut into the fabric, some extra fabric must be cut to finish this off. A small area of fabric can be cut to form a facing that surrounds the slit and lies on the WS. A continuous strip of fabric may be cut to enclose the raw edges as a binding and this is folded to the WS. A placket, such as that used on shirt-sleeve openings, may be cut to attach to one side of the slit, the other raw edge being turned under and neatened. All these are suitable for smaller openings.

Larger openings incorporated into seams must have some allowance made for an area of wrap-over, as an edge to edge finish is likely to gape between the points of fastening. Openings that lie at the side seams tend to have a facing attached to the back edge that lies underneath. Openings that lie at the CF or CB tend to be symmetrical about the centre line with the same amount of wrap added to each side. Always work with the original seam line or slit line as a base. Whatever methods of facing, placketing or neatening you choose, remember that these edges must come exactly together in their original position when the opening is fastened. Centrally placed openings often incorporate a facing which may be extended to include a neck facing. Openings that are positioned

77

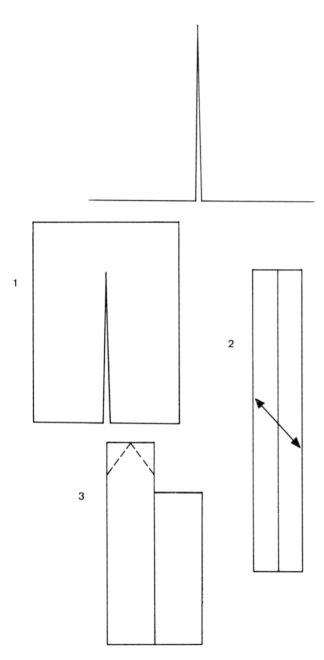

67 *Finishing slit in fabric with (1) facing; (2) continuous strip; (3) placket*

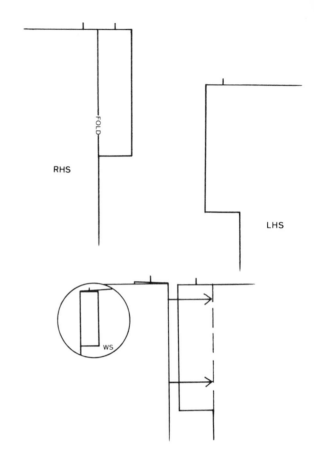

68 *Opening in seam with extension cut*

where a seam would otherwise be may have extensions added to the cut of the main garment piece to avoid unnecessary seaming (*Fig. 68*). Foldlines may well be incorporated where the extension is folded at the edge of the wrap allowed to the WS, or an interfacing is enclosed (*see p. 154*).

Where a button fastening is to be used, work with a few basic general rules as guidelines (*Fig. 69*). The button sits centrally on the seam or centre line from which you work. To this line add a minimum of the total width of the button for the wrap. This means that half the button width will extend beyond the edge of the button to the fold edge of the wrap, as the button sits in its correct position, whatever the size of the button. The wrap edge will most probably be cut as a foldline, to which a facing will be added. If the buttons sit on a band, again work from the centre line on which the buttons sit, so that an equal width is added to each side of the button. Remember that the buttonhole is made on the top wrap and the buttons stitched to the under-wrap. Areas of opening may be designed so they are as inconspicuous as possible or stylish, incorporating clever design features (*Fig. 70*).

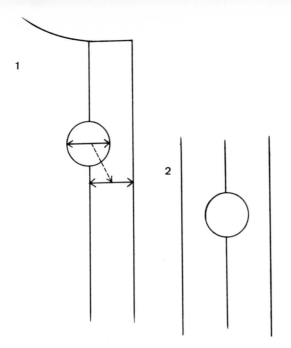

FACINGS

A facing is an area of fabric that is either cut in one with the main piece, or cut separately and joined to a raw edge that requires neatening, and then turned, usually to the WS, to give an area of double fabric. This, with the addition of a suitable interfacing, gives the area greater stability, increasing considerably the strength and durability of the garment. It provides a sufficiently firm base for sewing buttons and button-holes, or for taking top-stitching. The appearance of the garment is also improved, so long as the facing is cut well and the correct interfacing has been chosen.

The facing is cut to match the raw edge to which it is to be joined (*Fig. 71*) and kept at an even width from this edge. The finished width is generally about 6 cm (2¼ in.). Where the line of the seam may change direction sharply, as at a corner, the outside edge of

69 *Principle of wrap allowances for button fastenings: (1) fold edge; (2) button band*

70 *Examples of openings: (1) facing with ties; (2) loop applied; (3) button/loop fastening at faced opening; (4) extended facing; (5) centrally placed zip in dart at lower edge of sleeve; (6) placket opening with detachable jabot*

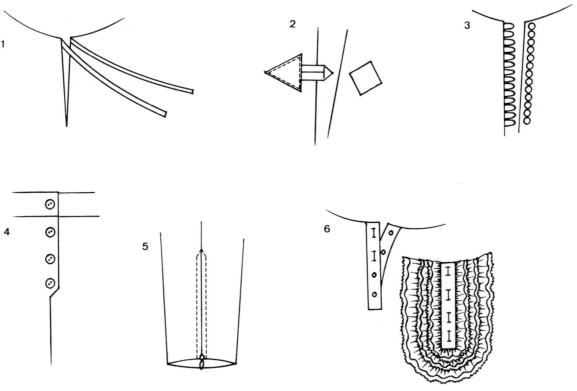

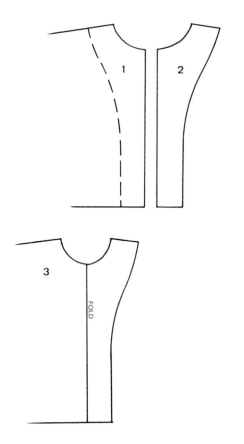

71 *Front facing: (1) area of bodice to be faced; (2) facing cut separately; (3) facing cut in one with bodice*

the facing takes the line of an extremely smooth and gradual curve; a sharp edge would be far more apparent, disturbing the fall of the top fabric and making the facing obvious from the RS.

Consider the following points: the general cut of the garment and the weight and type of fabric; any specific purpose the facing may have in addition to those previously mentioned; the particular area of garment that is to be faced; any sensible action that should be taken to avoid possible conflict with another area of the garment, such as where multiple thicknesses of fabric might occur; considerations that might depend on top-stitching or other feature that the facing might assist. Having taken these points into account, do not cut the facing so narrow that it continually flaps out of place and shows on the RS, or so unnecessarily wide that excessive bulk will give an unpleasant appearance to the RS. Remember that a facing that has no top-stitching and that is intended to be invisible from the RS can only be anchored on

the WS where convenient seam allowances are positioned.

Alternative construction methods may avoid the need for a facing. This may be preferable where a sheer fabric is being used. See p.131 for other ways to finish raw edges. In cases where they are unavoidable, remember there is no reason why they cannot be turned and stitched to the RS, and used as a decorative design feature. Here, the facing is cut with the RS of the fabric on the same side as it is for the main garment piece. Where the facing is cut to be turned to the WS of the garment, the opposite is the case, so that the RSs of the fabric can be placed together when stitching.

NECKLINES/COLLARS

Plain neck edges
It is a good idea to cut a standard, fitting, round neck edge on the main garment pieces and, where possible, cut your neck edge when the garment is at a stage ready for fitting. You must always remember to allow for seam turnings, except where a binding is to finish the neck edge, so what you see is at least 6 mm ($\frac{1}{4}$ in.) higher than the finished neck edge will be. Decide on the depth at the CF and CB, and on the width that is to be cut at the shoulder seams. Then cut the shape that you want in between, making certain that the cut is symmetrical about the centre lines, if it is meant to be. Cut on the mean side, as you may be surprised when you try the garment on: more can always be taken away, but you can never add. Most neck edges will have an area of wrap where the opening is to be. Be careful that the wrap lies together when the opening is closed, with the neck edge shaping following a continuous line so that the top and under-wrap neck edges match exactly.

Neck facings are cut to match the neck edge, usually with a back neck facing and a front neck facing which are joined at the shoulder seams. Often a CF opening is faced with a single facing that includes the front neck facing, cut to the shoulder seam.

Flat collars
The easiest collar to cut is a flat collar which has no 'roll' but sits on the bodice flatly, as its name describes. The collar is cut with the neck edge exactly as the neck edge of the garment and the other edge styled to sit flat on the bodice of the garment (*Fig. 72*). The neck edge of the garment may be cut to any shape as may the size and outer edge of the collar. The collar is cut twice, so that it is made up in double fabric. In some cases a different fabric may be

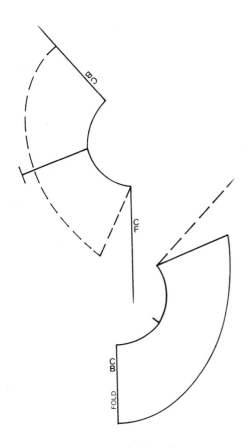

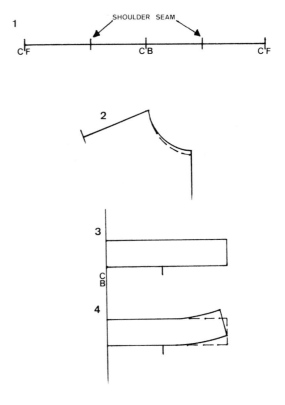

72 *Example of the cut of a flat collar*

73 *Cut of a stand collar: (1) neck measurement; (2) re-shape front neck; (3) depth of stand required; (4) shaping given to stand to shorten upper edge*

used – for instance, if a thick velvet collar is placed on a soft, wool, challis dress, the under-collar may be cut in the main fabric or in one that is much finer than the velvet. The collar may be cut in separate sections, so much so that it is reduced to a neck trim. Wherever the openings that run into the neckline occur, ignore the wrap. The collar is cut to fit the finished neck edge; where there is a CF opening the collar will fit to the CF point on each side, so that, when the opening is fastened, the collar meets edge to edge at the CF.

Stand collars

The cut of any collar is worked from the measurement of the neck edge to which it is to be attached. This measurement can be clearly divided into four sections: from CB to shoulder seam and from shoulder seam to CF on each side of the garment. These can be represented on a straight line (*Fig. 73*). The problems arise when the collar must sit properly around the cylindrical neck. Stand collars are usually

attached to a standard, round neck edge, which is lowered by about 1 cm ($\frac{3}{8}$ in.) at the CF, and the curve re-shaped. The depth of the stand is usually between 2 and 4 cm ($\frac{3}{4}$ and 1$\frac{1}{2}$ in.). Mark in the depth required. The back neck section remains straight but the front neck area of the collar must be shaped so that its top edge has a shorter length than the neck edge at the same area. The collar will then sit properly around the neck at the front. Raise the neck-edge point about 2.5 cm (1 in.) and shape a curve to run into the straight section of the neck edge at the shoulder. The top edge will be curved parallel to the neck-edge curve. Mark the shoulders and centre back with nips in the seam turnings. This is the basic shape that all stand collars should follow. Cut away the excess fabric to give the styling required at the CF. If the collar is to wrap over, simply add the necessary amount to the end of the collar as a straight section – i.e. without continuing the curve at the neck edge. Mark the CF position carefully with a balance mark. The stand is cut twice, so that it is made up in double

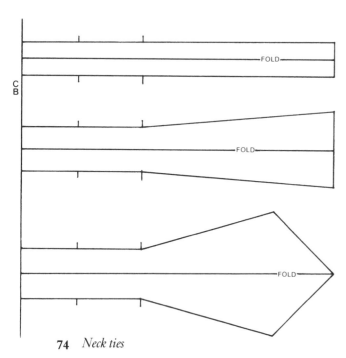

74 *Neck ties*

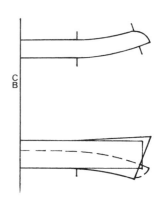

75 *A standard cut for a shirt collar*

fabric, together with an interlining. The CB line may be cut on a fold of the fabric if this is convenient to the lay. The collar is then automatically cut symmetrically.

A simpler stand can be cut as a straight strip which continues in length to incorporate ties (*Fig. 74*). These may have shaping added. Often, the collar is stitched to the neck edge to within about 2 cm ($\frac{3}{4}$ in.) from the CF, or wherever the edges of the opening meet, on each side, so, when the ties are fastened, the knot or bow sits properly in line with the stand and is not forced forward on to the bodice.

Shirt collar
The standard shirt collar consists of four cut fabric pieces, plus two interfacings (*Fig. 75*). The stand part of the collar is cut as already described, with a wrap added to the CF of the same width as that added to the shirt front. Mark the CF with balance nips at the top edge of the stand as well as the neck edge. The interfacing is cut to match. The collar section meets edge to edge at the CF. The depth of the collar is usually a little more than the depth of the stand (1–1.5 cm [$\frac{3}{8}$–$\frac{5}{8}$ in.]) so that the seam is covered. Begin at the CB, with a straight section as on the stand. The edge that is to be joined to the stand is curved in the same way as the stand but is reversed, being concave and not convex, as on the stand. To do this, simply lie the stand on the collar with the shoulder points

and CB together, but with the stand turned upside-down, so that the curve can be cut to match. The outer edge of the collar for the front section is cut according to style. Two pieces are cut as for the stand but, on one collar, trim away 3 mm ($\frac{1}{8}$ in.) from the outer and side edges. This slightly smaller piece is the under-collar. Cut interfacing to match the top collar. Again, symmetry is of the utmost importance so, preferably, cut the collar with the CB placed on a foldline of the fabric.

Roll collars
A collar that stands and rolls requires correct shaping (*Fig. 76*). To begin with, mark in the neck shape and the collar shape, as for a flat collar. If the outer edge of the collar is then shortened, the collar will automatically sit with its outer edge nearer the neck edge, so causing the collar to lift and roll. (This is what must be avoided when cutting a flat collar.) By darting away the excess fullness evenly around the collar, the total measurement decreases and the shape of the neck edge of the collar is altered, so becoming a more gradual curve than the curve of the neck edge cut on the garment. This is suitable for a reasonably shallow amount of stand. Obviously, the more the outside edge is shortened, the further up on the bodice it is forced to sit, and so the higher the collar will stand before rolling over. Remember you must allow extra depth to the cut of the collar so there is enough fabric to include the height of the stand, a little to allow for the area of roll, plus the fall of the collar, which must be enough to cover the seam at the neck edge where the collar is joined. As for the shirt collar, trim away about 3 mm ($\frac{1}{8}$ in.) around the outer edges on one piece, to give an under-collar.

If the principle of giving a collar roll is followed

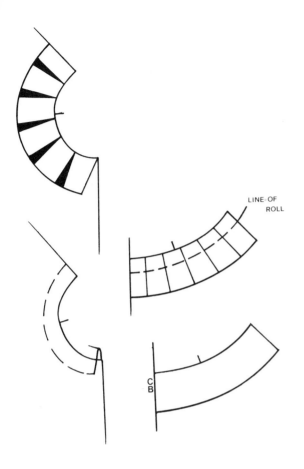

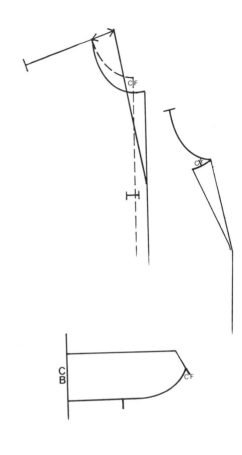

76 *Cutting a collar with roll*

77 *Cutting a revers collar*

through, where a high stand is required on a collar that rolls and just covers the neck edge, the outer edge of the collar will obviously measure fractionally more than the neck edge itself. Such collars will be cut straight. Mark up the collar with the relevant balance marks and cut the depth a little more than twice the height of the stand required. A little extra depth should be allowed for the area of roll. On finer fabrics, as little as 3–5 mm ($\frac{1}{8}$–$\frac{1}{4}$ in.) roll allowance will be sufficient, but on thicker, more bulky fabrics, anything from 1–1.5 cm ($\frac{3}{8}$–$\frac{5}{8}$ in.) may be needed. The garment edges of the collar that meet at the opening on the garment can then be cut with the styling desired. Again, cut an under-collar a little smaller than the top collar, together with an inter-facing.

Completely straight collars that have square edges with no additional shaping can be cut on the cross. This gives an attractive roll as well as a soft look to a turtle-neck. A soft interfacing may be cut, also on the cross, if the fabric needs it.

For more floppy, cowl-type collars which may be larger, cut the neck edge of the garment a little wider at the shoulder seams. The collar can then be cut straight, doubled over with a foldline and rolled down casually when worn. The excess fabric may be gathered on to a narrow band at the neck opening, so that the fullness falls around the neck with more control when fastened. Soft fabrics that drape well need no interfacing for this kind of collar. Experiment with the possibilities of how to control larger amounts of fabric around the neck and the effects that larger collars can give when only partially fastened, for instance.

Revers collars
A revers collar is relatively simple to understand and easy to cut (*Fig. 77*). Read the instructions for its

construction carefully before attempting to cut, so that the meaning of each cut edge is clear in your mind. This collar is always used on a garment with a CF opening. Whether a wrap-over closure or edge-to-edge zip fastening is chosen, a facing must always be cut up to the shoulder seam. It is this facing, which is folded back from the top of the fastening, that shows on the RS and forms the revers. The neck edge is lowered at the CF by at least 2.5 cm (1 in.) and a new curve shaped from the shoulder seam. This varies according to style. The front edge of the bodice often remains straight, so that the facing is cut in one with the bodice and turned to the WS on a foldline. A larger revers may be shaped, in which case the facing will be cut separately, the joining seam incorporating the necessary shaping. Decide the position of the top of the fastening first. Then work out the roll and shaping to give the desired effect. Cut a section on paper, including the shoulder seam, the lowered neck edge and straight bodice edge. Fold back the paper along the line along which the collar will turn back when worn. Extend the shoulder seam by the height of the stand. Draw a line from here to about 2.5 cm (1 in.) above the height of the top button or to the top of the zip. You can then draw in any shape for the revers. To cut the collar, mark in at the CB and the shoulder seam the height required for the stand, roll and fall. For the front collar area, the neck edge is cut to the same shape as the neck edge on the garment – as an upward curve which reduces the collar depth. This length will stop short of the end of the neck edge to form the 'nick' in the styling that is characteristic of the revers collar. This position must be marked carefully on the back edge with a balance nip. Now add any shaping required for the front edge and outer edge of the collar, remembering to consider carefully the balance of the finished shape. No back neck facing is necessary, but cut a top and under-collar as well as interfacing for both the whole of the front facing and the collar. The facing, or the top collar, or both, may be cut in a contrast fabric to that of the main garment pieces, to give additional interest.

Wing collars

Wing collars are cut in the same way as the revere but, instead of a collar at the back, a back neck facing is cut to give a plain back neck edge (*Fig. 79*). The front facing folds back to the RS from the top of the fastening to just in front of the shoulder seam. A CF opening is necessary if the point where the collar begins to fold back is deep enough to allow the head to pass through. A button/loop fastening may be used to close the opening a little higher. If the

78   *Cut pieces required for a revers collar*

shaping of the collar comes beyond the CF line minus a 6 mm ($\frac{1}{4}$ in.) seam allowance, a CF seam will be necessary in the bodice and the facing, so that it is possible to cut the collar. The front and back neck facings will require interlining.

Shawl collars

The shawl collar is a little more complicated to cut well, so experiment with calico or some old sheeting to ensure correct cutting. Read the instructions for the construction of this collar to help understand this cut.

As with the revers collar, a CF opening is necessary, and it is the turned-back facing that gives

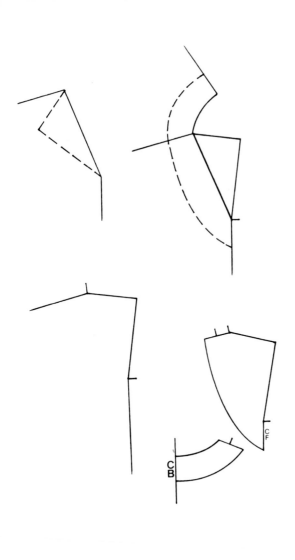

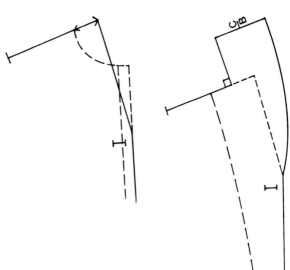

80 *Cutting a shawl collar*

81 *Cut pieces required for a shawl collar*

79 *Cut for a wing collar*

the top collar. The work is mainly concentrated on the bodice, and the facing is simply cut to match, as shown (*Figs. 80 and 81*). Extend the shoulder seam the distance of the height of the stand of the collar at the CB and, as for the revers, mark from here to the appropriate point at the CF to indicate the position of the roll of the collar. Measure exactly the distance of half the back neck, from shoulder seam to CB and, from the original point of the shoulder seam, mark a straight line of that length, at right angles to the shoulder seam, as indicated. This seamline is half the back neck edge of the collar, and the next seamline runs up the CB line of the collar. Mark it in, at right angles, to include the depth of the stand, any allowance for roll and the fall required at the

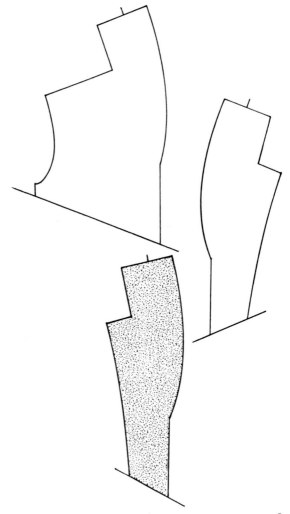

85

CB. This point reaches the outer edge of the collar. From here to the top of the opening where the roll begins, the outer edge of the collar is cut depending on the style. The back section remains the same width until the shoulder is reached, but take care to mark at right angles from the CB seam so that the outer edge of the back collar has a smooth line with no dips up or down. As the collar is stitched to a facing, there is wide scope for shaping – a scalloped edge, for instance, is not particularly difficult, but requires some care in construction. The facing is cut to match the outer edge and comes up to the shoulder seam and on to include the back collar. It is cut in two separate pieces and seamed at the CB. Contrast fabric may again be used for the facing to emphasise the collar. Cut interfacing to match the facing in two pieces. You may wish to trim away a minimal amount around the outer edge of the under-collar – i.e. the collar edge cut on the bodice of the garment – to allow the collar edge seamline to be out of view.

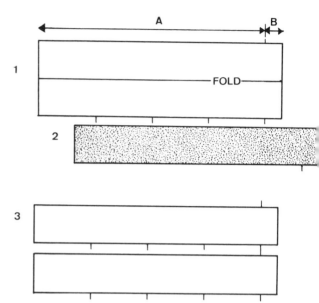

82 *(1) Straight cuff; (2) interfacing; (3) straight cuff cut in two pieces*

CUFFS

Usually, a cuff is cut as a straight strip the width of the wrist measurement plus an extra centimetre ($\frac{3}{8}$ in.) or so, for comfort (*Fig. 82, measurement A*), and with a wrap added for the fastening (*measurement B*) as on the waistband of a skirt. The cuff is cut double the finished depth, with a foldline clearly marked, which forms the lower edge of the cuff. An interfacing is cut the size of the finished cuff, wrap included (*Fig. 82 [2]*). There is rarely a need to cut a plain cuff in two pieces, with a separate top cuff and under-cuff seamed around outside edges (*Fig. 82 [3]*), unless the top cuff has been crossway-cut for decorative purposes. A straight-cut under-cuff will prevent the cross-cut fabric stretching out of shape, although in many firmer fabrics, the interfacing may give an adequately firm base. A seam may also be required around the outside edge, where an insertion is to give a decorative feature to the cuff.

Turn-back cuffs can be cut in two, three or four pieces (*Figs. 83 and 84*). The part that is stitched to the sleeve is cut as a plain cuff, with a wrap for fastening. The section that is turned back does not usually have a wrap, so that when the cuff is fastened, the turned-back part of the cuff meets edge to edge. This part may be cut separately, in which case the cuff that fits to the wrist must be cut in two pieces so that there is a seam into which the turned-back section can be stitched. This part may be cut with shaping according to style, either in one piece with a foldline forming the edge, or in two pieces, where a

seam may be necessary for insertion. This part of the cuff need not be the same depth as the plain section. It may be cut deeper, so that it sits over the seam that joins the cuff to the sleeve, hiding it altogether, or less deep, so that it leaves a strip of the under-cuff showing. This can be an attractive feature where the under-cuff has been cut in a contrast fabric.

When a cuff is cut deeper than about 7 cm ($2\frac{3}{4}$ in.) it will require shaping to sit comfortably around the wrist and lower arm (*Fig. 85*). Measure the arm at the level at which the top edge of the cuff is to sit and mark up the cuff at the width and depth required. Now take the difference between this and the wrist measurement and dart away evenly this amount at the lower edge of the cuff. This gives the correct wrist measurement at the lower edge. Form a smooth curve at both the top and lower edges and add the wrap required as a straight strip. This type of cuff must be cut in two pieces with an interfacing to match.

In all cases where a standard button/buttonhole fastening is used, the wrap is added to the under-arm seam side of the back edge of the cuff – i.e. the end of the cuff that is to be attached to the back quarter of the sleeve (*Fig. 86*).

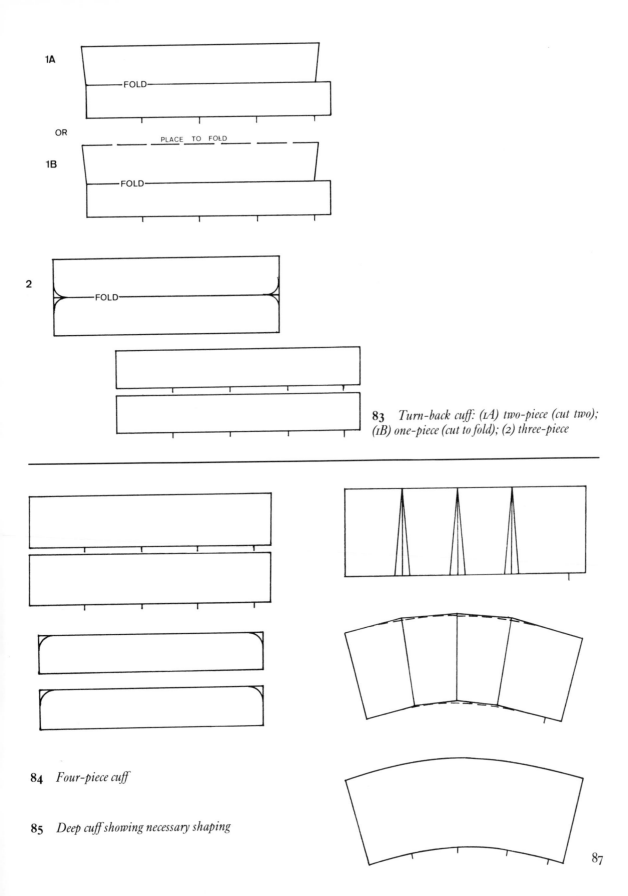

1A

FOLD

OR

1B

PLACE TO FOLD

FOLD

2

FOLD

83 *Turn-back cuff: (1A) two-piece (cut two); (1B) one-piece (cut to fold); (2) three-piece*

84 *Four-piece cuff*

85 *Deep cuff showing necessary shaping*

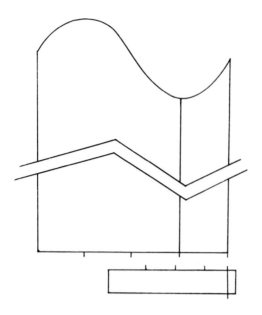

POCKETS

Whatever type of pocket is cut, it should be large enough to be useful and should be placed in a suitable position on the garment.

The most inconspicuous pockets are those with openings that are simply gaps in a seam, the pocket consisting of a bag attached to a small extension added to the original seam allowance (*Fig. 87*). The seam is then joined as far as the pocket, continued around the two pocket bags and then on for the continuation of the seam. The bags remain on the WS of the garment. The opening must be large enough to allow a hand to enter without placing strain on the seam. These pockets are usually placed

86 *Sleeve section showing cuff position with corresponding balance marks*

87 *Pocket bags and extension cut at side seam*

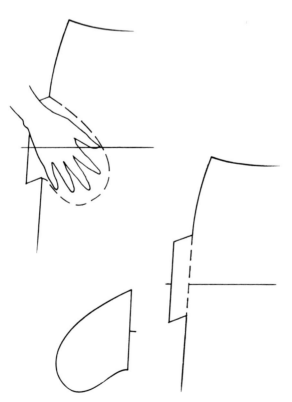

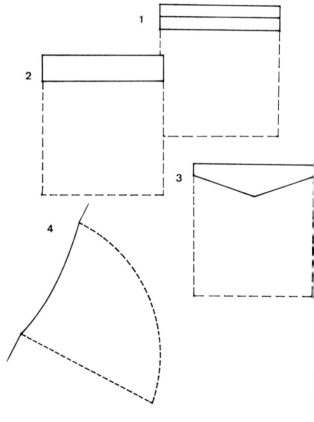

88 *(1) Piped pocket; (2) welt pocket; (3) flap; (4) single bag stitched to WS of opening left in seam. Dotted lines show position of bags on WS*

in the side seam of a garment. If the garment fabric is too bulky, cut the pocket bags in a lighter-weight fabric.

Patch pockets are equally simple to cut, but are more decorative. Cut to any shape and add a facing to the WS of the pocket. This forms a stronger area where there is likely to be most strain, as well as giving a neat finish along the top edge. The pocket is applied to the RS in a suitable position on the garment.

Other pockets may consist of a slit in the fabric which is finished with piping or a welt with pocket bags, which hang loosely inside the garment (*Fig. 88*). A flap may be stitched to the top edge of the opening. Alternatively a single pocket bag may be stitched to the WS of the main garment piece where the stitching line will show on the RS. This is also true for pockets with an opening that has been left along a seamline.

A slightly more complicated method of cutting a pocket is to cut away a section of the garment (*Fig. 89*). A facing is cut to finish this edge which includes the front pocket bag shape, the back pocket bag shape and the remaining section of the garment that was originally cut away. Divide these areas with a balance nip on each seam in the correct position, as indicated in the example. The front pocket bag may be cut in a lighter-weight fabric if it is necessary to reduce bulk.

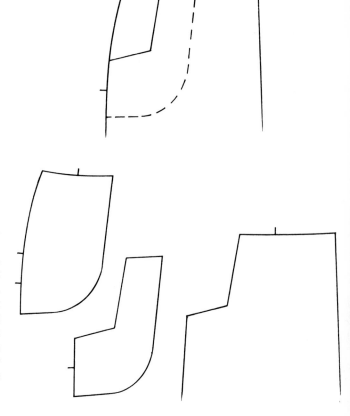

89   *Cut of a section pocket*

CHAPTER NINE

Practical cutting: general information

This chapter is intended to help with the practical problems of cutting out. So far, only the principles of why a certain shape should be cut have been discussed.

SEAM TURNINGS

Seam turnings or allowances have been omitted from the cutting instructions to avoid confusion between stitching and cutting lines arising. The actual width of the seam turning may also vary from seam to seam, depending on the type of seam to be stitched and also on the fabric used. Suggestions for suitable widths for seam turnings are given throughout the construction section.

All seam turnings are cut parallel to the seamline, whatever width they may be. If a seamline changes width for some reason a small step will be cut. Although you should always think of the position of the stitching lines which determine the finished size of each piece, you must get used to including seam turnings automatically, especially as you consider the fabric width available and the positioning of all the pieces on the fabric prior to cutting. As a garment may be cut with turnings of varying widths, the width of each turning is indicated by a nip at the beginning and end of each stitching line.

SEAM-TURNING SHAPING

Many seam turnings require shaping to be cut at each end of the seam. This may seem a small point but the need for a little extra thought here cannot be over-stressed. You must first be certain of every detail of the construction methods to be used so that the direction in which each turning will lie when the garment is made up will be quite clear. Each seam turning will have one of only two alternatives: to be pressed back from the stitching line or be left to lie flat. In Fig. 90, turnings A, B and C are pressed back; turning D remains flat. Fig. 91 shows the necessity to cut shaping at the end of a seam turning so that it lies correctly in line with the continuous cut edge that results when two fabric pieces are seamed together. Note that for diagrammatical purposes, the turnings are shown fractionally short of the cut edge: in reality, these will lie exactly together. Fig. 92 shows what happens if shaping is omitted. Example A is cut with the edge of the seam turning too short in length. Whilst this may be caught in the next seam, a narrower turning and a more extreme angle may make this impossible. It is also easy to pull the seam turning up in the direction of the arrow when stitching the seam across the top. This will then tighten the seam turning and badly pucker the fabric on the RS. Example B shows too much fabric protruding beyond the edge; this requires trimming away. Fig. 93 shows further examples of shaping cut on seam turnings.

90 *Direction of pressing seam turnings*

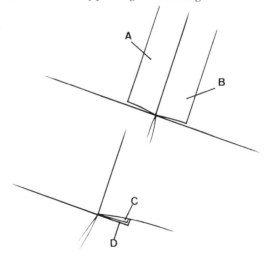

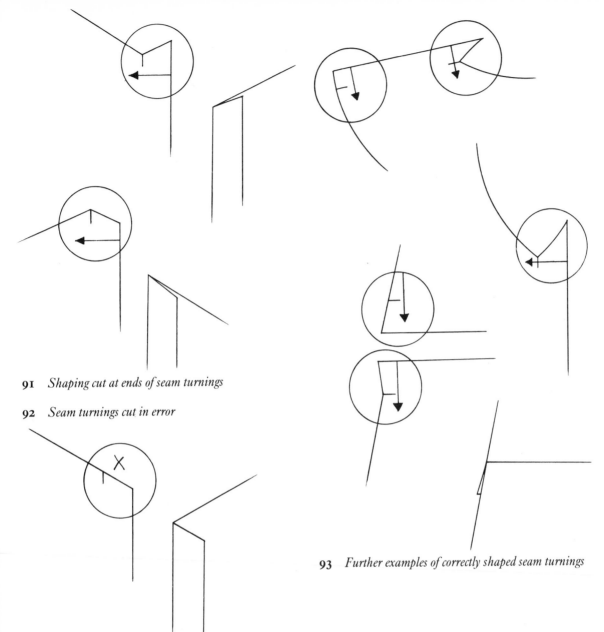

91 *Shaping cut at ends of seam turnings*

92 *Seam turnings cut in error*

93 *Further examples of correctly shaped seam turnings*

DIRECTION OF STRAIGHT GRAIN

The straight grain – i.e. the direction of the warp threads – must be carefully positioned in the right direction for each cut piece. This is important when you come to lay the pattern pieces on the fabric length.

The original centre front and centre back lines are almost always placed on the straight grain as is the centre line of any sleeve (*Fig. 94*). Where, for instance, a skirt has been cut in panels with, perhaps, flare added, the straight grain may be positioned down the centre line of each panel. Facings are cut with the grain in the same direction as the main

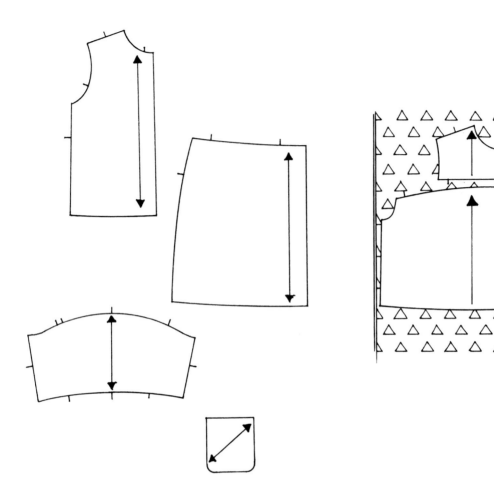

94 *Examples of direction of straight grain*

95 *Example of one-way fabric and positioning*

garment piece on to which they are to be joined. Collars and cuffs may be cut with the straight grain running along the width of the piece, as this takes more strain in wear. Similarly, long ties or straps usually have the straight grain running along their length, so that the maximum stability of the fabric is in the direction where the most pull or strain is likely to be. A dirndl skirt has the straight grain running horizontally around the skirt, parallel to the hemline. This is to achieve more bulky, springy gathers around the waist and to avoid seaming several fabric widths to create the fullness. If a symmetrical piece is to be cut on a foldline, the foldline almost always follows the line of the straight grain. The direction of the straight grain is marked with a double-ended arrow. An on-grain foldline is marked with the ends of the arrow pointing at the fold edge.

Fabrics that for reasons of print, pile or weave must have the top of each pattern piece the same way up have the straight grain marked with an arrow with a single head (*Fig. 95*). Each piece has the arrow pointing in the same direction. Before beginning to cut, always be certain if this positioning will be necessary.

The direction of the straight grain is much more obvious on some fabrics than on others. Woven, vertical stripes are easy: the straight grain can be determined by measuring accurately an equal distance in from the selvedge and joining two or more of these points. Never rely on a printed stripe as being an accurate indication of the straight grain and check this before using such a fabric. (An off-grain print is often not worth using and should be discarded as faulty unless it will not be glaringly obvious when

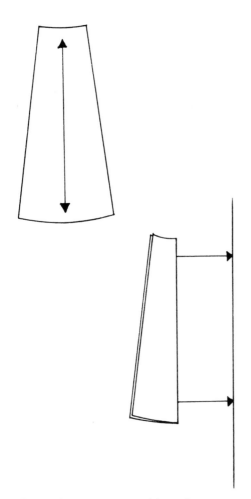

96 *Positioning pattern on straight grain*

centre of what is to be a garment piece but is useful for marking cutting edges or dividing up accurately fabric widths. Never be tempted to tear a fabric along the grain: the stress caused by the pull distorts the nearby weft threads considerably.

Practice and experience will help you to sense the straight grain of any fabric, not only with your eyes but with the feel of the scissors as you cut. When you cut a garment directly from the fabric without a pattern, the straight grain almost invariably lies along the first line that you build the whole of the cut around – i.e. parallel to, or at, the centre line.

BALANCE MARKS

Balance marks are used to help identification of a fabric piece or to indicate even distribution of ease or gathers etc., size of darts or tucks and width of seam turnings. They are also used for correct positioning of two pieces before seaming. Little nicks are made in the seam allowance which stop short of the seam line and they must be positioned accurately. Whilst the omission of a single necessary balance mark can cause problems at a later stage of the making up, too many balance marks will only confuse the issue. Accuracy is the key to success; a balance mark that is positioned maybe only 6 mm ($\frac{1}{4}$ in.) out is far more misleading than a total omission.

Measure each section along the stitching line, *not* the cutting line. The nip is then placed exactly opposite the appropriate position. Nip the fabric at the correct angle, using the tips of the blades only, as a safety precaution. Where possible, mark the nips for the RHS and LHS through double fabric. A small nip of about 3 mm ($\frac{1}{8}$ in.) should be large enough to see clearly with the help of a gentle pull on the fabric, although thicker fabrics or those that fray readily need more care and consideration. On narrow turnings, never nip more than half the total turning width.

Users of commercial patterns will be familiar with the triangles that serve as balance marks. Cut straight through the centre of these. You will then be saved the awkwardness of cutting around them and have what is likely to be a more accurate balance mark.

PLACEMENT MARKS

The only time when balance marks are not helpful is where placement marks would be used instead on a pattern – for instance, to show the position of a patch pocket. These are not important so far as the pattern is concerned and, if you use a commercial pattern, they should only be followed as a guide. Wherever

made up.) These points are easily marked with pins picking up a single thread, or double threads on finer fabrics. You may then find it helpful to press lightly one or more foldlines to indicate the straight grain. If you are to position a pattern piece that does not have at least one edge cut on the grain, first place it at roughly the correct distance from the selvedge (*Fig. 96*). Now fold back the pattern piece along the arrow indicating grain direction. Mark the straight grain as described already and lay the folded edge against this line. Anchor the pattern in position and fold back the other section, where it will lie correctly in place.

With certain fabrics the straight grain may be indicated by picking up a single warp thread with a pin and jerking it sharply. This will pull up a line of puckers, clearly indicating the line of the straight grain. This should, of course, not be done down the correct placement is important, it is better to position directly on to the fabric when the garment is at a stage where it can be tried on, and the markings shown with pins.

The point of a dart is marked on the WS of the fabric with a small pencil dot that is exactly 1.3 cm ($\frac{1}{2}$ in.) up from the actual point to which the dart is stitched.

RECORDING PATTERNS

You will probably wish to keep a record of the pattern of the garments you make and, as you build up a collection, you will find them an invaluable source of reference. The following suggestions may help you to keep your patterns in a logical and tidy manner, making them all the more easy to refer to in the future. Individual preference and the particular methods you use to cut will influence the way in which you record the necessary information, and the information itself may well have come from several sources for the one garment. It is a good idea to keep all the information used for one garment together in a suitable envelope. Sketch the design on the front or, if you prefer, label it and attach a scrap of the fabric used so that the contents are clear.

Whatever form the pattern itself may take, you will always require a written sheet containing important notes. Some things may seem pointless to record but, six months later, you may be thankful for the reminder. Ideally, you should make a sketch of the garment, clearly showing its structure and particular design features. This need not be large, or contain a body, but should provide a record of the details in a diagrammatical form. Make any explanatory notes alongside. You should then list clearly every pattern piece that is cut, with a number, name, cutting instructions and where the information or pattern piece may be found. Now total the actual number of cut pieces the garment takes. Make a separate list in the same way to include the interfacing pieces to be cut. You should also record the details of the materials used. This will include the fabric width, the length of fabric actually used, including any contrast fabrics, the approximate amount of interfacing and any specific haberdashery requirements, such as lengths of elastic. Make notes or draw a diagram of the layout used, especially where more unusual positioning made good fabric savings. The diagram need only divide the area of fabric up with straight lines, each section being labelled with the appropriate pattern piece. Notes of any special problems encountered in the cutting and the making up of the garment are useful.

The pattern itself will either include cut paper pieces or a list of detailed written instructions giving method and measurements, or be a combination of the two. *Always include details of all seam turnings, so they cannot possibly be forgotten.* Making a set of huge paper pattern pieces is not necessary although, if you have the facilities and prefer to cut from full paper patterns, do so. Use a reasonably strong paper that will not tear or crumple too easily. Avoid newspaper at all times, as the print soils fabric easily. You will need a reasonable width, so that joining with Sello-tape does not become a major task. Commercial pattern paper, marked with a grid, is useful but expensive. Suitable pencils and pens, a metre rule and a shorter rule, a large and small set-square and some decent paper scissors will be needed.

It is helpful to keep a selection of paper patterns of the more complicated but standard areas – such as a rounded neck edge or a fitting armhole and sleeve head – or of any particular detailing you like – such as a standard shirt collar, shirt-sleeve placket or side-seam pocket bags – for future use. Only the relevant section of the pattern is necessary, but use strong paper for pattern pieces that will be used often. Keep these together in a large envelope, with a list of the contents on the outside.

A well-fitting, standard blouse pattern is worth keeping as a full paper pattern. Keep the various collars, cuffs, pockets, etc. in smaller envelopes inside the large one. The main pattern pieces are then easily found for repeated use.

Always make complicated sections of pattern in paper. Intricate tuck shaping, for instance, needs cutting in paper, although only the top area of the full pattern piece need be included. Where a part of a pattern piece is made, cut a jagged edge or tear the paper along the line where the fabric continues. Mark bold arrows to indicate a continuation. You can also write the instructions and measurements for the cut of the remainder on the pattern itself. Otherwise, the instructions should be included on an information sheet listing the details and methods used to cut each garment piece. Some patterns may consist entirely of such a sheet with written instructions; others will include this sheet directing you to particular 'stock' pattern pieces in another envelope. You may have used part of a commercial pattern, in which case, the relevant tissue pieces should be enclosed. If you prefer not to split up a commercial pattern, indicate the pattern name and number where appropriate on the written instructions.

If you find you tend to cut patterns with information from several sources, you may then find it helpful to list on the envelope what the exact contents should be. After re-using the pattern, it is easy to check that all the correct information is returned to the envelope.

LIE

Lie refers to the positioning of the various garment pieces required on the length of fabric to use the least quantity of fabric possible. As the majority of patterns are cut for the RHS of the body only, by cutting through a double thickness of fabric, with either its RSs or WSs together, opposites will result, giving the correct number of RHS and LHS pieces (*Fig. 97*). Most garments are cut in this way with the fabric double. Where the design allows, cut the pattern to make the most of the fabric width. This is easier when the garment is cut straight from the fabric, as the available fabric area is spread before you as you work. The diagrams (*Fig. 98*) show the ways in which you can easily 'block' up a fabric area by working, to begin with, from the maximum dimensions of each piece. Lengthwise and widthwise folds and areas of single fabric may be used, or a carefully planned combination. One-way fabrics should not present extra problems and these too are included in the examples. More careful thinking is necessary when planning the lay on a fabric with a bold print or stripe. There may be no alternative but to cut every piece individually, from single fabric, to ensure accurate placement. A simple skirt can be cut, for instance, with its hemline 2 cm (¾ in.) below the top of a yellow stripe or through the pink blob next to the black speck in the centre of the cabbage rose, but more complicated patterns may cause difficulty and should be avoided until you are reasonably experienced.

MARKING UP FABRIC

Ideally, you should use a table large enough to lay out flat a reasonable area of fabric. Let the remainder rest on a chair, and use some heavy weights to hold the fabric in place. If you have no suitable table, then resort to working on the floor. A carpeted surface is preferable, as the fabric will not slip about. When you are cutting directly, with no pattern, you will probably find it easier to lay out the full fabric length on the floor, while you make decisions about the layout. It may then be possible to cut away some areas and work on the details of each piece individually at a table in greater comfort, rather than crawling on the floor for a more complicated cut.

Always take the trouble to press the creases and crumples out of the fabric length before you begin. Unless there is a good reason for the RS of the fabric being visible, fold the fabric with the RSs together. Although marking up should never show after cutting, even on the WS, the RS is generally kept cleaner and more protected. Remember that when cutting double fabric, if either both the RSs or both the WSs are facing uppermost, two identical fabric shapes will be cut. You may not need two left fronts, so check! RSs together or WSs together will result in a left front and a right front. If the RS of the fabric is not immediately apparent, indicate the WS with small chalk marks or pins at appropriate places along the fabric. As each piece is cut, and so separated from the main fabric length, a similar mark in a seam turning will be useful when checking that the correct pieces have been cut as well as when making up. If you think there is no difference between the RS and WS, do not be tempted to ignore this and cut regardless. From a distance, or in certain lights, it may be all too obvious when the garment is made up.

Foldlines must always be exactly along a warp or weft thread. Carefully measure in from the selvedge to check that each piece will be cut with the straight grain in the correct direction. Once the correct foldline has been positioned, it may be helpful to pin the fabric together at intervals along the selvedge, or

97   Cutting double fabric with RSs together

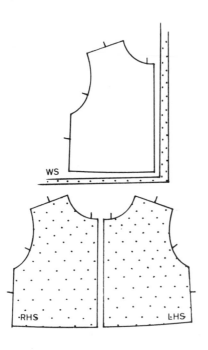

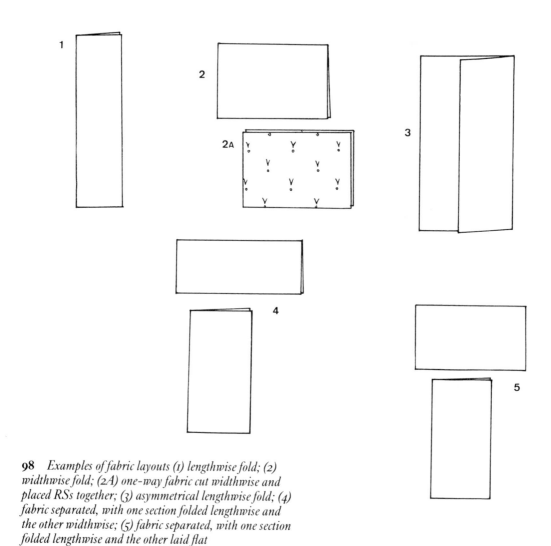

98 *Examples of fabric layouts (1) lengthwise fold; (2) widthwise fold; (2A) one-way fabric cut widthwise and placed RSs together; (3) asymmetrical lengthwise fold; (4) fabric separated, with one section folded lengthwise and the other widthwise; (5) fabric separated, with one section folded lengthwise and the other laid flat*

hold it in place with small bulldog clips. Check that the fabric is flat top and bottom, in case of twist occurring. If there should be ripples, gently smooth them away little by little. Do not tug or pull sharply on the fabric as you will then find you have to start again.

It is better not to place pins in the fabric where the garment pieces will be placed, as it can be difficult or impossible to remove the pin holes. It is probable that you will not make up the complete garment straight away, and the longer pins remain in the fabric, the more likely they are to mark it. Therefore, pin only where you are certain the fabric will be waste. Where garment pieces are pinned together to anchor the double fabric together prior to cutting, use as few pins as possible and place them in the

areas of seam turnings. The same rule applies to pinning paper patterns to fabric. Be careful that pins do not cross the cutting line as this can ruin an expensive pair of shears. If pins are used to indicate measurements when marking up without a pattern, carefully pick up the minimum number of threads practicable. If you are using a crisper fabric that marks particularly badly, use this to your advantage and poke pin holes to indicate the cutting lines.

You may choose other methods of marking the fabric. These will depend on the type and colour of the fabric itself. Soft pencils (B or 2B), tailor's chalk (always kept sharp) and pens that do not 'spread' into the fabric are useful. Any line that you mark up will itself have some width so should be thin and clear for accuracy. Do not bother to mark areas of fabric where it is not vital to obtain the correct cut, but always mark every corner. Place a pin at each corner and wind a taut thread around it to mark straight edges. Curves may be marked in with a dotted line. You may decide to leave particular areas uncut so that you can decide the final shape at a later stage when fitting. Every balance nip should be cut, having been positioned by accurate use of the tape measure; stand it on edge to measure around curves.

Always work with a list of every cut piece that you need to complete the garment, and use this as a checklist as you mark and cut. Make sure you will have the correct number of LHS and RHS pieces. Immediately before you cut, check once more the direction of the straight grain.

CUTTING TECHNIQUES

Extremely sharp, good-quality shears are essential. If you have always struggled with second rate, paper-damaged blades, the difference must be tried to be believed. It is little wonder that so many people hate 'cutting out' as they have never used the right tool for the job.

Cut into your fabric with confidence. Problem fabrics may need extra pinning. It is always a good idea to cut in from the edge of the fabric where possible, if you are not certain of how it will handle; you will then have some idea of what you are up against.

For a smooth, accurate line, cut with long, rhythmic strokes. Your arm must feel comfortable and the rest of your body positioned so that you can see directly above the area as you cut. Keep your eye just ahead, so that you have a more complete image of the shape the cutting line follows, rather than concentrating on the blades themselves. Be careful to cut the fabric, without excess pressure that would cause the blades to 'shear' through. Unless the blades are keen, the weave may be distorted and the scissors difficult to control. When cutting into corners, slits in the garment, or balance nips, always use the ends of the blades only; this way accidents cannot happen if you should slip. When cutting a corner, cut slightly beyond the point wherever possible so that, as you change direction and begin to cut up the next edge, the blades will sit comfortably in position to continue cutting without pulling at the fabric.

ALTERNATIVE SOURCES OF INFORMATION

Ways in which different sources of information may be used when cutting a garment have been mentioned where methods of recording patterns are discussed. Cut your own designs from your own measurements and use as much information from other patterns as you need.

Commercial patterns
One of the main purposes of this book is to discourage the use of the commercial paper pattern. The idea is to promote dressmaking skills which should be understood clearly, so that a garment can be made right from the initial conception of a design idea. The cutting principles are elementary, but are directly linked with the finished size of the garment, with emphasis placed on body measurements of the individual. You may still prefer to work from commercial patterns but, if you understand some of the reasoning behind the cut of a pattern, you should find it easier to avoid some of the pitfalls of a bad fit.

Where you choose to include the cut of part of a commercial pattern in what is otherwise your own design, remember it is exactly that. Check for suitable guide markings on the tissue pattern so that you are not misled by its positioning. The waist level is usually marked in at the CF with a line or large dot if there is not a seam that sits on the shoulder. Look for these or other markings that indicate the underlying body measurements which are often overwhelmed by authoritative-looking print or instructions, as you are in a position to question and alter them. Do not necessarily comply with the blanket 1.5 cm ($\frac{5}{8}$ in.) seam allowance but cut to your own widths, and always include shaping – something which most patterns trust to luck. Ignore meaningless balance marks, marking in your own where necessary.

Existing garments
If the garment you wish to take a cut from is worn out, you may not mind cutting it up and using the pieces directly as a pattern. First press the garment well. Cut exactly along the stitching lines, from the RS or WS, whichever is easier. The seam turnings can be discarded. Darts, tucks or any other stitching that has been used for reasons of suppression will need to be carefully unpicked so the fabric may be spread flat. Alterations to the cut can then be made to improve the fit, make allowances for the use of a different weight fabric, or change the original styling or detailing as required. Add your own seam turnings and balance marks and identify the direction of the straight grain in the original cut.

If you do not chop the garment up, a pattern may be transferred directly to the fabric by taking measurements from the garment. Begin by determining the direction of the straight grain. Take the longest and the widest measurements from stitching line across to stitching line along and perpendicular to the straight grain. Mark these points with pins. Continue to work from this base, by measuring at suitable intervals parallel to either of these first two lines, until the appropriate seam lines have been marked up. You will find it necessary to mark the areas measured on the actual garment with pins, even if it is only at the stitching lines. Mark them in step by step as you work so that each distance measured is transferred to the fabric at the correct position in which it lies on the garment. Never under-estimate the amount of fabric width suppression and ease may take up. These areas will require careful measurement and cutting of the seam with the correct shaping. Refer to the directions included in the cutting section (*see p. 68*).

Further sources of information

You may also find a use for industrial patterns (often used for mail order) or those given in magazines. Do not be surprised to find scant printed information, and check to see whether seam turnings have been allowed. If so, make sure the widths are suitable. If multiple sizing is included, take extra care. It may be helpful to mark around the cutting line applicable in a coloured pen to avoid possible confusion.

Other patterns to be found in books and magazines may be shown scaled down on a grid. These can be marked up directly on to the fabric in much the same way as you would work from your own body measurement when transferring information from an existing garment. The only difference will be in applying the relevant multiplication factor. If a scaled-down version has no grid, make up your own on tracing paper to the appropriate scale, and this can then be placed over the diagram. Be sure that the diagram is intended to be read to scale and that it is not serving illustration purposes only. Any scale diagram will usually have the scale marked against it.

Part III:

Construction

Introduction

Construction methods need to be understood before a design can be cut and made up successfully. The methods shown here are based on industrial processes but, as the home dressmaker lacks industrial machinery, they have been necessarily modified. The object has been to eliminate most of the time-wasting that is often such a prominent feature of dressmaking. At the same time, this results in a more professional finish. As efficiency is the basis for what is included, the machine is used as widely and as often as possible in place of tacking and hand-finishing.

Making up fabric in this way requires an appreciation of how to handle the fabric at the machine in any given circumstance and includes using the eye for judgement of accuracy. Several of the basic methods are very different from 'home dressmaking' ideas; this makes machining easier and, therefore, quicker, and also has the result of omitting much hand-finishing.

A little practice may be necessary. Try out ideas that are new to you on scraps of fabric first. You will than appreciate any difficulties for yourself and see how best to overcome them. Time spent trying new methods is never wasted and the more you practise, the more expert you will become. Pins should be used to aid control when machining and their particular usage is suggested where relevant but, where it is possible to control the fabric with the fingers only, refrain from relying on pins too much or the skills of controlling fabric will take longer to acquire. The iron will save time, too; if it is used to prepare fabric prior to machining it makes the fabric much easier to handle. Have the iron set up as close to the machine as possible and keep pins, scissors and a tape-measure handy while you work. When the necessary item has been left on the other side of the room, it may be tempting to skip doing a job properly.

For the beginner, the best advice is to practise. Take time to work things out and do not try too many complicated methods at first. Try something new each time you make a garment and, as your experience increases, you will find ways of dealing with difficulties as they occur. Set yourself high standards from the beginning and bad habits will not then develop. Many of the construction processes shown are a slight variation of one basic method so, once this has been mastered it can often be applied to several garment areas.

If you are used to working from the making-up instructions given with commercial patterns you will soon realise how time-consuming and awkward to achieve they often are and that they often result in a poorer finish on the inside of the garment than more professional methods. You will have the advantage of being able to combine and develop the skills you already have to improve your standard of work.

Particular construction techniques are suited to different fabrics; they will be affected by the weight, handling qualities under the machine, draping or stretch abilities and the print or weave of the fabric. The success of a garment depends not only on good cutting and sewing but knowing which are the most suitable methods of construction for the chosen fabric. Insensitivity to the enormously varied properties of fabrics will result in a frustrating waste of effort and this can only be truly appreciated through experience. Use scraps first to see how a fabric should best be treated and how it is most easily controlled when being machined. While it is true that some fabrics demand far greater care when machining than others, beware of 'fighting' the fabric. Generally, the easier it is to control and work on a fabric the better the finished result will be.

Whilst the limitations of showing an intensely practical subject in this form are many, it is hoped that the following rules and guidelines will provide an insight into a certain approach and attitude towards the construction of clothing. To this, add inspiration and individuality and you will derive pleasure and satisfaction from your work.

CHAPTER TEN

Handling techniques

Handling techniques are fundamental to the achievement of efficient and high-standard clothing construction. Different fabrics will demand variation in the way they are controlled with the fingers, but the following descriptions cover the more general points and will be helpful in most instances. Further advice is given where more difficult fabrics are concerned.

SEAMING

Where two layers of fabric are passed through the machine, several problems will arise if the correct control is not applied. To begin with, the pieces of fabric must be placed together accurately, with the edges exactly together. The fabric will be placed just in front of the needle with both layers level at the start of the seam, and at a distance from the cut edge to give the correct width of seam turning. The main bulk of the fabric will always be to your left, so that it will not be forced through the limited space available on the machine to the right. You must make sure there is sufficient table area to support the fabric both to the left and behind the machine.

Begin every row of machining with a back tack (*Fig. 99*). Remembering to hold the threads behind the needle, machine two or three stitches. Make sure the last stitch is complete – i.e. that the needle has risen as far as it goes and you see it begin to come down again to form the next stitch. Now lift the foot and pull the fabric gently towards you until the needle is back at its starting position. It may be necessary to release a small amount of thread to prevent it pulling. Having formed a secure end to the seam by back-tacking you can begin to stitch the seam, making sure the first few stitches lie on top of the back tack. The thread ends may be neatly cut off with this type of finish, which is repeated in reverse at the end of the seam. Avoid the balance nip by starting just to the turning side of it.

The object is to machine a smooth line of stitching which runs parallel to the cut edge. If the cut edge is completely straight, so must the stitching line be. You should learn to use your eyes, to gauge the correct seam allowance. Until your confidence increases, work with a tape-measure, and use it as often as necessary to check the correct width is maintained. Watch the width of fabric beyond the right-hand edge of the machine foot as you sew. When machining around a curve, keep your eye on the width from the edge of the foot that is opposite the needle. As you practise, you will learn to judge this distance by eye (*Fig. 100*).

By machining at a reasonable speed, it is easier to maintain a correct and even seam width. Keep your eye on the edge of the machine foot to gauge a constant width of protruding fabric as described above, and a straight and even line of stitching will result. When you stop to adjust the fabric, always check that the needle is in the down position, right through the fabric, so that the fabric will not slip and cause a 'step' in the stitching line. The pressure of foot alone is not enough to prevent this occasionally happening; if it is, reduce it slightly, for it will be too great. It is equally important to exercise correct control of the fabric, so that both layers are joined in the right position.

Common problems to avoid include the following: the two cut edges do not remain exactly together; the fabric is stretched or distorted; the top layer of fabric is pushed progressively forward so that it protrudes beyond the fabric underneath at the end of the seam; tiny, unintentional pleats catch in the seam where creases in the fabric underneath pass unnoticed through the machine. These and other less common difficulties can be prevented by the way the fabric is held immediately prior to stitching.

The machine feeder has to be allowed to take up the amount of fabric for each stitch that has been set by the adjustment of the stitch-length dial. While

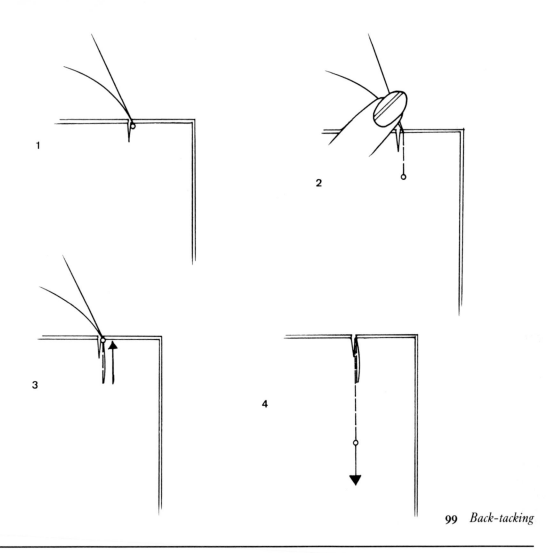

1

2

3

4

99 *Back-tacking*

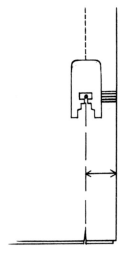

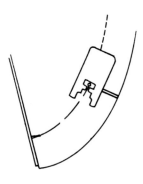

100 *Machining parallel to the cut*

machining, the fabric should neither be held too tightly at the front of the needle, thus preventing sufficient fabric from passing through the machine, nor should it be pulled from behind, causing too much fabric to pass. The result will be a respectively smaller or larger stitch than that set, a considerably weaker stitch, and the strong possibility of bending or breaking the needle and causing damage to the feeder mechanism. You may think it unlikely that you may ever do this, but it all too easily occurs when concentrating hard on other matters. It is also far more likely to happen when the machine is set at a larger stitch length.

Every balance nip must be exactly matched to its corresponding mark. To keep the two fabric layers aligned correctly, pinch them together tightly between the thumb and forefinger of the right hand. Hold the fabric firmly together in this way not only at important balance marks, but as you work along the seam. You can also ensure that the cut edges remain exactly together by using the thumb and forefinger to correct the position if the fabric slips. When you are sure the fabric is evenly placed, pinch it tightly and do not release it until you can machine no further. Your hand must, therefore, be free to move from the elbow towards the machine foot as the seam progresses, especially avoiding any interference with the feeder mechanism, as previously described.

This often removes the need for the repetitive use of pins or time-consuming tacking but, with particularly difficult fabrics, use pins when helpful. Always pin in the seam turning, with the pin lying perpendicular to the seamline, so that it prevents slipping; pins placed parallel to the seamline do not. The left hand must both lift and move the bulk of the fabric along as the seam is worked to avoid any pull or strain occurring on the area of fabric close to the seam as it is stitched. It should also smooth out the fabric in preparation for the next section of seam to be stitched and help to keep the cut edges together. Spread your fingers out lightly to the left of the seamline and, for comfort, stick your left elbow out so that the lower arm sits naturally in line with the fingers. If the under layer of fabric tends to protrude and it is difficult to keep the cut edge exactly together with the right hand, place the left hand in a similar position between the fabric layers and gently claw the under layer back until it lies together with the top fabric, as it should.

TOP-STITCHING/EDGE-STITCHING

Top-stitching is often included either in single or multiple rows both for decoration and to add strength. Edge-stitching is a row of stitching placed very close either to a folded fabric edge or to a seam, and often replaces the need for hand sewing. Top-stitching and edge-stitching show on the RS and, therefore, adjusting the machine to sew the best possible stitch is important. Achieving an accurate stitching line is easy as there is a seam or fabric edge with which the machine foot can be kept in line.

Top-stitching is almost always machined through double fabric, often the top fabric and the seam turning. This tends to give a much better machine stitch. Only on fabrics that are bulky will this not be so. If multiple rows of top-stitching are to be included, consider where they may pass through varying fabric thicknesses and test to see whether this makes a noticeable difference; it may be sensible to increase an area of double fabric so that each row has a uniform appearance. The most likely problem to arise is when the area of fabric between the seam and the top-stitching bubbles or puckers slightly. This is not because of ease, as any fabric to have been eased into a seam is certainly unsuitable for top-stitching for this very reason, but because the top layer of fabric has been pushed forward by the machine foot. This can be avoided firstly by ensuring that the area of fabric and seam has been carefully pressed and is placed under the machine flat with no distortion and, secondly, by holding the main fabric area in the correct position with the left hand as the stitching progresses. Keep the left-hand fingers comfortably close to the foot and, as you machine, check that the angle of the threads in the fabric to the seam do not alter. Where you suspect this might be happening, pull slightly on the fabric with the fingers so producing a little tension, coming at the correct angle from the seam, immediately in front of the foot, to counteract its 'pushing' action and to keep the position of the fabric correct. You can imagine how too great a pressure on the machine foot will intensify the problem and where difficulties of this kind are likely to present themselves. This is often the reason why distortion occurs in the first place.

When edge-stitching, the most common difficulty is caused by the same factor. The folded edge must not be allowed to stretch to any degree and must remain, as when cut, exactly matching the corresponding seam on to which it is to be stitched. If this is likely to happen because of the nature of the fabric or a crossway cut, then take steps to avoid it by applying interfacing, a row of stay-stitching (a row of smaller stitches running next to the fold edge, just inside the seam turning) or, in extreme cases, stitching in a narrow stay tape, cut to the correct length. Be especially careful to avoid stretching the fabric when pressing; you will find it easier to control and will achieve a better finish if the fold edge is pressed to give as sharp a crease as possible. It may be sensible, especially on longer strips, to pin the fabric down in the correct position at intervals. When machining, do not run the needle right on the thread before the fold edge, but about 2 mm ($\frac{1}{16}$ in.) away so that the stitching line 'beds down' properly into the fabric. It may be helpful in some cases to use a zip foot as this both reduces foot pressure and allows increased visibility. The fingers of the left hand may be used to control the fabric as when top-stitching, and you can use your right-hand fingernails to hold the fold edge firmly in place prior to stitching. Be especially careful, as you are more likely to place a finger under the needle when using a zip foot.

APPLICATION

When applying a fabric shape on to a main fabric area, the basic principles for top-stitching and edge-stitching will be relevant. An accurate stitching line is important for visual reasons and dangers where distortion might arise must, similarly, be avoided.

Use pins plentifully to ensure correct placement, starting from the centre area. Pinning around the extreme edge, where the stitching is to be, may then not be necessary. Rather than back-tacking, begin and finish stitching accurately and pull the top threads through to the WS to tie off or darn in. To do this, turn to the WS and tug carefully on the bobbin thread in the direction of the stitching line. A small loop will appear at its base into which you place a pin and so draw through the top thread.

Before beginning to stitch, always make sure that a large wayward fold has not appeared underneath or that part of a sleeve is not trapped under the foot unknowingly. When such a mistake arises and you find you have machined through and caught part of the skirt into the back of the pocket on the bodice that you have just so meticulously stitched in place with not one, but three rows of top-stitching, summon all your patience. Defy any expert to say the same thing does not occasionally happen to them too! This is one problem that is avoided by working on the garment as much as possible while it is still 'flat'. Apply to the fabric at the earliest stages of construction.

CHAPTER ELEVEN

fabrics: suggestions for handling

HEAVY-WEIGHT FABRICS

Do not be put off using heavy-weight fabrics because you fear handling them. More simple styles do not require expert tailoring methods and an appreciation of the bulk involved is the main consideration. The following points include the most important aspects of working with such fabrics.

Cutting

1   Cut larger seam turnings (2 cm [¾ in.] at least). This is so they will lie flat on the WS.

2   Cut all measurements on the generous side. Remember that an amount of fabric is used up with bulk. Where, for instance, there may be a foldline, the fold itself will take possibly 5 mm (¼ in.) to 'roll' around the crease. At seams, especially where they may meet, there will be bulky areas, so ensure a loose fit for comfort.

3   Be careful when cutting balance nips. It is tempting to cut far into the turning so that they are easily visible, but heavy-weight fabrics are often of a loose weave and two fraying threads could mean a loss of 5 mm (¼ in.) of fabric.

4   To ensure accuracy, it is often necessary to cut every piece individually, rather than cutting through double thickness fabric. Heavier-weight fabrics are more expensive, so it is worth spending more time and making an excellent job.

5   Choose flat seams or those with least bulk: an overlaid seam with a decoratively bound edge instead of a fold is ideal.

Machining

1   Use a larger machine needle (90 or 100) and thicker thread (40).

2   Adjust to a slightly longer stitch for straight stitching – about 3–3.25. It may be necessary to loosen the tension for the perfect stitch.

3   Work with less pressure on the machine foot. This will make the difference between easy, successful work and a difficult, frustrating struggle. The main problem when working with heavy-weight fabric is trying to keep two fabric layers accurately together when seaming. As the fabric passes beneath the foot the top layer is pushed forward and, with a thicker fabric, this is exaggerated. By releasing foot pressure, the top layer of fabric is not squeezed forward and the fabric can be controlled as easily as any other. Even so, it may be that the top layer of fabric should be positioned back a little on purpose – say 3–4 mm (⅛–¼ in.) – so that a minimal amount of forcing forward will push the fabric into the correct position. This is especially useful to remember when matching stripes in a heavy-weight fabric where accuracy is critical.

4   It is helpful to use larger pins so they do not disappear amongst the fibres. Glass-headed pins are ideal as they remain easily visible and you can be sure of removing them before one breaks the machine needle.

JERSEY FABRICS

Fabrics with a knitted construction are widely available in varying weights and types. They differ from woven fabrics where handling is concerned in that they are liable to stretch, and the raw edges do not lie flat but roll up and, instead of fraying, will run into ladders.

Cutting

1   When laying the fabric out in preparation for cutting, be especially careful that it is not stretched or pulled in any direction.

2 Be careful that the damaged point of a pin does not catch and snag as this can ruin a fabric instantly.

3 If the fabric tends to roll out of position immediately it has been cut into, use weights to keep it in place. Plates or saucers are useful.

4 If a fabric runs badly, do not cut nips into the seam turnings: use a pen to mark all balance points instead.

Machining

1 Use a ball-point machine needle of a size suitable for the weight of the fabric. These pierce the fabric so that a proper stitch is made. An ordinary needle may 'bounce' off the fabric, resulting in missed stitches.

2 A synthetic thread is preferable, whatever the fibre content of the fabric. These are stronger and so less likely to snap; this is an advantage where a fabric may stretch and so put strain on the stitching.

3 Because of the ability of the fabric to stretch slightly, it may be helpful to set the machine at a very slight zig-zag setting. This is barely noticeable in the appearance of the stitch and should not affect the seamline on the RS. It will, however, help the stitching line take the strain that will be placed upon it if the fabric stretches, and so will prevent the stitches cracking. Loosen the tension a little, too.

4 When machining, gently stretch the fabric by pulling it towards you as it passes under the foot. This, too, will stop seams from breaking, but is not advisable if the fabric distorts.

5 Unless the fabric is of a particularly heavy weight, finish plain seam turnings together. This will help prevent them rolling up. If you have a three-step zigzag, this will also be useful for keeping the cut edges of jersey fabrics flat.

PILE FABRICS

Fabrics with clipped fibres such as velvets require special attention to certain points when being used but otherwise should cause no real difficulties.

Cutting

1 Check the direction of the nap. These fabrics require a one-way lay. The pile is smooth when brushed along grain in one direction and rough when brushed in the opposite. The true richness of any pile fabric is seen when the fabric falls, so that on a velvet skirt, for instance, the fabric feels rough when brushed from waist downwards to the hem.

2 Be especially careful not to pin through any fabric that is not a seam turning. Even so, do not leave pins in the fabric for any length of time as pin marks are difficult, if not impossible, to remove.

Machining

1 Do not machine against the pile. If this cannot be avoided, use a zip foot so that the foot passes over the fabric on the turning side of the stitching line.

2 Reduce the pressure of the foot so that the pile is not crushed even when machining in the 'smooth' direction.

3 If the fabric is constructed with a jersey base, which you can see by looking at the WS, follow the instructions given for jersey fabrics.

4 Top-stitching or edge-stitching are not suitable.

Pressing

The difficulty with pressing a pile fabric is that the fibres are easily squashed. Always press on the WS only. You may have a needleboard (a long strip of short spikes rather like a mini bed of nails) which is specially for pressing velvets, where the fabric is placed RS down on the needleboard and can then be pressed normally with no fear of crushing the pile. Otherwise it is possible to lay the fabric face down on to another piece that is face up, so that the two pile surfaces lie together. Apply minimal pressure at all times using steam where helpful.

STRETCH FABRICS

The main problem with making up fabrics that stretch is that the stitches crack and so the seams fall apart. Consider the suggestions given for jersey fabrics. It is possible on some machines to set a triple stitch which sews every stitch three times. This is impossible to break in everyday wear, but be sure to machine right first time as unpicking such a seam is an unenviable task. A three-step zigzag is ideal for any other machining. Where you do not want the fabric to stretch at all, stitch a narrow tape of the correct length along the stitching line. A normal stitch can then be used.

SLIPPERY FABRICS

Certain fabrics have a particularly smooth surface which makes them difficult to control as they slip and slide out of position.

Cutting

1 Lay the fabric up on a carpet rather than a smooth table surface.

2 When cutting double, hold the selvedges together with small bulldog clips placed at intervals along the fabric length.

3 Hold the fabric down with weights as much as is practicable and use pins plentifully in the seam turnings.

Machining

1 Pin closely, perpendicular to the stitching line. As you remove the pins, hold the fabric firmly, watching that the cut edges remain in place as the fabric is taken up by the feeder.

2 Increase the pressure on the machine foot a little.

FABRICS WHICH FRAY READILY

Fabrics of any fibre and weight may be constructed in such a way that the threads at a raw cut edge will quickly begin to come away. Steps can be taken to avoid this causing problems.

Cutting

1 Allow perhaps 3 mm ($\frac{1}{8}$ in.) extra to every seam turning so that if some threads should be lost it is not critical.

2 Do not cut balance nips, but mark them in with a pin.

3 Do not be tempted to trim off any little hairy ends where several threads may be coming away together.

4 Choose seams and construction methods that enclose all the raw edges: French seams are the ideal example.

5 Avoid all hand sewing in the construction of the garment.

6 Cut the garment out as quickly as possible. If you are not going to make it up immediately, fold the cut pieces up, enclosing all the raw edges.

7 Beware of trimming closely.

Machining

1 In cases where the fraying is extreme, machine a long stitch around the edge of every cut piece.

2 In places that will need trimming, machine small reinforcement stitches just outside the stitching line.

3 Make the garment up as quickly as possible. Get away with as little pressing as you can while there are still raw edges.

4 Machine with a slightly shorter stitch than usual (2–2.25).

LIGHT-WEIGHT, FLOATY FABRICS

These are, perhaps, the most difficult of all fabrics to control. It is wise to go along with their nature as much as possible, so do not try to force them into styles which are unsuitable.

Cutting

1 Follow the cutting suggestions for slippery fabrics.

2 In extreme cases – chiffon, for example – lay tissue paper between the two fabric layers.

3 Pin through all layers together.

4 Cut out slowly, placing your free hand down on the fabric with your fingers spread, so that as large an area as possible is held down close to the cutting line.

Machining

1 Use the finest machine needle available (60 or 70) and fine thread (50–60).

2 Work with the pressure on the machine foot either normal, or slightly increased.

3 Use small, fine pins as regularly as you need.

4 Hold the fabric edges extremely firmly together. Make sure the bulk of the fabric to the left of the machine foot is lifted along in the correct position as the seam progresses.

5 Use a very narrow stay tape if helpful.

further suggestions for good results

TRIMMING

To obtain a good-quality finish to your work it is as necessary to clip and trim during the construction of the garment as it is to stitch neatly and accurately. Many believe that the good needlewoman 'sews with her iron' but, unless the work has been carefully trimmed and adequately clipped, no end of pressing will help even the neatest stitching to look good. Sharp scissors that are comfortable to use are essential if the job is not to be a chore. It is important that there is no excess bulk left on the inside of the garment so that there is nothing unattractive on the RS to draw attention to the fact that there are seam turnings beneath. Where two fabric pieces have been seamed together and turned through so that the seam turnings lie together, completely enclosed, it is even more necessary to trim away all excess fabric. If there are several thicknesses of fabric lying together it is better to trim these away by grading each one, otherwise a stiff edge will result in a 'lumpy' finish on the RS or an unsightly ridge will show. Leave the widest turning lying against the fabric that will show on the RS so that the latter lies on as smooth a finish as possible. A non-fusible interlining may still be trimmed away right up to the stitching line (*Fig. 101*).

Make every effort to trim seam turnings as smoothly and evenly as you can. It has previously been emphasised that it is more efficient to cut garments out in the first instance with seam turnings that are the finished width required and, if you do this, much time can be saved by avoiding the need to trim. Where fabric is stitched with RSs together and turned through, trimming cannot, however, be avoided and this is where careful cutting pays surprising dividends. Trimming that leaves a wavering cut edge, however slight, will never turn through to give such a high standard of finish as one which is cut with care. Examples are shown of a curved turning and a pointed turning (*Fig. 102*). The curved

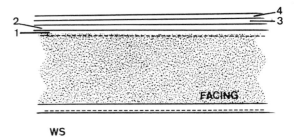

101 *Graded trimming. Example shows back neck, collar and back neck facing seam: (1) facing; (2) top collar; (3) under-collar; (4) bodice back*

edge should be cut in a smooth line that grades gradually closer to the stitching line as the curve increases and then comes gradually back out to run into the original cut edge. How close you dare cut to the stitching line will depend on a combination of what the weight of the fabric demands and the closeness of weave will allow. From a standard 6 mm ($\frac{1}{4}$ in.) seam turning it is possible to trim as close as 2 mm ($\frac{1}{16}$ in.) on a medium-weight, reasonably closely woven cotton fabric. To cut this close on a loose-weave or jersey fabric, especially of a more slippery fibre, would be disastrous, but remember that a smoothly cut line will compensate for having to leave more seam turning for safety's sake.

Trimming away a point that is to be turned through is based on a similar principle of grading. First, trim across the point, again as close as 2 mm ($\frac{1}{16}$ in.). Now cut away the seam turning from the narrowest point as shown on each side. If necessary, trim away a further section, removing more fabric from the seam turning remaining in the area of the point, though not close to the point itself. The sharper the point is to be, the further up the seam the turning needs to be trimmed. Badly turned through

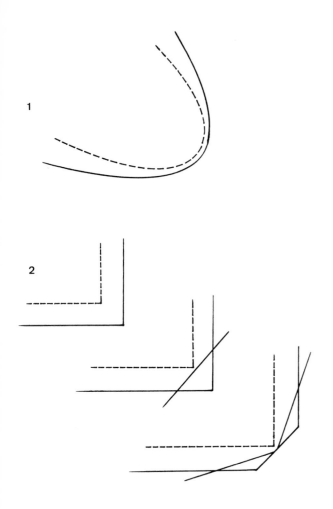

102 (1) Trimming a curve that is to be turned through; (2) trimming a corner that is to be turned through

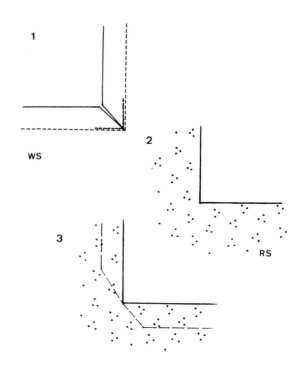

103 Clipping a corner: (1) seam showing reinforcement stitches; (2) seam turned through to RS; (3) position of seam turnings indicated

points are disappointing and will spoil what might be an otherwise beautifully made garment. Once the turnings have been trimmed away sufficiently, place a pointed object – blunt not sharp – to the corner of the stitching: an old plastic knitting needle is ideal. Holding it in position, turn the corner through to the RS. To achieve a good point, roll the corner between the thumb and forefinger so that the fabric is pushed gently down over the knitting needle until the point is properly turned through. It is tempting to push the knitting needle and poke at the point, but this may break right through the fabric and does not, in fact, give such a well turned out point.

Just as points must be trimmed away inside to reduce bulk, corners need to be clipped to allow the seam turnings to lie flat. Any corner must be clipped

into, as shown (Fig. 103), right up to the very point where the stitches turn. When turned through, the fabric will then sit flat. It is often wise to place a row of smaller stitches – known as reinforcement stitches – around the corner, where clipping causes an otherwise weak area. Fig. 103 shows the necessity for clipping into corners as well as the positioning for reinforcement stitches.

Curved seam turnings also require careful clipping. Where the seamline forms a convex curve, the cut edge of the turning is shorter than the position in which it will lie when in its final position. Clipping increases the length of the cut edge, so allowing the turning to lie flat inside the garment. Clip at regular intervals, right up to the stitching. Too many clips are preferable to too few.

Where a curved stitching line forms a concave curve, the cut edge will be longer than the position in which it will lie when in its final position. In this instance, the excess fabric must be removed to avoid bulk. Trim away V-shaped nicks at regular intervals, as indicated (Fig. 104), to reduce the amount of fabric in the seam turning.

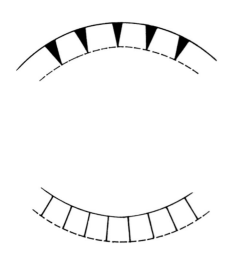

104 *Clipping curved seam turnings*

PRESSING

Unless you are working with a fabric that is particularly difficult to handle, it is not usually necessary to press at every step of each stage of the construction of a garment. Try to do so much in one 'sitting' at the machine and similarly save up jobs for pressing so you do not have to bob up and down constantly from machine to iron.

To begin with, you must meet the requirements of the fabric, so that you can treat it in a way that will give the best results. The most obvious point is temperature. So long as your iron has a thermostat you can trust, set the iron at the highest setting the fabric will take. The heat of the iron will then do much of the work – it is unnecessary to apply as much pressure as when the heat is insufficient. When testing fabric check that the surface texture of finish is not altered by the application of the iron. It is often sensible to wait for the fabric to cool right down before comparing it with a piece of 'control' fabric that has not been pressed. Certain fabric dyes, for instance, react dramatically to heat. As the fabric cools, the colour rapidly returns to normal. You must also test fabric to see whether to use steam or not. Some fabrics should never be pressed wet as this will cause water marks which cannot be removed – so beware. With other fabrics, steam is unnecessary as a dry iron alone is good enough. When steam is helpful, it may either be used directly from the jets of the iron, where it can be controlled in some irons, or

where much steam is required a dampened cloth can be used. If a small amount of dampness is all that is needed, a gentle spray from a mister can be used and is also easy to direct on certain areas. Even if you do not usually use steam when pressing, it may sometimes be helpful, particularly where there are any creases to be set.

Be careful not to cause a shine by being too heavy-handed or using too high a temperature. Be especially careful with lighter-coloured fabrics, as even the slightest singeing will cause yellowing, and bear in mind that many synthetic fabrics will shrink away if over-heated.

When to press
Pressing is as important before you machine as it is afterwards. In the construction methods given here, 'preparation' pressing is included where it is necessary during the making up of a process. This often means that pins or tacking are dispensed with as it is possible to control the fabric with the fingers as you machine.

Each cut piece may require a light pressing on the WS before you begin work. Then try to reach a stage where the garment can be hung as quickly as possible so that it is not creased needlessly. While it has been suggested that saving up pressing to do in batches is a good idea, this is only possible as far as the construction will allow, and cannot be applied to all circumstances. For example, an elasticated skirt is made up of four panels which are to be joined with French seams. The first stage of the four vertical seams is stitched. Each seam can then be pressed ready for the second stage. The four seams are then completed and must now be pressed before the waistband/casing can be attached. This is an over-simplified instance, but shows how you can work within the confines of the construction methods to press in stages. It requires a little thought beforehand on more complicated garments where it is not quite so obvious, but can be worth the effort if time-saving is important to you.

Pressing technique
The secret of successful pressing lies in using the iron in a careful and gentle manner. Often you will not be ironing a large fabric area to remove creases, but working on a small area to improve the finish of each stage of construction. It follows that it is not always necessary to use the whole of the base of the iron flat but that the sides and toe areas alone will give better results. Use the iron patiently: you are not ploughing through a mountain of family laundry. Delicate touches will often suffice. Hold the iron still

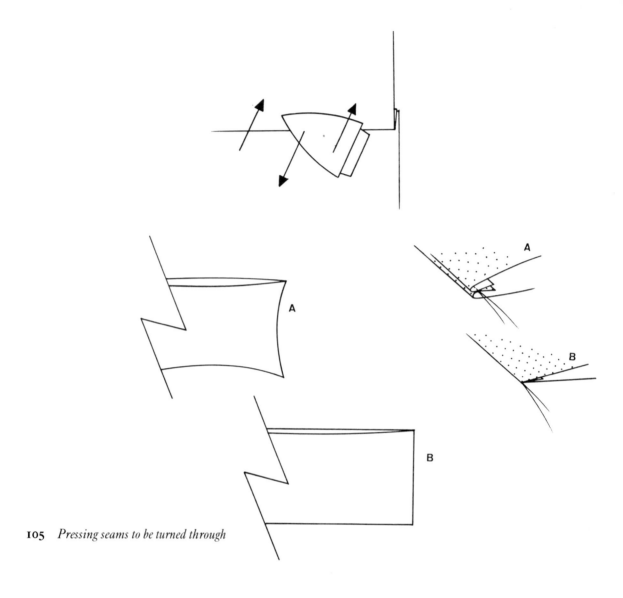

105 *Pressing seams to be turned through*

in one place for a few seconds, preventing the full weight of the iron from pressing down on the fabric. This allows heat rather than pressure to 'set' particular areas of the work. Collar points, finished patch pockets, corners of cuffs are instances where this is preferable treatment.

First, run the iron smoothly over lines of machining to embed the stitches in the fabric and so 'set' the seam. Certain fabrics will show indentations of seam turnings, etc. on the RS more readily than others and this is one of the reasons why heavy or unnecessary pressing should be avoided. To prevent this, try the following. Press a flat seam open from the WS with as little pressure as possible and with the back of the iron raised. Run only the toe area along the stitching line. In order to remove any marks which may still appear, run the side of the iron along, next to the stitching line but underneath the seam turnings. This should mean you do not need to press the seam from the RS.

When seams are turned through to the RS, leaving the turnings enclosed, it can sometimes be awkward to press a neat, crisp crease along the stitching line. To give a good finish, first press the seam flat from the RS, with the seam turnings lying together in the seam direction (*Fig. 105*). It may be difficult to get to the seams, but try to reach as much as possible by using the toe of the iron. It will now be much easier to turn through and to press along the edges, as the fabric does not roll up inside.

INTERLININGS

The correct use of interlinings will give your work an extremely professional finish. Exactly where you use an interlining and the effect you wish it to have on the garment is entirely up to you. Collars, cuffs, facings, openings, waistbands and other areas where strain or heavy wear is bound to occur are all the usual places where an interlining is used. When reinforcement is needed for various reasons, or a firmer fabric area is required, the use of an interlining will give control and a high standard of finish.

Choosing the most suitable interlining for the fabric should not be a problem. Often an interlining of similar weight to the fabric gives a good result and this is a useful guide to follow when faced with a wide choice. Use a heavier interlining if that is what you need but always be careful to avoid too stiff a finish if this is not specifically required. It does not matter that more than one type of interlining is used in the same garment, so long as the most suitable type is used for each job.

Interlining fabrics are woven or non-woven. The latter is bonded or felted and, therefore, has no grain. Either type can be bought as fusible or non-fusible. Iron-on interlining may seem a wonderful time-saving boon but there can sometimes be problems that make a non-fusible interlining – one which needs to be sewn in position – a better choice. Fusible interlining is literally 'fused' to the fabric by applying heat and pressure with the iron. The dried adhesive then melts and the interlining and fabric stick. This is a relatively quick process but it must be done properly. If the interlining does not stick properly, it will soon begin to come away inside when the finished garment is washed. This can also result in bubbles appearing on the RS. Fusible interlining may also begin to become unstuck after repeated washing even when applied correctly, especially if the fabric has a slight surface texture. If the fabric is one which will not withstand a high temperature or will be damaged by fairly heavy pressure then it is not possible to use fusible interlining successfully. When you test a fusible interlining with scraps to decide whether it gives the desired effect, wait for it to cool right down before seeing how stiff it makes the fabric because, as it cools, it stiffens.

Applying fusible interlining

Make sure the iron is right up to temperature before you begin. The fabric is laid WS up and the interlining placed with the adhesive side down. Position the interlining accurately. Begin at one end and work slowly across the fabric to the other

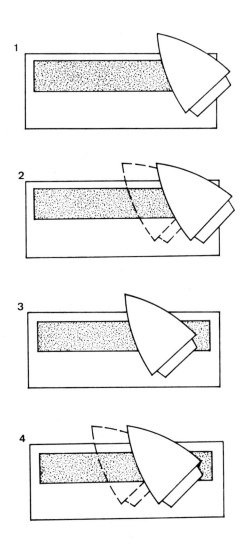

106 *First stages of applying fusible interlining: (1) hold; (2) move across; (3) hold; (4) move across*

(*Fig. 106*). Do not lift the iron – if you do, put it down where you have already pressed. Only apply normal pressure at this stage. The idea is to soften the adhesive sufficiently to hold the interlining in the correct position and to remove all the air that is trapped between the two layers of fabric: allowing air to remain is the main reason why fusible interlinings are found unsatisfactory by many. Check that the edges, particularly the corners, are stuck down. Once you are satisfied that the interlining is correctly positioned and that all the air has been removed, you are ready to fuse the interlining. At this stage you have a chance to correct any mistakes as the interlining will still peel off; once fused it is too late.

Position the iron at the same place as you began for the first stage, but you can now cover a greater area at a time (*Fig. 107*). With the iron on hot, or very hot, press it down hard. Hold in one place, maintaining pressure for about ten seconds. (This is why it is important to ascertain how well the fabric withstands heat before deciding to use fusible interlining.) Lift off the iron. Allow this area to cool slightly before continuing, because there will be an area of overlap. When you have covered the whole area in this way, iron thoroughly over both RS and WS. Allow the fabric to cool right down, leaving it flat, before machining. Before you make it up, check the edges and corners to see if they will pick away. If they do, repeat the second stage.

Applying non-fusible interlining

Non-fusible interlining is used when the fabric will not withstand heat or pressure, when the specific weight, colour or type of interlining required is not available in fusible material, or because of personal preference.

Wherever it is used, it must be anchored in position before the fabric can be made up. This is done by machining it in place with a 'hold' row of stitching – i.e. machine tacking that need not be removed. It is vital that the interlining is attached so that it lies exactly flat on the fabric, not causing rippling, twisting or any other distortion, however slight. To ensure against this, first press every tiny crease out of both interlining and fabric. Now position the interlining accurately, and hold it in place with pins (*Fig. 108*). Start pinning from the centre and work towards the edges. Leave a 1.3 cm ($\frac{1}{2}$ in.) margin around the edges free of pins. The object is to machine the interlining in place 2 mm ($\frac{1}{16}$ in.) outside the stitching line so, depending upon the seam turnings allowed, machine around the edges of the interlining at 2 mm ($\frac{1}{16}$ in.) less than the turning from the cut fabric edge. Remove the pins. Now trim off any excess interlining that would otherwise cause unwanted bulk in the seam turnings, cutting as close to the stitching as possible. Press flat on both sides, checking that there is no distortion of either the fabric or interlining.

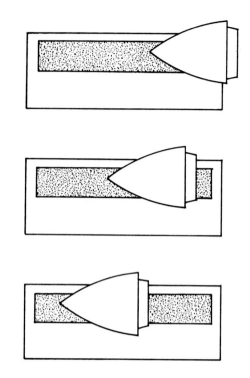

107 *Moving iron across interlining in stages to complete fusing*

108 *Machining non-fusible interlining in position*

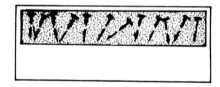

CHAPTER THIRTEEN

Seaming

When deciding what particular seam to use, consider the following: the type of fabric; the neatening of the inside of the garment; its suitability in relation to the chosen construction method; the time involved; the strength required – its position on the garment and, therefore, how much strain will be placed upon it; ease of construction and the visual appearance.

FLAT OR PLAIN SEAM

The quickest and most basic seam is the plain seam which leaves the appearance of a single line or crease on the RS (*Fig. 109*). The RSs of the fabric are placed together, with the edges exactly level, and the stitching line runs parallel to the cut edge, leaving a seam turning of suitable width. This seam is the most commonly used as its size/width can be varied so much to suit many fabrics, and there are many ways to neaten the raw edges of the seam turning on the inside.

Seam turnings

A narrow, 6 mm ($\frac{1}{4}$ in.) seam turning can be left on all fabrics where a finish is not necessary as the raw edges will be enclosed, either by turning the work inside out or for some other reason. Any seam where trimming would normally be necessary may just as well be stitched at this width to begin with, saving time and fabric. Beware of cutting such a narrow seam on loosely woven fabrics that are likely to fray, and be careful not to stitch any narrower than the full 6 mm ($\frac{1}{4}$ in.) by mistake. When in doubt, test a scrap and then pull on the seam to see how well the turnings cope with the strain. On many machines, running the foot edge along the cut edge will act as a guide to give a 6 mm ($\frac{1}{4}$ in.) seam turning.

1.3 cm ($\frac{1}{2}$ in.) is an average width turning suitable on most fabrics for most major constructional seams on the garment. This will give sufficient wear with a minimum amount of bulk. It also leaves enough

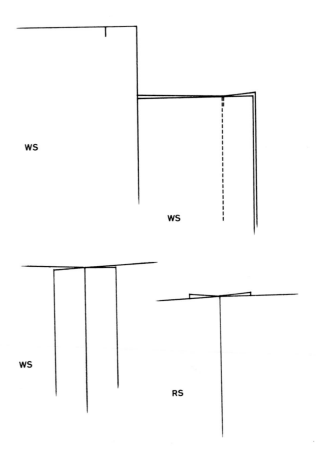

WS

WS

WS

RS

109 *Flat or plain seam*

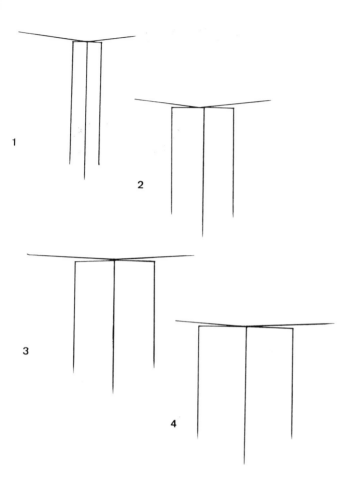

1

2

3

4

110　*Common seam turning widths: (1) 6 mm (¼in.); (2) 1.3 cm (½in.); (3) 1.7 cm (⅝in.); (4) 2 cm (¾in.)*

fabric to finish off the raw edges reasonably, although always decide on the method of finishing first and cut accordingly.

Wider seam turnings than this may be needed when extra fabric is necessary to achieve a particular neatening method. Certain fabrics may fray particularly badly or simply need a wider turning to hold securely. At other times, an extra wide seam turning can be used to form a casing, act as an interlining or be used for some other functional purpose. It may also be that only one of the seam turnings will require this extra width which will mean that the cut edges will lie not together, but parallel to each other, when being stitched. In these instances the narrower seam turning is always uppermost, so that accurate stitching is possible.

Neatening flat seams

Pinking

Pinking shears cut a zigzag finish which is intended to prevent raw edges fraying (*Fig. III [1]*). A good, sharp pair of shears is essential to prevent an untidy, chewed edge. This is only satisfactory on firmer fabrics that really do stop fraying when pinked and, as this does not give a particularly professional finish, it is more suitable on garments that are to be lined. Many fabrics will soon fall apart along the pinked edge and look worse than if they had been left raw in the first place. Closely woven fabrics, certain brushed fabrics, medium- to heavy-weight wools and other fabrics with a rough surface are examples where pinking may be satisfactory.

Machine finish

A zigzag stitch run along the edge of the seam allowance will prevent fraying and is useful where an attractive appearance is important (*Fig. III [2A]*). Keep the stitch length proportionate to its width. A long stitch will look untidy and not serve its purpose so well and a very wide stitch will not always give the best finish. Try a smaller, more dainty stitch as this will prevent fraying much more successfully and look altogether neater. The correct tension is vital so that the fabric edges do not roll or pucker.

A three-step zigzag stitch (*Fig. III [2B]*) will give a firmer finish and the seam turning will lie flatter than with an ordinary zigzag stitch. This is also suitable for fabrics with any give or stretch in them.

Modern machines offer a multitude of other utility stitches which are useful when machine-neatening raw edges and give alternatives to the industrial overlock stitch. Always make sure the tension is perfect. When stitching through a single layer of fabric you will need to take care and reduce the machine speed. In fact, a far better result can often be achieved by pressing the seam allowances together in the same direction and finishing them off through the double fabric (*Fig. III [3A and B]*). Generally, seams that run vertically are pressed towards the back and seams that run horizontally are pressed in whichever direction is most suitable. So long as this does not cause too much bulk, there is no reason why all seams suitable for machine-neatening should not be pressed and finished together, saving time and thread and increasing the strength of the finished seam. Finish any seams that have turnings with edges of unequal length, such as where there are gathers, tucks, etc. A straight row of stitching close to the turning edge to begin with will give greater control and often a flatter finish.

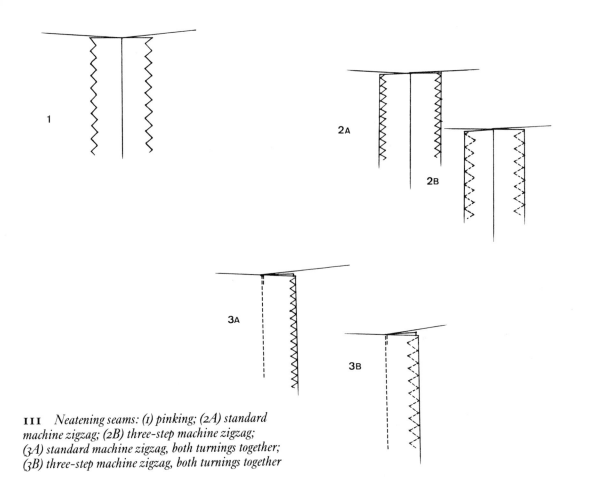

III *Neatening seams: (1) pinking; (2A) standard machine zigzag; (2B) three-step machine zigzag; (3A) standard machine zigzag, both turnings together; (3B) three-step machine zigzag, both turnings together*

Edge-stitched

The raw edge of the seam turning can be narrowly turned under and a row of machining stitched virtually along the foldline to give a crisp, neat edge (*Fig. 112*). This is more suitable for straight seams as it cannot be clipped to allow curved seams to lie flat. It is often more suitable to cut a 1.7 cm ($\frac{5}{8}$ in.) seam turning so that 1.3 cm ($\frac{1}{2}$ in.) is the finished width of the turning. Be careful not to stretch the raw edge as your index finger of the right hand rolls it over as this will distort the seam turning. A stretched edge will give a fluted seam turning that will not press flat and will give a lumpy look to the RS. Too tight a tension will lead to a puckered seam and cracked stitches. When machined correctly, this is an attractive finish and a small zigzag stitch may be used as an alternative to the straight stitch. Any light- to medium-weight fabric that is reasonably easy to handle in this way can be machine-neatened along the right kind of seam.

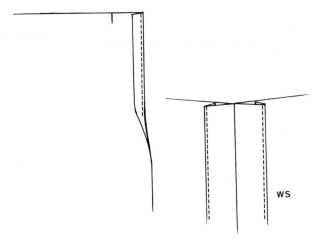

112 *Edge-stitched flat seam turnings*

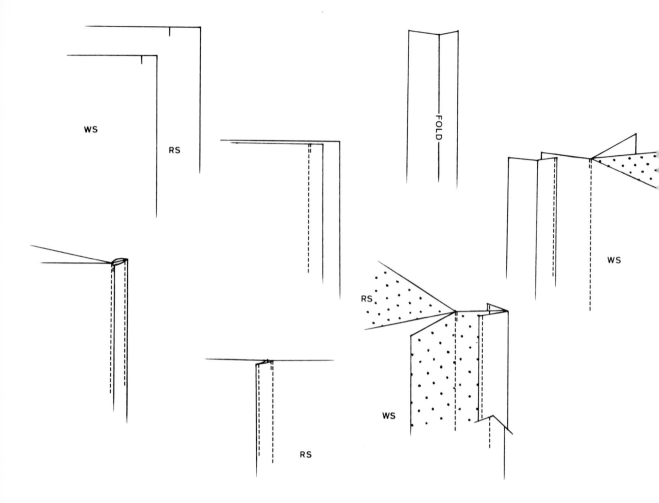

113 *Self-bound (mock French) seam*

114 *Binding seam turnings*

Self-bound (mock French) seam
Where both seam turnings are pressed together in the same direction, the uppermost allowance can be folded over the allowance underneath and edge-stitched, giving a bound appearance (*Fig. 113*). The allowance to be enclosed should be trimmed away to the finished width of the seam turning, to reduce bulk. This may be especially suitable if the turning to be enclosed has been gathered or has extra bulk for any other reason.

Binding
Bulky fabrics may need to have their raw edges enclosed in a tape or binding, especially those more closely woven and likely to disintegrate quickly (*Fig. 114*). A 1.7 cm (⅝ in.) seam turning is suitable. Hand-sewing a binding should be unnecessary.

Press the tape lengthwise with one side 2 mm (1/16 in.) wider than the other. Place the foldline to the raw edge (not right up against it, as the tape will strain over the bulk and a crisp edge will not result) with the wider half uppermost. Now machine the narrow half to the WS of the seam turning, stitching close to the edge of the tape. Stitch the top half down in the same way. Be careful that the tape is cut with sufficient length to avoid accidentally easing the seam turning on to a short tape that will then pull tight, distorting and puckering the seam. Alternatively, a wide zigzag stitch will hold down both edges of the tape in one row of stitching. In this case, the tape can be pressed exactly in half. It is well worth binding the seam turnings in certain garments, such as unlined jackets, where the inside of the garment may sometimes show, or where heavy wear is to be expected.

FRENCH SEAM

This seam is ideal for light-weight and soft fabrics although it was traditionally used for very fine or sheer fabrics, giving a very narrow and dainty finish (*Fig. 115*). Its use can be extended to many medium-weight fabrics and is extremely useful as all the raw edges are enclosed in the seam, which is constructed with only two rows of machining. Careful handling will result in a very neat finish that will remain so after constant washing and wear. The finish width of the turning is 5 mm ($\frac{3}{16}$ in.). Cut a 1 cm ($\frac{3}{8}$ in.) seam turning.

1 Place fabric WSs together. Machine 5 mm ($\frac{3}{16}$ in.) seam. Trim down close to the stitching. To avoid trimming down, cut a narrower seam turning to begin with. Press WS flat, leaving turnings lying together and then, placing RSs together, press a crisp foldline exactly along the first machining row.

2 With RSs together, machine along the final stitching line, which should fall 6 mm ($\frac{1}{4}$ in.) from fold edge (first stitching line).

Trim the first turning away evenly and with care.

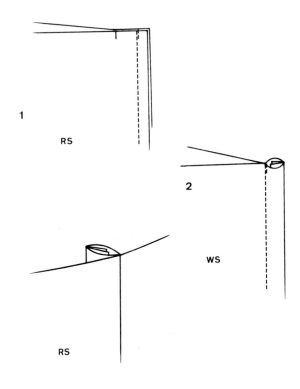

The finished allowance will then lie smoothly and little fuzzy threads will not poke out on to the RS where they have been caught in the second line of stitching. Careful pressing will make a great difference to the success of this seam. Once you understand its construction, you will be able to adjust the width to suit the fabric. It is not advisable to make the allowance of this seam very much wider than 6 mm ($\frac{1}{4}$ in.) simply because it is not necessary. A fabric that needs any wider allowance is too bulky to be suitable for this type of seam.

FLAT-FELLED SEAM

This is an extremely strong seam where the stitching lines show on the RS, and an example can be commonly found on the seams of jeans. It leaves no raw edges. The seam turnings of the pieces to be joined are not equal. Usually, one has a 6 mm ($\frac{1}{4}$ in.) turning and the other a 1.3 cm ($\frac{1}{2}$ in.) turning (*Fig. 116*).

1 Place WSs together, with the narrower 6 mm ($\frac{1}{4}$ in.) turning uppermost and the stitching line matched exactly, and machine first row of stitching.

2 Press the seam on the WS with the turnings on the RS lying together so that the wider turning falls on the top. Press this carefully in half.

3 With the RS facing, edge-stitch the folded edge down through all fabric thicknesses.

Use a fabric that is reasonably crisp and firm. Accuracy in the positioning of the fabric for the first row of stitching is important as this is the finished seamline of the garment. The remainder is basically a neatening process. With some practice, and a suitable fabric, it may not be necessary to press the foldline in place in preparation for edge-stitching. Instead, run the raw edge under with the fingernail of the right-hand index finger. Press the seamline on the WS carefully so that, as the second row of stitching is worked, there is no excess fabric on the underside which might bubble in the area between the two stitching lines. Follow the suggestions given for edge-stitching to avoid problems of distortion arising. The straighter the seam, the easier it is to sew this process. On slightly curved seamlines, cut the wider seam turning on the concave curve so that the fold edge can be stretched around the curve to lie flat on the wider edge of the curve. This is preferable to attempting to ease away excess fullness along the folded edge as it is edge-stitched down which, even with the best possible handling, would still look untidy.

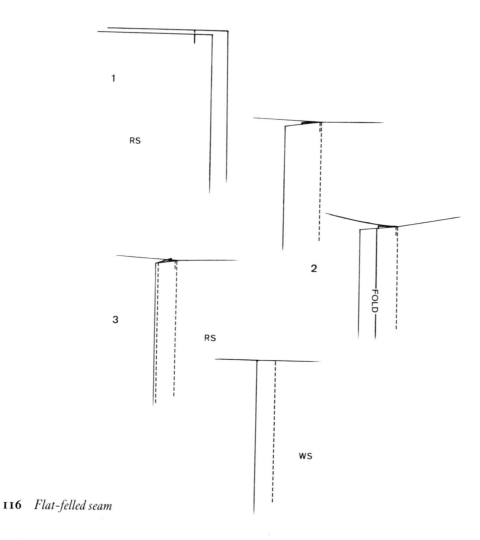

116 *Flat-felled seam*

It is much easier to work this seam on the flat, as difficulties arise when trying to join up cylindrical areas of the garment. If there is plenty of width it is possible. The main problem is to avoid catching any other part of the fabric under the machine when edge-stitching the second row in place. The longer a seamline is, and the narrower the total width of the fabric being joined up, the harder it becomes to avoid this and, in many cases, it is impossible. This is the reason why the inside leg seams of jeans are stitched as plain seams.

The finish of the WS of this seam may be worked so that it appears on the RS, giving a reversed flat-felled seam. The one basic difference is that the fabric is placed, in the first instance, with the RSs together. The edge-stitching is then automatically worked with the WS of the garment facing. The seam retains all the advantages, but may be worked on softer or more springy fabrics, where it is not

possible to achieve an extremely neat, crisp finish and is, therefore, better hidden on the WS.

OVERLAID SEAM

This type of seam construction is not commonly used, but it can be extremely useful and offers many possibilities for incorporating design features (*Fig. 117*).

1   Press the seam edge to be overlaid firmly along the stitching line on the pattern (the actual edge-stitching will be about 2 mm [$\frac{1}{16}$ in.] to one side of this).

2   Position the fold edge against the corresponding stitching line, pinning as required (the raw edges should lie exactly together on the WS).

Take the greatest care not to stretch the fabric along the fold edge when pressing, and follow the suggestions given for edge-stitching. This method can be used to incorporate decorative pleats or tucks and so the existence of a seamline may be disguised. This is simply achieved by adding the extra amount required to the top seam turning where double the finished tuck overlap is needed. This is obviously only possible on straight seamlines. This may be attractively used when overlaid where gathers have been included, or a piping cord may be inserted, so achieving two processes quickly and simply. Unusual and decorative processes can be experimented with once these basics are understood. The most important point is always to keep in mind the position of the actual seamline.

An alternative method is to finish the raw edge of the top fabric, instead of folding it under (*Fig. 118*).

1   Finish both seam turnings as required.

2   Matching the balance nips, place the top fabric in position. It is usually necessary to pin this in place along the seam, as once the fabric is under the machine it is difficult to check for accurate positioning.

This type of seam is suitable for bulky fabrics or where a decorative finish or feature is made of the seam.

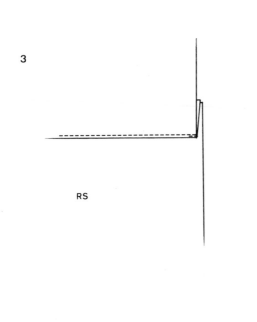

117   *Overlaid seam*

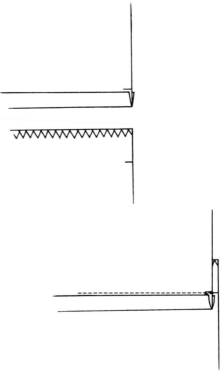

118   *Overlaid seam: alternative method*

CHAPTER FOURTEEN

Suppression

There are several ways to control the fullness of a fabric so that it is permanently held in position when made up. The choice of the method of suppression used is made at the design stage.

In order that the correct amount of fullness is held in the right position along the seam, the use of accurate balance nips is essential. In some instances the suppression is not placed along a seam but across a piece of fabric. Here, pins will be necessary to indicate the correct placement of the suppression.

EASE

Ease describes the process whereby a seam is joined with the appearance of a plain seam on the RS, but where one fabric piece has a greater seamline length,

119 *Distribution of ease with pins*

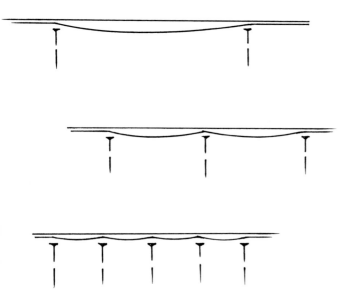

and therefore more fullness, than the corresponding seamline. With many fabrics it is possible to squash the threads more closely together on one side, so incorporating an amount of extra fullness into an ordinary seam. This is an important process and is invariably needed at some stage of construction. The stitching line of the longer fabric piece is 'eased' away on to the shorter length, which is the correct finished seam length. Ease commonly occurs on shoulder seams, where it is necessary to cut the back shoulder wider than the front to allow for a comfortable fit and greater movement across the back shoulder, and the sleeve-head of a set-in sleeve, so that the head seam is longer than the armhole and the head of the sleeve fits comfortably around the arm muscle, again allowing greater movement.

One difficulty that often arises when attempting to ease away excess fabric is that small pleats form. Then tucks may be accidentally stitched into the seam, and the amount of fullness is not distributed evenly. To avoid this happening, pins should be placed at the beginning and end of the seam length where the ease is to lie (*Fig. 119*). The centre point of the longer seamline is matched to the centre point of the shorter seamline, and pinned. Repeat this for the quarter marks and, if necessary, continue until the pins are about 5 cm (2 in.) apart. Mark these corresponding points with nips and remove the pins. When you are practised, the frequency of the nips can be lessened. Work at the machine as follows.

The fabric with the longest edge should be placed underneath. Stitch the seam to the first pair of nips. Place the three middle fingers of the left hand (with the fingers slightly apart) on the under fabric at the seamline, just ahead and to the left of the machine foot. Gently draw your fingers together and watch the fabric ripple. The closer your fingers become, the greater the amount of fabric drawn up will be. You will see how much fabric is being eased away and experience will help to judge the correct amount.

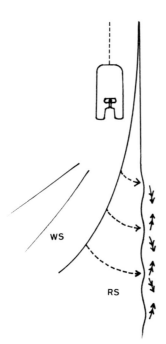

WS

RS

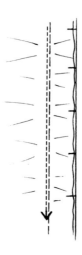

121 *Machining ease pulled up by a line of stitching*

Hold the top layer of fabric up in the right hand so that you can see how much ease you have drawn up underneath, and bring it down into position with the top fabric still held by the left hand by stroking the ease gently with a slow, left to right sideways movement, gradually bringing the edges together in the correct position. Machine each section, matching the balance nips and controlling the fabric, as described (*Fig. 120*).

The key to success is to maintain an even drawing-up of ease in the left hand and a stroking, sideways movement in placing the top fabric in position. If you are too heavy-handed in placing the top fabric down on top of the under fabric, you will flatten the ripples and small tucks will appear in the seam. Certain fabrics will ease away far more readily than others and with softer, loosely woven fabrics, it is possible to ease away far greater amounts satisfactorily.

Be careful not to stretch the top fabric by pulling on it as you hold it up and bring it down. This results in a puckered fabric and a distorted seamline. Keep a smooth and even stitching line and ensure that both fabric pieces are positioned correctly when the feeder takes them up.

Do not expect to be able to ease away fabric correctly without practice. This is one of the more difficult skills to acquire but one of the most time-saving. Co-ordination of the hands and eyes must be perfected so that lengths and distances can be judged quickly and accurately. Begin with softer fabrics, as stiffer ones will fight against you and you will need experienced hands to control the ease. Become familiar with the movements of the hands first, without worrying too much about keeping a straight stitching line when practising. Try easing a relatively small amount away and gradually increase this amount. Begin with easing 1 cm ($\frac{3}{8}$ in.) over 10 cm (4 in.) and increase to 2 cm ($\frac{3}{4}$ in.), 3 cm ($1\frac{1}{8}$ in.) and then 4 cm ($1\frac{1}{2}$ in.). 10 cm (4 in.) will be the length of the finished seam in every case but you will cut corresponding seam lengths of 11 cm ($4\frac{1}{8}$ in.), 12 cm ($4\frac{1}{2}$ in.), 13 cm ($4\frac{7}{8}$ in.) and 14 cm ($5\frac{1}{4}$ in.) respectively.

With fabrics that are difficult to ease away, run a line of full-length machine stitches just outside the stitching line the length to be eased (*Fig. 121*). A slightly tighter tension might help, as this row of stitching will pull up quite a large amount of ease automatically, acting in a similar way to the fingers. You may prefer to use a row of stitches every time ease is required. Cut sufficient balance nips in the same way. Secure the end of the machining and pull the thread taught, until it has pulled the excess fabric length in to fit the finished seam length. Adjust the ripples gently with a pin so that the ease is even, and machine, holding firmly together with the left hand. If the normal foot pressure for a particular fabric is reduced, the chances of pleats becoming accidentally stitched in the seam are lessened. Slackening off the pressure too much will, however, tend to cause more problems as the fabric is liable to slip and slide under the foot when the needle rises out of the fabric, so beware. Where a stitching line is used to pull the fabric up, you may prefer to machine the seam with the ease uppermost.

GATHERS

A section of seam which is to be gathered up is marked with balance marks. There will also be additional nips to help with the correct distribution of the fullness. There are two basic ways to gather up fabric ready for seaming. Whichever method you prefer to use you must make sure that the following points are observed.

1 The fabric gathers are even – there are no sparse areas or parts where the fabric is particularly bunched up.

2 The gathers lie straight and are held in place neatly (*Fig. 122*). This is important both in terms of finished appearance and to prevent gathers which cross untidily from catching in the seams.

3 Enough pins are used to hold the gathers in the correct position. As the pins lie across the stitching line it is easy for them to get lost amongst the gathers so make sure you remove every one as you machine.

Gathering up on a thread

The easiest way to gather up fabric is to run a line of stitching just outside the seamline: loosen the tension a little and use a larger stitch than is used for seaming. Increase the stitch length more for less flimsy fabrics.

Secure the threads at one end and pull the fabric up along the stitching to the correct width (*Fig. 123*). Bend the finger and thumb so that your nails pull on the fabric and the gathers are not flattened by this action. Distribute the gathers as evenly as you can as the fabric is pulled up, then it needs only to be checked and adjusted and the gathers are fingered as little as possible. Anchor the thread end and adjust the distribution lightly with a pin.

Machine the seam with the gathering uppermost. The gathers can then be seen to lie straight. You may like to run a second row of gathering stitches further up the seam turning and so pull the fabric up on both rows together, as this helps the gathers to lie straight. It is, however, not too difficult to make minor adjustments at the last minute when sewing the seam. Use a pin in preference to the finger to keep the gathers neatly side-by-side and lying straight.

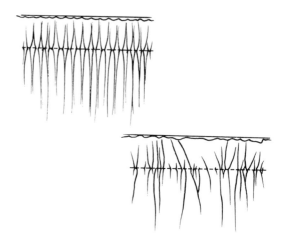

122 *Correct and incorrect gathers*

123 *Gathering up on a thread*

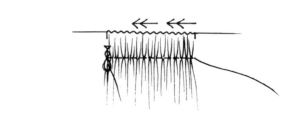

Pre-gathering

With this method, the gathers are stitched in place and so held in the final position immediately. There is no later chance to adjust their distribution or alter the direction in which they lie. This technique is well worth mastering for those occasions when large amounts of fabric are to be gathered as the effort is reduced drastically as well as the amount of time it would otherwise take.

Position the fabric at the machine so that the stitching runs just outside the seamline. Use an average-length stitch. Machine a few stitches up to the first balance nip. Using the forefinger of the left hand and something pointed, such as a pair of scissors, in the right hand, push an amount of fabric up under the foot. The quantity of fabric to be pushed up determines the size of the gathers and so how much fabric in total will be gathered away. It is important to push up an equal amount of fabric each time so that the gathers are even. Machine a few stitches at a time, pushing the gathers up as you proceed (*Fig. 124*).

The only difficulty with this method is knowing how much fabric is going to be gathered up in total. This is very important as the resultant seamline must, obviously, match up accurately to fit the corresponding seamline. Practice is the only real solution. Try out a 10 cm (4 in.) section of scrap fabric to see what is necessary to reduce the finished seam length to 5 cm (2 in.). Once you are able to judge this correctly, you will then be able to utilise this method.

UNPRESSED PLEATS

Where gathers are not intended as part of a design, unpressed pleats may provide a suitable alternative: the excess fabric is simply folded away into pleats which are then caught into the adjacent seam (*Fig. 125*). Two balance marks indicate the amount of fabric that is taken up by the pleat. It is not necessary to mark in the foldline that lies on the WS as this automatically comes down the centre of the pleat. Hold the pleats in position with a row of machining placed just outside the seamline.

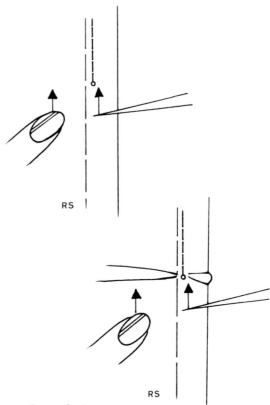

124 *Pre-gathering*

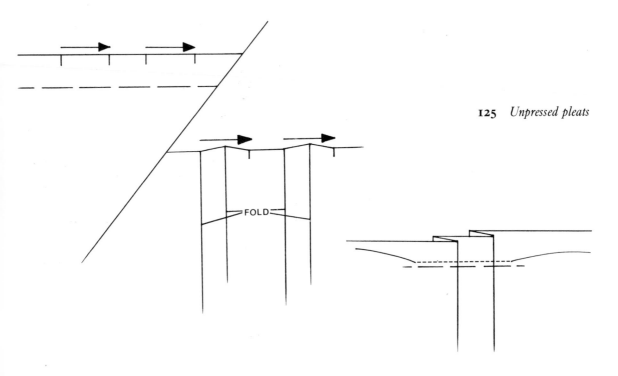

125 *Unpressed pleats*

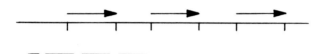

TUCKS

A tuck is marked in the fabric in the same way as an unpressed pleat – i.e. with two balance nips that indicate the amount of excess fabric that is to be folded away (*Fig. 126*). When the fabric is folded so that the nips are together, the nips then indicate the stitching line. Press the fold in place the full length of the tuck, with a pin to indicate the end of the stitching line where there are multiple tucks which are pressed to the right (*Fig. 127*). Work from left to right, so that the fold edge of the previous tuck can be used as an additional guide. If the tucks are pressed to the left, then work from right to left. Back tack at the beginning and end of each stitching line.

Tucks may be stitched so they fall on the RS or WS of the fabric. They may be pressed in either direction or pressed flat with an equal amount on each side of the stitching line. The direction of pressing affects the appearance at the base of the tuck where the fullness is released (*Fig. 128*). Top-stitching may be incorporated to hold the tuck either down or across one or more tucks for decoration. The possibilities are limitless, but whatever the size or direction of tuck, absolutely straight stitching and crisp fold edges are essential.

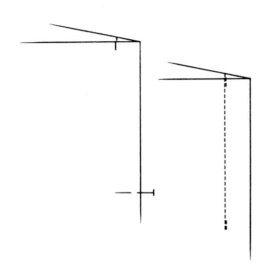

126 *Tuck sizes marked in fabric*

127 *Stitching multiple tucks*

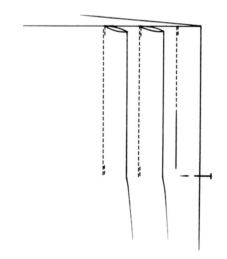

DARTS

1 Matching the balance marks, press the fold of the dart in position to the marked point, which is 1.3 cm (½ in.) above the finished point of the dart.

2 Stitch two stitches with the needle passing through the fabric thread on the very edge of the fold, beginning 1.3 cm (½ in.) below the mark. Back tack with extreme care and continue the next few stitches close to the edge, widening minimally until the mark is opposite the needle.

3 Lift the machine foot and swing the fabric until the direction of the foot is in line with the balance nips. Continue to stitch in a completely straight line to run into the nips, finishing with a back tack.

Pressing

Do not fold the fabric back without first pressing the dart. Be especially careful not to press beyond the point of the dart. Use the toe gently to 'set' the stitches. Trim the thread at the point leaving short ends. Now press the fabric on the RS with the dart lying in the correct direction (*Fig. 130*). If an impression of the dart should show on the RS, turn the fabric over and press under the dart to remove the mark. Fig. 131 shows how to finish a particularly wide dart, or a dart stitched in a bulky fabric.

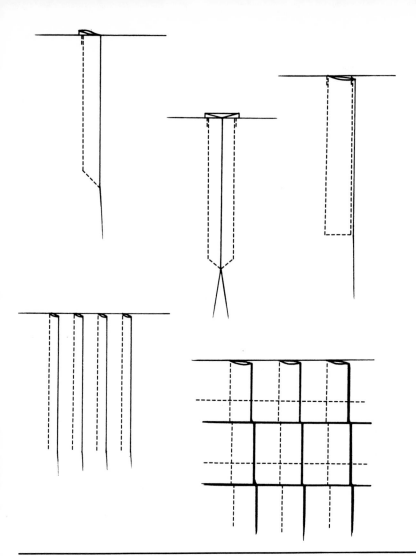

128 *Various tucks showing effects achieved by direction of pressing*

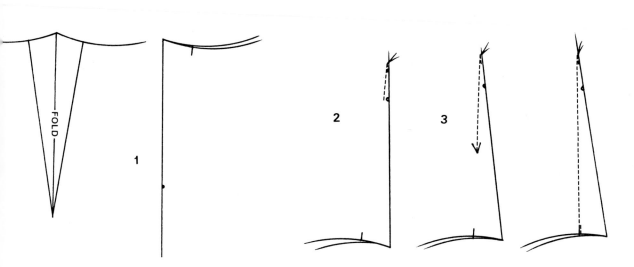

129 *Stitching a dart*

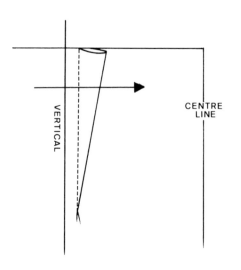
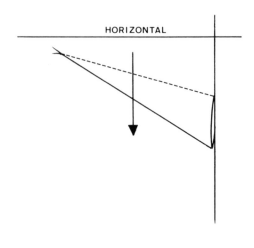

130 *Pressing darts*

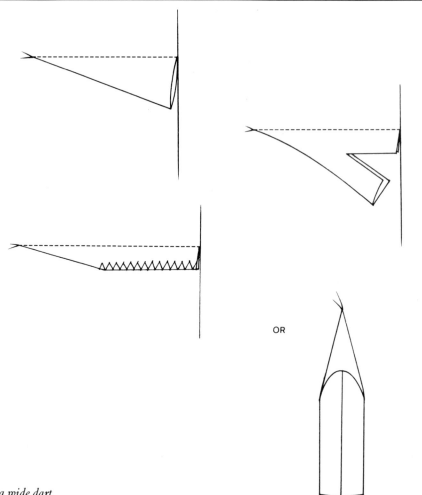

OR

131 *Neatening a wide dart*

ELASTIC

The most usual place for elastic to be used to control fullness is around the waist. A channel is stitched in the fabric through which the elastic is threaded and so held in position. Alternatively, the elastic is machined straight on to the fabric.

The ways a channel may be structured are varied. The following suggestions show how the solution depends on the design and the chosen method of construction.

Casings (*Fig. 132*)

Usually, a channel is stitched when the garment is in a 'tube', so that all relevant seams have already been stitched. The side seams of a dress or skirt would be completed as would the under-arm seam of a sleeve. There is a small area of overlap at one point where an applied casing is used. Exceptions might be where only a part of the garment is to be elasticated – e.g. across the back waist. Here, the raw ends of the elastic and casing can be neatly concealed in the side seams when they are stitched at a later stage.

1 The most obvious method is to cut a tape and edge-stitch both sides to the WS. This is adequate where the casing is straight. It is more satisfactory to use bias binding or crossway strip with the raw edges pressed under, as this will sit flat when it follows a curve. Apply in the same way as tape, edge-stitching both sides. There is no reason why contrast fabric may not be used and the casing stitched to the RS.

These two methods require careful placement. Try the garment on and use a tie or belt to hold it in position. Adjust the amount of blousing until the silhouette is satisfactory. Pin at regular intervals to mark in the position for the casing.

2 A casing for elastic can be included in a seam

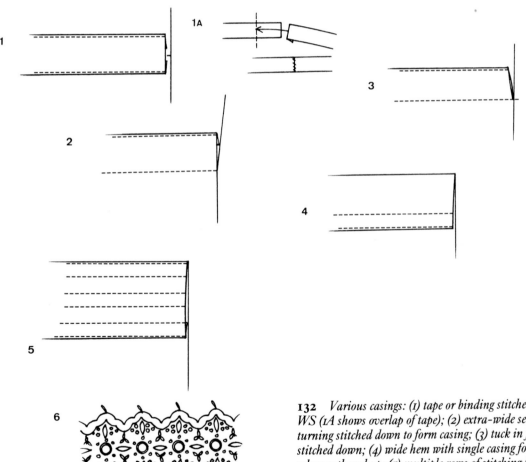

132 *Various casings: (1) tape or binding stitched to R or WS (1A shows overlap of tape); (2) extra-wide seam turning stitched down to form casing; (3) tuck in fabric is stitched down; (4) wide hem with single casing forms frill when gathered up; (5) multiple rows of stitching form triple casing; (6) lace is applied to fabric and eyelet holes are threaded*

turning if a seam follows the part of the garment to be elasticated. Edge-stitch the larger seam turning around the seam. This may be on the RS or WS.

3 If a straight channel is required it is possible to stitch a tuck in the fabric which can then be edge-stitched down. This is more suitable for finer fabrics. Waistbands, sleeves and trouser legs may all have elasticated finishes.

4 A narrow machine hem will provide the simplest casing of all (*see p. 159 for examples*). A deeper hem can be machined, with an additional row to form a casing with the hem row. Here, there will be a frill when the casing is elasticated (*see p. 179 for examples*).

5 A waistband can be attached to a skirt with no petersham or interlining. Rather than use a stiff, wide elastic, stitch multiple rows for narrower elastic. This is more time-consuming, but gives a good finish.

6 An alternative, decorative casing can be made by applying lace to the fabric and threading elastic through the eyelet holes.

Threading elastic

In all these instances, a space must be left for the elastic to enter the casing. Use a safety pin stuck through the centre of the elastic as far up the elastic as the safety pin will allow. This will minimise the chance of the elastic fraying away before the threading is finished. Pull the elastic through, gently gathering the fabric as it goes. Try not to lose the loose end up into the casing. As soon as the threading is complete, pin the two ends together, taking care not to twist the elastic.

Joining elastic

Allow a good overlap of at least 2.5 cm (1 in.). First machine down the centre of the overlap. Turn and stitch back down one side, turn and stitch up the other. With the needle up, adjust the machine to a suitable sized zigzag stitch. Now machine either down the centre or down one and then up the other side, depending on the width of the elastic. Re-set the machine to straight stitching, sew two or three stitches and trim the thread ends off. This method of joining will last longer than the elastic (*Fig. 133*).

All that remains is to stitch up the opening left in the casing. Overlap several stitches at the beginning and end, and trim off the thread ends close.

Stitching elastic directly on to fabric

When elastic is stitched directly to the fabric it is cut to the finished length required, plus an allowance either for enclosing the ends in seams or for an overlap. The elastic is then stretched to fit the fabric and machined in place while stretched. A zigzag stitch is preferable and if you have the choice, use a three-step zigzag.

Mark the elastic with pins to show the half and quarter marks, unless there are any other more suitable distances to mark, for instance where corresponding seams may be. Stretch the elastic, matching the balance markings as you proceed section by section, so that the 'stretch' is distributed evenly. As the fabric passes under the machine, the tension on the elastic is lost and so the fabric behind the foot is pulled up into gathers. It makes the job of machining that much easier if this tension remains, at least until the fabric is well clear of the foot. Hold the elastic taut at the back of the work so the fabric remains flat immediately behind the foot. As you have to handle the fabric firmly, it is important to let the feeder take up the fabric properly so that the stitch length is not distorted.

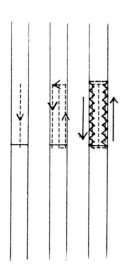

133 *Joining elastic*

finishing off raw edges

There are many occasions that arise in the construction of a garment where a raw edge remains to be finished because that particular cut edge is not enclosed in a seam. Some edges are finished neatly when double fabric is stitched RSs together, turned through to the inside and hemmed.

All the fabric 'edges' of the garment need to be hard-wearing, practicable and neat. The finish may be as inconspicuous as possible or be a feature of the design. Raw edges that are not finished in the ways already mentioned are either faced or bound.

A facing is either stitched with RSs together to the main fabric and then turned completely to the WS, or may sometimes be cut in one, together with the main garment, and is then simply folded to the WS. It is not visible from the RS.

A binding is stitched to the fabric and folds to enclose the raw edge. It remains visible on the RS and WS (*Fig. 134*).

CROSSWAY-CUT STRIPS

Strips of fabric, either self or contrast, that are cut on the cross in varying widths can be used to bind raw fabric edges or as a substitute for a facing where it is impracticable or unnecessary to cut a separate facing.

Single binding and facing strips
Single strips of binding are cut with a narrow 6 mm (¼ in.) seam turning, twice the width of the finished binding and a further 6 mm (¼ in.) for turning under (*Fig. 135A*). Single facing strips are cut with a 6 mm (¼ in.) seam turning, the width of facing required (not usually more than 2.5 cm [1 in.]) and a further 6 mm (¼ in.) for turning under.

Double binding strips
Double binding is a crossway strip that is folded in half lengthwise (*Fig. 136*). It is cut with a 6 mm (¼ in.) seam turning and twice the width of the finished

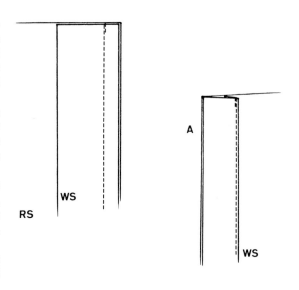

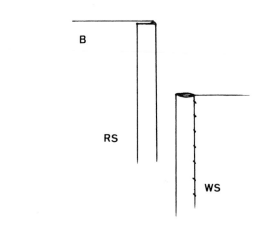

134 *The difference between a facing (A) and a binding (B)*

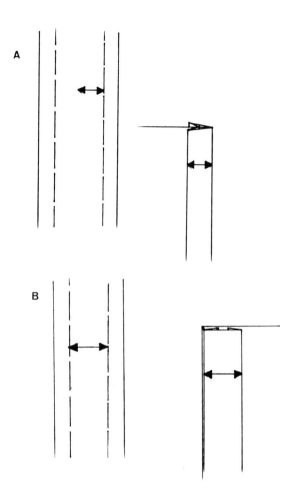

135 *Crossway strips cut for binding (A) and facing (B)*

binding required. Double this total measurement and add 1–3 mm ($\frac{1}{16}$–$\frac{1}{8}$ in.) extra to allow for the amount of width taken in 'roll' where the double binding folds around the raw edge. No allowance is needed for turning under as the fold edge of the strip forms a neat finish.

Double facing strips

Double facing strips are cut with a 6 mm ($\frac{1}{4}$ in.) seam turning and the width of facing required (not usually more than 2.5 cm [1 in.]). Double this total measurement for the width to cut the strip. As with the binding, no allowance is needed for turning under as the fold edge of the strip forms a neat finish.

Joining crossway strips

Crossway strips often need joining to give sufficient continuous length. Before you begin to stitch the strip to the raw edge, make sure it is long enough to complete the binding or facing as any necessary joining should be done first. The joining seam is stitched on the straight grain, therefore the ends of the strip are cut on-grain. The positioning of the strips is important; in order that the binding continues with a straight edge when it is pressed open, it is essential that a right angle is formed between the two strips. Machine a 6 mm ($\frac{1}{4}$ in.) seam, back-tacking at beginning and end. Press the seam open. Trim off the protruding points of the seam turnings (*Fig. 137*).

Facing a raw edge with a crossway strip

If single crossway strip is used, press under the raw edge. With RSs together, stitch the strip in place. Clip the seam turnings if necessary and press the strip to the WS. Press the seam turnings together in the direction of the strip. Stitch the strip to the seam turnings close to the seam; this will stop the strip from rolling on to the RS and encourage it to lie flat on the WS (*Fig. 138*).

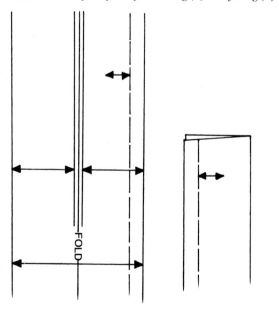

FOLD

136 *Double crossway strip*

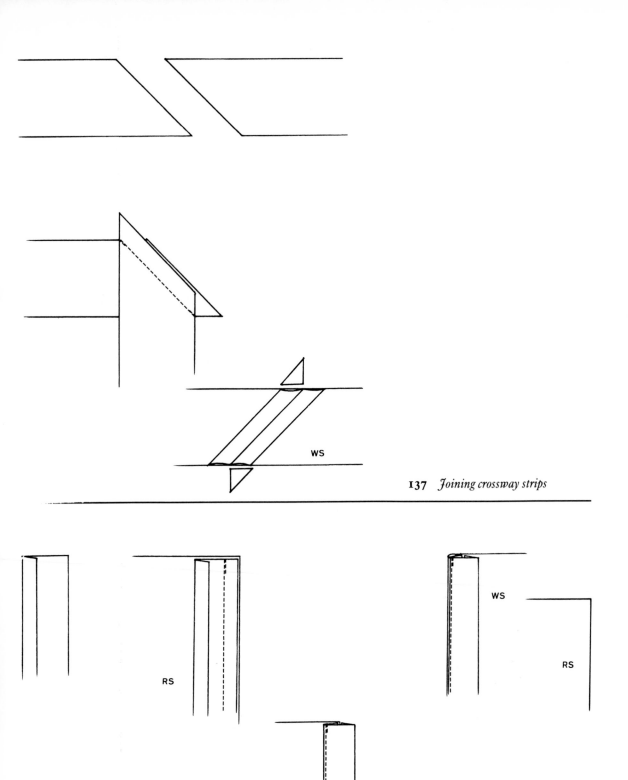

137 *Joining crossway strips*

138 *Facing a raw edge with a crossway strip*

Binding a raw edge with a crossway strip

Method 1 (Fig. 139)

1 Press under the raw edge.

2 Lay the strip on the fabric with both WSs up. Stitch the strip in place. The width of seam turning will be the finished width of the binding.

3 Press the strip around the raw edge to the RS.

4 Edge-stitch the loose edge in place from the RS.

With this method, the stitching shows on the RS. A contrast thread or decorative stitch could be used to hold the binding down.

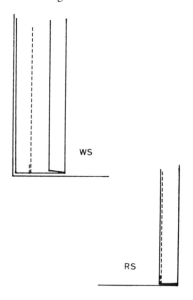

139 *Binding a raw edge with a crossway strip*

140 *Binding with a hand-stitched finish*

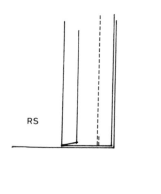

Method 2 (Fig. 140)

1 Place the strip with RSs together and stitch in place.

2 Press the strip around the raw edge to the WS.

3 Catch the binding down by hand on the WS to the first row of stitching.

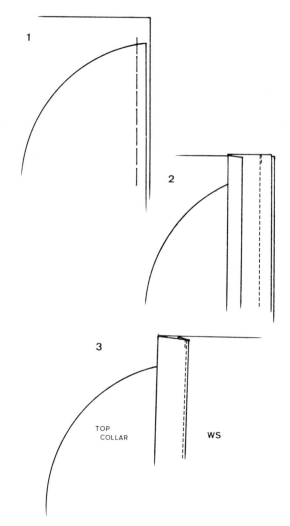

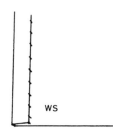

141 *Binding on a flat collar with a crossway strip*

'Binding on' with a crossway strip

This method is very useful for joining a separate piece of fabric to a raw edge and neatening it at the same time. The fabric being joined will be 'finished' – i.e. a frill will be hemmed or a flat collar will be turned through, top-stitched and pressed. A collar is used as an example (*Fig. 141*).

1 Place the collar in its finished position along the seamline on the RS. Machine it down just inside the seam turning.

2 Lay the crossway with RSs together as shown. Stitch the binding along the seamline.

3 Press the binding back to cover the seam turnings and, from the WS, edge-stitch down the binding.

Bind and apply method

Crossway is used to neaten the raw edge of fabric that is to be applied on to the main fabric. This is usually for decorative purposes. A patch pocket is used as an example (*Fig. 142*).

1 Fold the crossway in half lengthwise. Place around the pocket as shown and machine in place around the stitching line. Turn the seam turning to the WS and press the pocket from the RS.

2 Position the pocket and pin down.

3 Stitch down around the edge of pocket, making sure the needle passes exactly through the binding seam. It will be necessary to pull back the pocket fractionally as the fabric will 'roll' slightly towards the

seam. If the stitches lie exactly in the groove formed by the seam, this minimal rolling action of the fabric hides the stitching completely. Back tack at beginning and end.

FACINGS

A facing is either cut in one and folded to the WS, or cut separately, sometimes in more than one piece, and stitched RSs together, to the raw edge it is to neaten. All facings have an interlining fabric applied to stiffen and strengthen (*see p. 113 for how to apply interlinings*). The facing is stitched to the garment with a narrow 6 mm ($\frac{1}{4}$ in.) seam to avoid the necessity to trim. This seam must always be clipped. It does no harm to clip too often, but inadequate clipping will always spoil what would otherwise be a neat, flat finished edge.

The facing is always made up prior to being attached to the garment. All seams are narrow and are pressed open. The outer edge of the facing must be neatened. Fold over the raw edge once and edge-stitch down from the WS (*Fig. 143 [1]*). An alternative method is to place the interlining to the facing with RSs together and stitch a narrow seam. Turn the interlining to the WS of the facing (*Fig. 143 [2]*). This is ideal when the facing itself is cut in one piece, such as a CF facing.

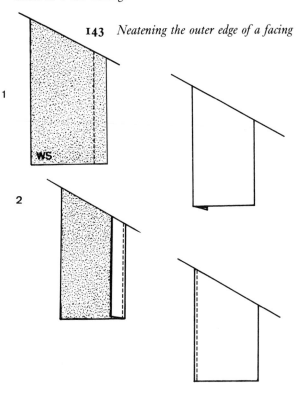

143 *Neatening the outer edge of a facing*

142 *Patch pocket shows example of 'bind and apply' method*

Most facings lie on the WS and are not visible from the RS. So that they stay flat, press the seam turnings towards the facing and edge-stitch around the seam, machining the facing to the turnings. It will then be unlikely that it will ever turn itself through and show on the RS while being worn.

A standard CF opening is used as an example to illustrate most of these points (*Fig. 144*). The method of construction is as follows:

1   Neaten the loose edge of the facing. Place the interlining to the facing with RSs together. Stitch around the edge with a narrow seam. Turn the interlining to the WS of the facing. Press, if non-fusible interlining is used; otherwise, fuse the interlining.

2   Turn back the facing down the foldline with RSs together. The CF balance nips match together. Stitch around the neck to the shoulder seam. Clip and trim at the corner. Turn through to the RS and press.

3   Fold back the seam turning and catch this down by hand to the seam turning of the bodice shoulder seam.

The lower edge of a facing that finishes at a hem is finished as follows (*Fig. 145*):

1   Fold the facing back with RSs together. Cut away the excess fabric as shown. Do not cut right back to the edge of the facing. Stitch the facing to the garment at hem level. Trim away the corner.

2   Turn the corner out and fold up the hem. Tuck the raw edge of the side of the hem under the facing and catch the facing edge down by hand.

There are many occasions where a facing is, in some way, an integral part of a construction method. This is included under the relevant headings.

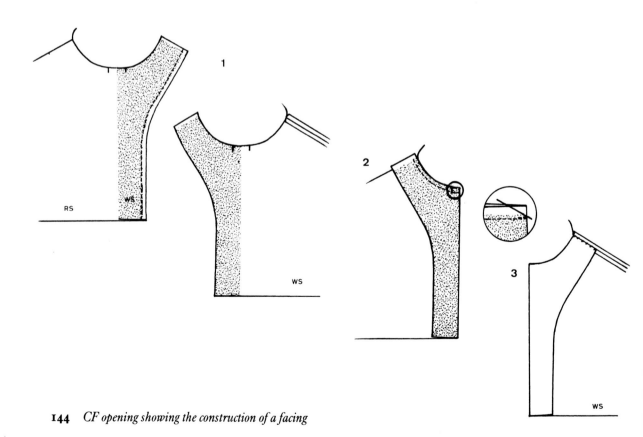

144   *CF opening showing the construction of a facing*

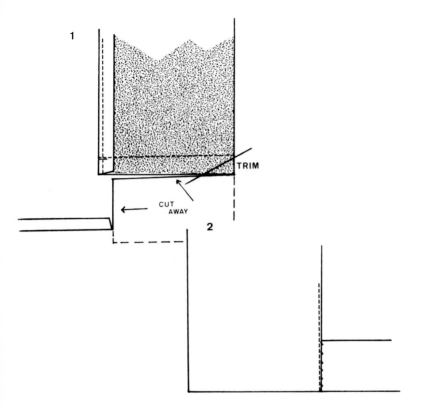

145 *Hem finish for facing*

CHAPTER SIXTEEN

Pockets

POCKETS SET IN SIDE SEAM

The pocket bags are first stitched to the main garment pieces. This is done when you are ready to join the side seams of the garment (*Fig. 146*).

1 Place the front pocket bag to the garment front at the extension with the RSs together. Stitch in place for the full length of the extension, back-tacking at each end. Join the back pocket bag in the same way.

2 Press the seam turnings together towards the pocket and neaten them together.

3 With both front and back prepared in the same way, place the side seams with RSs together. Begin from the top, stitching the seam to the pocket opening. Pivot carefully and continue to machine around the pocket bags. Be careful to match the extension seams exactly – pinning here is helpful. When you reach the bottom of the pocket opening, pivot carefully and stitch down the remainder of the side seam.

The most suitable seam finish is one where both turnings can be neatened together and pressed in the same direction. If this is not possible, the pocket bag seam will be neatened together but the side seams will require clipping so that it is possible to press the turnings flat. As this creates a weak area, reinforce each corner with tiny stitches placed just outside the stitching line (*Fig. 147*).

PATCH POCKETS

These pockets may be of any shape or size and are applied to the RS of the fabric. Accurate positioning is important.

The pocket
The pocket must be prepared before being stitched on to the garment. The raw edges need turning under and the edge which is to form the open edge must be finished suitably. There is often an area of double fabric across the top edge of a patch pocket which forms a facing to increase strength and stability in this area where a pocket has the most wear. An interfacing is applied to the facing at the earliest opportunity, when required.

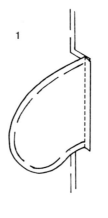
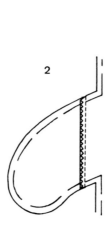
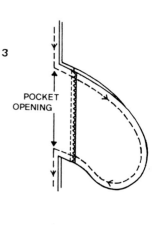

POCKET OPENING

146 *Pocket set in side seam*

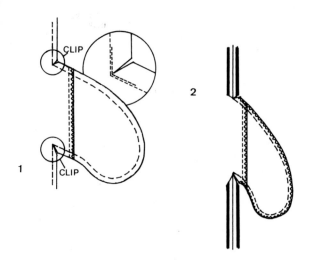

147 *Finishing side seam and pocket bags*

Finishing the top edge of the pocket

Facing cut in one with pocket (Fig. 148)

1 Turn under a narrow single hem. Edge-stitch or just leave a sharply pressed crease.

2 Fold the facing area down with RSs together. Machine from the fold to the facing edge on both sides. Trim away excess seam turning to leave 3–5 mm ($\frac{1}{8}$–$\frac{1}{4}$ in.), cutting a step as shown, just above the base of the stitching. Trim off the corners.

3 Turn through facing and press.

Facing cut separately (Fig. 149)
This is usually when the facing serves a decorative purpose.

1 Turn under and press the lower edge of the facing.

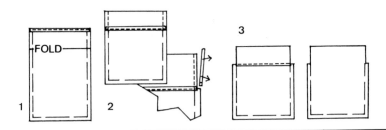

148 *Patch pocket: finishing top edge with facing cut in one with pocket*

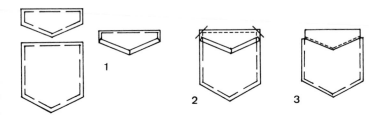

149 *Patch pocket: finishing top edge with facing cut separately*

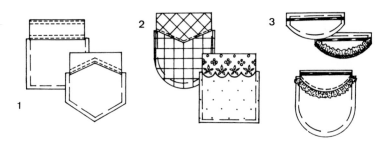

150 *Examples of patch pocket with facing cut separately*

139

2 Place the facing to the pocket with both WSs uppermost. Machine the facing to the pocket with a narrow seam. Trim away corners. Clip the seam turnings at right angles to the cut edge, just above the base of the stitching.

3 Turn the facing through to the RS. Press carefully. Edge-stitch down the loose edge of the facing.

The following are some examples of pockets with separate facings (*Fig. 150*).

1 The facing is finished with multiple rows of top-stitching.

2 The facing is cut in a different direction or in contrast fabric e.g. broderie anglaise.

3 The facing is decorated with lace and ribbon. First gather up the required amount of lace. Place to the raw edge of the facing with RS fabric and RS lace together. Edge-stitch in position. Apply ribbon or other trimming as required, positioning carefully. Now make up prepared facing as given.

Elasticated pocket with no facing (Fig. 151)
1 Hem the top of the pocket.

2 Attach elastic along placement line. Stitch to the WS of the fabric with a suitable zigzag or other special stitch. Stretch the elastic evenly across the fabric width.

3 Secure the elastic firmly in the seam turnings at both ends.

Preparing remaining raw edges (*Fig. 152*)
1 Press the seam turnings under to the WS. 1.3 cm (½ in.) turning width is the minimum that should be cut as any less will form a weak finished pocket edge. With a crisper fabric, pressing alone may be sufficient. Trim away excess fabric at corners if this gives a neater finish. If the pressed edges will not stay in position, pin them back.

2 It may be acceptable to top-stitch the seam turnings down from the RS, keeping an even distance from the fold edge. (A) shows a pocket with the facing on the WS and (B) a pocket with the facing on the RS. In (A) the top-stitching will begin at the top edge of the pocket, through the facing. In (B) if the top-stitching is not intended to continue across the facing, then top-stitch the seam turnings in place before the facing is edge-stitched down. This makes it possible to top-stitch a few stitches beneath the facing edge, as can be seen on the WS of the pocket.

3 Curved pocket edges can be more easily turned under if you first run a row of longish stitches around the pocket just inside the seam turning. This then helps to ease away the excess fabric in the seam turning on the curve. The smoother the line of stitches, the better the finish on the curve edge will be. (*See p. 135 for how to bind on a patch pocket.*)

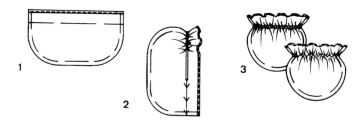

151 *Elasticated patch pocket with no facing*

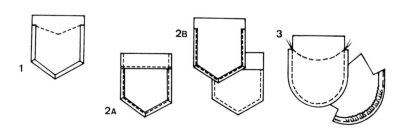

152 *Preparing raw edges of a patch pocket*

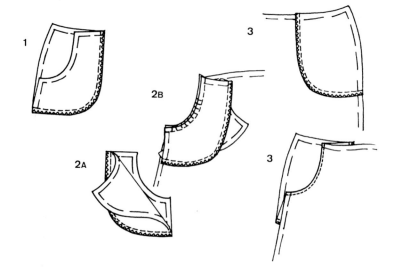

POCKET CUT IN GARMENT (SECTION POCKET)

The example shown is cut on a skirt front. The top edge is the waist seam, and is to be enclosed in the waistband (*Figs. 153 and 154*).

1 Place the pocket bags RSs together and machine around the bag edge. Neaten both seam turnings together.

2 Fold away the back bag section and place the front pocket bag only to the skirt front. Stitch in place, clipping the curve adequately. With particularly stretchy fabrics it is advisable to machine a narrow tape around this seam, so that the pocket edge remains firm with wear.

3 Turn the pocket to the WS and press, being careful that an indentation of the bag does not appear on the RS of the skirt front. Top-stitch the pocket edge if required. This will increase the strength of the pocket edge and is advisable, especially if a stay tape has not been used.

4 Lift the skirt front up out of the way and stitch the sides of the pocket bag together.

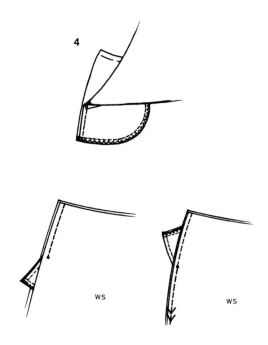

The triple thickness fabric at the top of the pocket can be held in position with a row of stitching just inside the seam turning, ready to be enclosed in the waistband. The side seam is a little more difficult to finish properly. If the sides of the pocket bag are caught in the side seam of the skirt, when the pocket is used it is possible that an ugly 'pull' will distort the hang of the skirt at the side. To stitch the side seam without catching in the pocket, it must be machined in two stages. First, machine the top section of the side seam down to the pocket opening or, if there is top-stitching, to the level of the top-stitching. Finish with a back tack. To machine the lower section of the seam, fold back the pocket bag as far as possible, either to the top-stitching or to the pocket opening, wherever the base of the first row of stitching reaches. Begin the lower section of the side seam

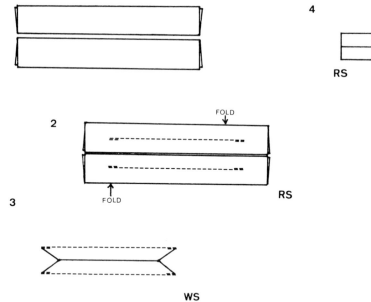

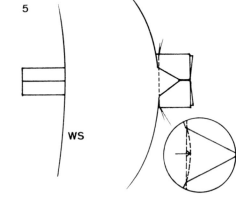

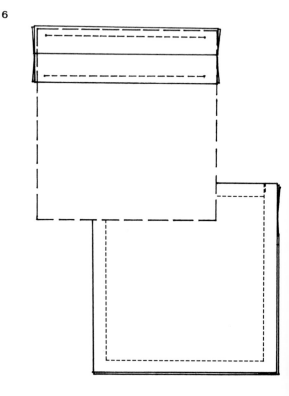

155 *Construction of a piped pocket*

156 *Completing a piped pocket*

157 *Attaching pocket bags to a piped pocket*

with a back tack, so that the seam continues in a straight line. Do not overlap the stitching or leave a gap. Pin the pocket bag back and it will then not be accidentally caught in the side seam.

If the pocket is large, the fabric medium- to light-weight and the skirt of a fullish silhouette, you may find it is acceptable to catch the sides of the pocket bag into the side seam as it is at the top, when the side seam can be machined as usual.

PIPED POCKET (*Figs. 155–157*)

1 Press the pipes in half lengthwise with WSs together. The pipes are often cut as crossway strips, but this is not essential. Cut the strips the length of the pocket opening, plus 1.3 cm (½ in.). Once pressed in half, the strips will be twice the finished depth of each pipe, or the finished depth of the pocket opening.

2 Pin the strips in position as shown, and machine in place from the RS. These rows of stitching must be parallel and begin and end exactly in line. Fasten the stitching with back-tacking.

3 From the WS, cut the fabric in a straight slit down the centre of the pocket opening to within about 1.3 cm (½ in.) of each end. Cut diagonally into the corners, snipping right up to the first stitch. Press from the WS to set the stitching.

4   Turn the pipes through to the finished position. The fold edges of each pipe should lie together. If they do not, the stitching lines have not been placed at the same width from the fold edge of each pipe or this width is not exactly half of the finished depth of the pocket opening. The ends of the pipes are tucked through to the WS and the triangular section of fabric is folded back to lie over the pipes.

5   The sides of the opening are stabilised by machining the triangular section of fabric to the loose ends of the pipes. With the RS facing, adjust the pipes so that they lie together correctly. Hold them firmly in position (this is easy if the work is placed on a table) and fold back the fabric in order to pin the triangle to the pipes. You may not find it necessary to pin if you check the pipes from the RS immediately prior to machining and keep the fingers firmly on the pipes at the machine. Stitch as shown, being especially careful at the corners of the triangle,

making sure that the needle passes through at the end stitch of the first rows of machining. The following tip is useful if you are using a medium- or heavier-weight fabric and helps to give a 'square' finish to the pocket: machine across the triangle in a fractionally inward curve; this will compensate for the 'rolling' effect of the fabric bulk and give a finished fold that is straight.

6   Stitch the bags in place, one to the seam turning of each pipe. Now stitch the bags together and neaten the seam (*Fig. 157*). Use the iron carefully, as there is danger of over-pressing.

WELT POCKET

The welt (*Fig. 158*)
1   Interline the top side of the welt.

2   Fold the welt in half with the RSs together. Stitch the sides with a narrow 6 mm (¼ in.) seam turning. Trim the corner, turn through to the RS and press.

158   *Making up a welt*

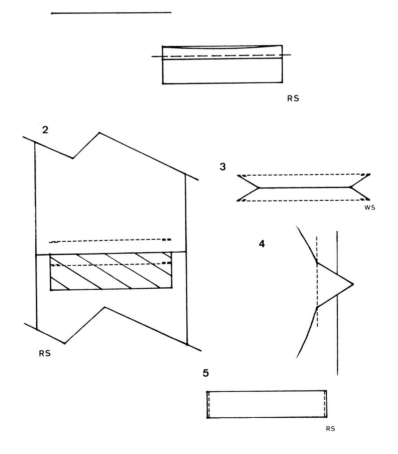

The pocket (*Fig. 159*)

1 The welt is placed with its seamline over the position of what is to be the lower edge of the finished welt pocket. Pin in place, and run a row of stitches across the welt, to hold it in position. Place these stitches just inside the seam turning.

2 Position the pocket bags as shown and stitch in place. The distance between these stitching lines should be slightly less than the depth of the finished welt. A 1.3 cm (½ in.) seam turning on the pocket bags will extend beyond each end of the finished welt. Begin and end these rows of stitching with a back tack. Note that the top pocket bag needs to be cut deeper.

3 Turn to the WS. Cut the opening as shown, snipping right into the corners.

4 Push the pocket bags through the WS. Fold back the top fabric and stitch the pocket bags to the triangular section fabric in the same way as you do for a piped pocket, but continue around the pocket, stitching the bags together. Neaten the seam.

5 On the RS, edge-stitch the sides of the welt down.

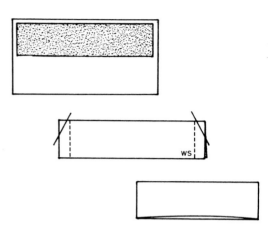

159 *Construction of a welt pocket*

CHAPTER SEVENTEEN

Openings and fastenings

INSERTING A ZIP

A zip is set into an opening in a seam with finished turnings of at least 1.3 cm ($\frac{1}{2}$ in.). The zip stop at the base of the teeth will sit at the bottom of the opening and the zip stop at the top of the teeth will sit 6 mm ($\frac{1}{4}$ in.) below the stitching line across the top.

1 Press the neatened seam turnings back at the correct width (*Fig. 160*).

2 Using a zip foot, edge-stitch the RHS of the opening down to the closed zip. Do not place the fold of the fabric right up to the teeth, but leave a narrow space to allow the runner to slide up and down easily. Back tack opposite the base stop.

3 Position the other side of the opening with the fold edge covering the first stitching line by no more than 2 mm ($\frac{1}{16}$ in.). Put in two or three pins to the zip tape as shown (*Fig. 161*).

4 Machine the second stitching line from the RS, working from top to bottom. Keep the stitching line parallel to the foldline all the way down with the width at a maximum of 8 mm ($\frac{2}{16}$ in.). Turn just below the base stop and machine across at a right angle until the needle enters the seam exactly. Adjust the last stitch if necessary. Turn and, holding the top fabric out of the way, stitch up three to four stitches over the first line of stitching. Finish with a back tack.

An alternative method at stage 2 is to place the RS of the fabric to the zip tape and machine in the fold from the WS (*Fig. 162*). Press the fabric back. This means there is no edge-stitching to cover with the opposite fold, but it is still a good idea to overlap the second side fractionally.

The top-stitching and edge-stitching are both important for a neat finish. The more crisply the seam turnings are pressed under, the easier it will be to achieve this. Once the zip is set in, it is impossible to press this area heavily as the zip teeth and stop will

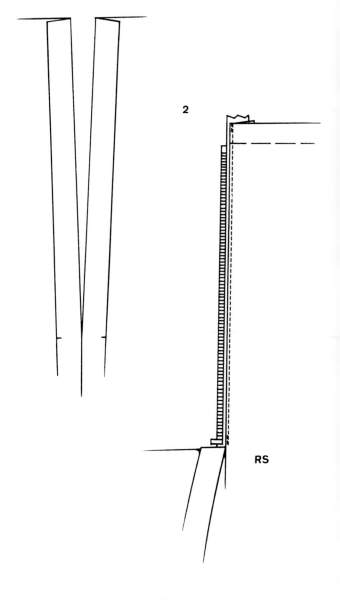

160 *Inserting a zip: stages 1 and 2*

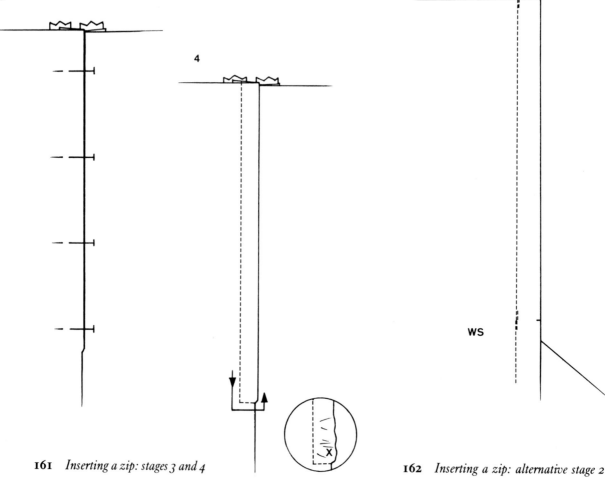

161 *Inserting a zip: stages 3 and 4*

162 *Inserting a zip: alternative stage 2*

cause indentations that will show on the RS of the fabric.

Apart from machining a wobbly line, the main problem to arise is the pressure of the machine foot distorting the fabric and pushing it forward so that it does not lie along the tape as it should. Concentrate on holding the fold edge down very firmly, bending the fingers to increase the pressure necessary to keep it in its correct position as the stitching progresses. This will prevent the excess fabric accumulating and forming a bubble at the base of the zip. Fig. 161 shows a badly stitched zip.

An alternative method of stitching the base of the zip is to turn 1 cm (⅜ in.) above the zip stop and stitch down to the seam at an angle.

Centrally set zip
This is a less attractive method to use generally, but may be more suitable on limited occasions. It is harder to achieve an excellent finish (*Fig. 163*).

1 Press the neatened seam turnings back.

2 With the fold edges meeting centrally down the centre of the teeth, pin the zip in position.

3 Machine parallel to the fold edge down one side of the zip, turn and stitch across the base, turn and complete the other side checking that the stitching is at the same width as the first side. Keep this width to 8 mm ($\frac{5}{16}$ in.).

Fig. 164 shows a neck facing finishing at the top of a zip.

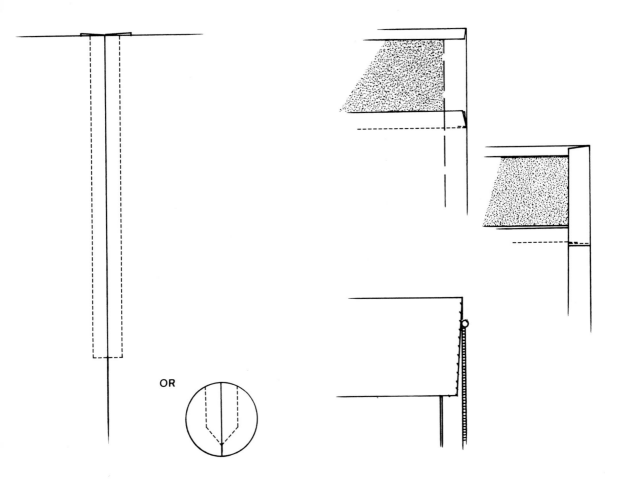

163 *Centrally set zip*

164 *Finish of a neck facing at the top of a zip*

BUTTONS/BUTTONHOLES

Buttons and buttonholes must be worked on fabric with adequate support and this is achieved by preparing double thickness fabric which is usually interlined. It is important that both the button and buttonhole are positioned correctly, so that the garment is the finished measurement required, and that the two sides are in line when the garment is fastened. The buttonhole is worked on the RHS of a woman's garment and the LHS of menswear. A side button fastening will have the buttonhole worked on the garment front.

Principles of positioning (*Fig. 165*)

1 The button sits exactly on the centre line of the wrap.

2 The buttonhole is positioned accordingly.

3 The buttonhole is cut to the diameter of the button, plus an extra 3 mm ($\frac{1}{8}$ in.) for ease of fastening. If the button is exceptionally thick, allow additional width to the buttonhole so that the button will pass through easily. The diameter measurement is placed to the fabric side of the centre line of the wrap and the extra width allowance is cut on the wrap side of the centre line. This allows the buttonhole to accommodate the button shank and, therefore, it lies flat when the button is fastened.

In order that buttons give a satisfactory method of fastening, they must be placed at adequate intervals in sensible positions down the opening. Any points where greater stress is likely must have a button at that level – for instance, opposite the bust point on a CF button fastening or at hip level on a button-through skirt. The buttons are then placed at equal intervals. Cuffs or waistbands of more then 3 cm

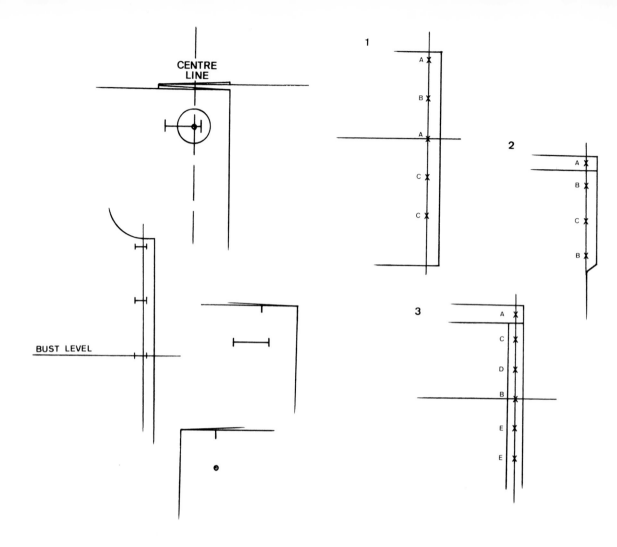

165 *Principles of positioning a buttonhole and button*

166 *Determining intervals between buttons*

(1⅛ in.) in depth will usually require two or more buttons, depending on their size.

The following examples show how to determine the measurement of the interval between the buttons (*Fig. 166*).

CF blouse fastening (Fig. 166 [1])
1   Mark the bust point level and the position of the top button with pins (A).
2   Determine half-way between these points (B).
3   Position all subsequent buttons (C) at measurement between A and B.

Skirt side fastening (Fig. 166 [2])
1   Position the waistband button (A) in the centre of the depth of the waistband.

2   Place the upper and lower buttons (B) at an equal distance from the waistband seam and the base of the opening respectively.
3   The centre button (C) is positioned half-way between buttons at B.

CF skirt fastening (Fig. 166 [3])
1   Position the waistband button (A) in the centre of the depth of the waistband.
2   Position opposite hip level (B).
3   Place roughly the same distance from the waist seam as button A.
4   Place D half-way between stage B and C buttons.
5   Position all subsequent buttons at the resulting measurement at stage D.

Do not position a button at or nearer than approximately 15 cm (6 in.) from the finished hemline.

Shirt front fastening

Follow the principle given for a CF skirt fastening but substitute the collar stand for the waistband and bust or chest level for hip level.

Buttons may be placed in groupings to give interest. Follow the same basic principles for their positioning.

Sewing on a button (*Fig. 167*)

1 Use double thickness thread. Pass through between the fabric layers about 2 cm (¾ in.) away from the point where the button is to sit and bring the needle up exactly in this position. Work two tiny stitches to secure the thread.

2 Pass the needle from the back to the top of the button and stitch from hole to hole placing the needle straight through all the fabric layers each time, not at an angle. Repeat this four or five times and finish on the RS. Do not pull these stitches tightly. Whichever direction the stitching follows in relation to the holes of the button, make sure they are all sewn in a similar way.

3 Wind the thread firmly several times around the threads between the button back and the fabric and pass the needle through to the WS. If a longer thread shank is required, leave looser stitches at stage 2 and wind around the thread to form a shank more often.

4 Finish the stitching off securely on the WS, sewing around the threads two or three times as shown. Fasten the thread by passing the needle through its own loop and pulling tight. Pass the needle between the fabric layers, pull through to the WS and snip off the thread.

Buttonholes (*Fig. 168*)

Generally buttonholes are placed horizontally, crossing the centre line of the wrap at right angles. The strain is then always placed on the end of the buttonhole by the button.

Vertical buttonholes are worked when the construction of the garment does not give a sufficient flat area of fabric on the WS to work a horizontal buttonhole. Band openings are one example, narrow facings on baby clothes or nightwear are others, where vertical buttonholes are quite acceptable. The buttonhole is positioned centrally down the wrap so that the diameter of the button is below, and the extra allowance for ease is above, the position of the button. The 'pull' is always in a downwards direction.

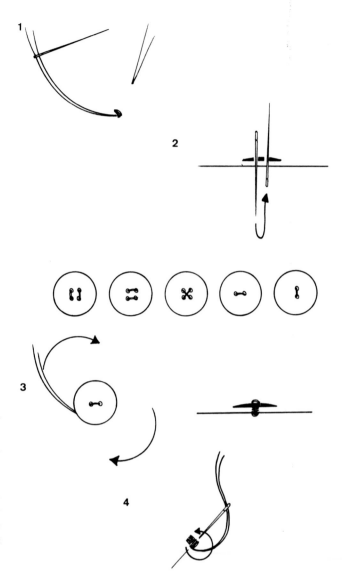

167 *Sewing on a button*

Machine buttonholes

Follow the instructions given in the sewing machine handbook for how to work a machine buttonhole. Use a 40 thickness thread and work two buttonholes in the same place if necessary. Do not overdo the bar tacks at each end of the buttonhole. Four stitches are usually quite enough.

Use a sharp, pointed pair of small needlework scissors. From the RS, poke through at the centre of the buttonhole and snip carefully to one end. Cut from the centre in the opposite direction to the other end. On a good automatic buttonhole, the two sides

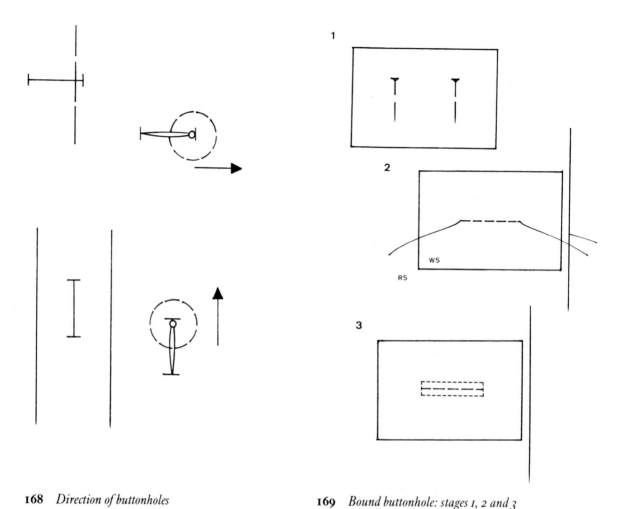

168 *Direction of buttonholes*

169 *Bound buttonhole: stages 1, 2 and 3*

of machine stitches will not meet, so there is a narrow space to cut into with no danger of cutting the stitches at the same time. If your machine works a buttonhole and leaves you responsible for the positioning of the needle at each stage, then make sure you leave 1 or 2 mm ($\frac{1}{16}$ in. or so) between the two rows of stitches so that cutting the buttonhole is not a traumatic experience. Work all the buttonholes first before cutting any of them, so that you can first check their positioning. Any mistakes can then be unpicked and re-positioned; a cut cannot. Finally, never cut a buttonhole in a hurry.

Bound buttonholes (Figs. 169 and 170)
It is not difficult to work bound buttonholes of a high standard with really very little practice. They will give a high quality finish to a garment and a good fabric deserves a little extra effort.

1 Cut a piece of fabric at least twice the width of the buttonhole and no less than 5 cm (2 in.) in depth for each buttonhole. On lighter-weight or more loosely woven fabrics a light-weight, fusible interlining will give a crisper, firmer buttonhole. Fabric that is cut on the cross to give striped effects, for instance, must be stabilised with interlining.

2 Place this centrally over the position of the buttonhole with the RSs together. Indicate the ends of the buttonhole accurately with pins. Machine a line to secure the fabric in place along the exact length of the buttonhole in the position of the cutting line. Leave loose thread ends.

3 Set the machine to a short stitch. Stitch around the line that indicated the cutting line, as shown. Begin along one long edge and overlap the stitches on completion. Stitch the long sides at the same width from the cutting line. This determines the

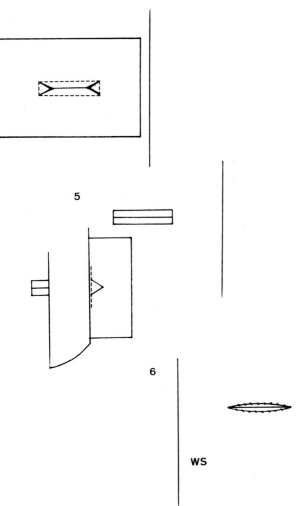

5

6

WS

170 *Bound buttonhole: stages 4, 5 and 6*

Loops are made out of crossway strips of fabric which are made up as follows (*Figs. 171 and 172*):

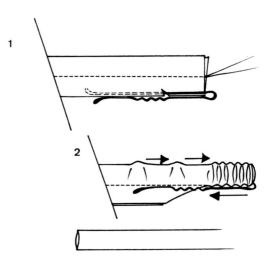

171 *Turning through rouleau loops*

172 *Stitching loops in position*

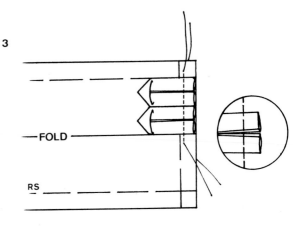

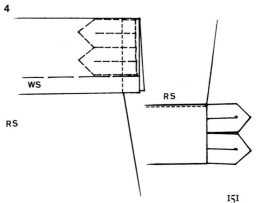

finished size of the buttonhole bindings. Keep them narrow and dainty for finer fabrics and about 6 mm ($\frac{1}{4}$ in.) for medium- to heavy-weight fabrics.

4 Cut along the original line of 'marker' stitches as shown, snipping right into each corner.

5 Push the fabric through to the WS. Press the buttonhole in place from the RS. Turn back the fabric and stitch through the triangular piece of turning and backing fabric to secure the sides of the buttonhole at both ends.

6 When the facing is folded back to its final position, cut a slit, tuck the raw edges inside and catch them down with tiny hand-stitching to complete the WS of the buttonhole.

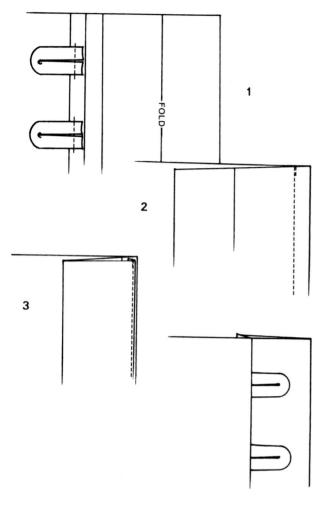

173 *Loops stitched into a tuck with a backing*

1 Cut strips 2 cm (¾ in.) wide (*see p. 76 for instructions*). The length of one loop will be the circumference of the button it is to fasten, plus 1 cm (⅜ in.). This allows 5 mm (³⁄₁₆ in.) at each end of the loop to be caught into the seam. Cut a long continuous strip.

2 Fold the strip in half lengthwise with RSs together. Machine down the centre, with a 5 mm (³⁄₁₆ in.) turning. Do not trim the seam turning away. Cut a small nick in the fold, about 1.5 cm (⅝ in.) from one end and pass a hair grip or hair pin through as shown. Turn the strip through to the RS by threading the hair grip along the strip. Tease the fabric over the end of the grip, using the thumb and forefinger nails to tug lightly and repeatedly at the fabric.

3 The finished strip can then be cut into loops of

the required length. The example shows two loops that are caught into a cuff. Place the loops as shown, with 5 mm (³⁄₁₆ in.) lying in the seam turning. Stitch the loops in position just inside the seam turning.

4 The cuff is then ready to be made up as normal. When the end of the cuff is stitched, the loops are automatically caught in the seam.

5 The buttons are sewn on so that the opening edges lie edge-to-edge.

There may be an occasion when you want to use a loop fastening but it is not suitable because of the possibility of the opening gaping, for instance, at the CF. It may be possible to include a backing behind the loops to avoid this problem. This should be cut in one with the garment (*Fig. 173*).

1 Position the loops in place and anchor with machining just inside the tuck.

2 Press the foldline of the tuck and stitch the tuck in place.

3 Fold the backing and catch down to the tuck by machine as shown. Press. You may wish to edge-stitch and/or top-stitch the tuck down from the RS. The opening meets edge-to-edge when fastened.

SHIRT BAND

Buttonhole band cut separately

Buttonhole band (Fig. 174)
1 Interface the top side of the shirt band. Press the seam turning of the top band under and press in half along the foldline.

2 With WSs uppermost, stitch the band to the front edge, matching nips as shown. Keep the seam turning edge parallel to the raw edge of the wrap, which is totally enclosed by the band.

3 Press back this seam and fold the band to the RS. Re-press the creases already pressed at the beginning if necessary. Pin the band together at intervals. Edge-stitch the band down from the RS.

4 Edge-stitch the fold edge to give a crisp band edge. The band may also be top-stitched.

Button band (Fig. 175)
1 Interface the band as shown.

2 Press to WS and press the raw edge under. Edge-stitch down from the WS. This row of edge-stitching should be covered by the buttonhole band when the front is fastened.

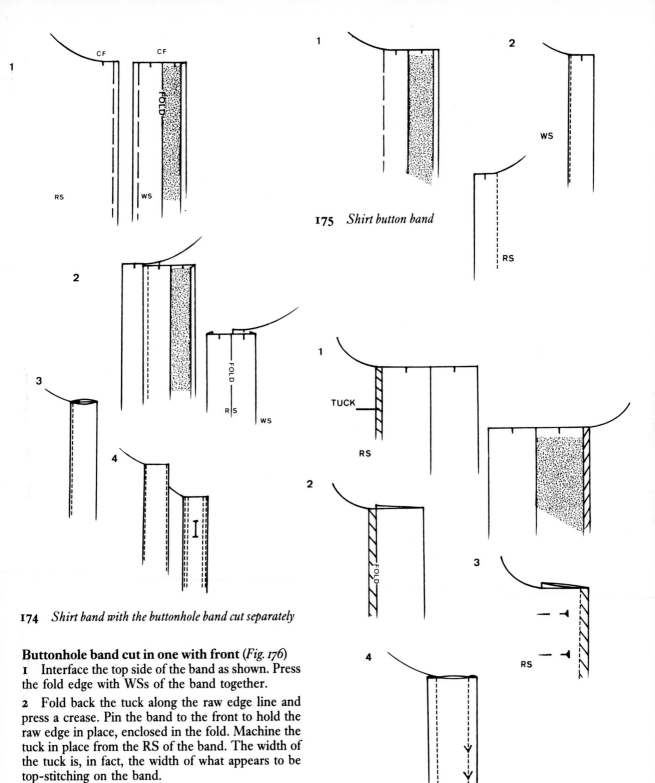

174 *Shirt band with the buttonhole band cut separately*

175 *Shirt button band*

176 *Shirt band with the buttonhole band cut in one with the front*

Buttonhole band cut in one with front (*Fig. 176*)

1 Interface the top side of the band as shown. Press the fold edge with WSs of the band together.

2 Fold back the tuck along the raw edge line and press a crease. Pin the band to the front to hold the raw edge in place, enclosed in the fold. Machine the tuck in place from the RS of the band. The width of the tuck is, in fact, the width of what appears to be top-stitching on the band.

3 Top-stitch the fold edge of the band at the same width, to match the tuck.

4 Finish the button band in the same way as given above.

153

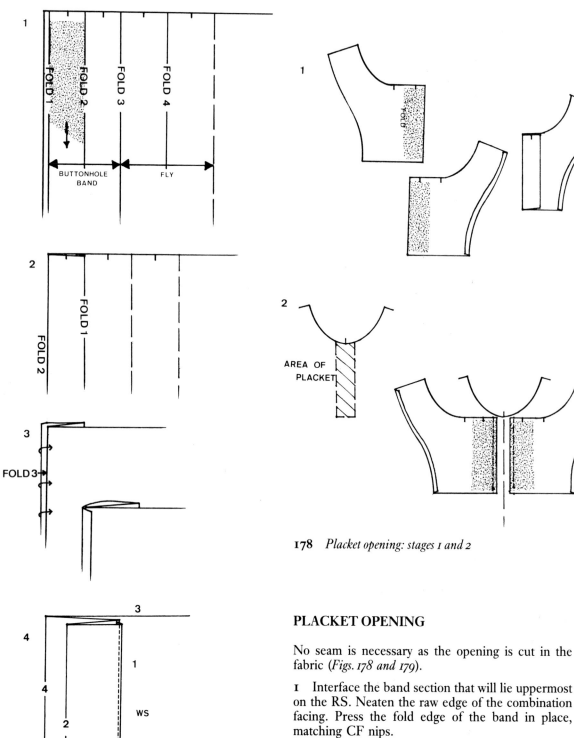

177 *Shirt fly front*

178 *Placket opening: stages 1 and 2*

PLACKET OPENING

No seam is necessary as the opening is cut in the fabric (*Figs. 178 and 179*).

1 Interface the band section that will lie uppermost on the RS. Neaten the raw edge of the combination facing. Press the fold edge of the band in place, matching CF nips.

2 Position the placket RSs together and machine down the stitching lines as shown. Finish with a back tack. Stitch the buttonhole band fractionally further than the button band.

3 Cut the opening from the WS as shown, snipping right into the corners. Trim away the excess fabric from the garment front as shown. Press the seam turnings together towards the band.

4 Turn the facings to the WS. Make sure the buttonhole band lies on top of the button band on the RS. Turn down the triangular section of seam turning towards the hem and, folding the garment front out of the way, secure both bands to the turning, stitching through all thicknesses. Trim away the protruding triangle of fabric and neaten across the base of the bands and facing as shown. It is worth pinning the base of the bands in place before stitching, so it is possible to check from the RS that the bands lie together correctly and the base is square.

3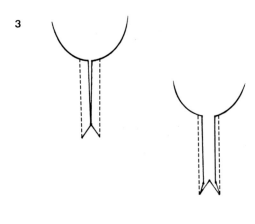

4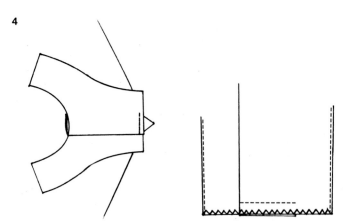

179 *Placket opening: stages 3 and 4*

CHAPTER EIGHTEEN

Waist finishes

WAISTBANDS

Straight waistband

Method of attaching waistband (*Figs. 180 and 181*):

1   Place the waistband to the waist seam with both WSs of fabric uppermost. Matching all the appropriate balance nips – the most usual are at the centre front, centre back and side seams – machine the waistband into place: a 1.3 cm ($\frac{1}{2}$ in.) turning is ideal. Begin and end with a back tack, leaving the seam turnings at the ends of the waistband loose. Press under the seam turning of the remaining long edge.

2   Machine the petersham or stiffening in place along the seam turning with the petersham edge 1 mm ($\frac{1}{16}$ in.) from the first row of stitching. The petersham is cut to the measurement of the finished waistband and it is, therefore, machined following the length of first row of stitching. If there is a wrap on the waistband only (this will protrude beyond the finished edge of the skirt opening if a wrap has not been included in the cut of the skirt) then cut a small section of petersham away with a step of about 2 mm ($\frac{1}{8}$ in.). This will allow the turnings of the waistband wrap more room inside and reduce bulk, allowing the wrap to lie flat when finished.

3   Stitch up the ends of the waistband to turn through. Mark the foldline of the top edge of the waistband with a nip. Place the garment at the machine with the WS uppermost. Fold the waistband at the nip, with the RSs coming together. Making sure that the garment is not caught into the stitching, machine as shown, back-tacking. If there is a separate wrap, fold back in the same way and machine as shown. Rather than stitching the base of the wrap exactly level with the waist seam, allow a fraction more fabric, stitching just outside the seamline. Fig. 181 shows an exaggerated version of this but, in reality, no more than 1 mm ($\frac{1}{16}$ in.) is necessary. When turned through this will compensate for

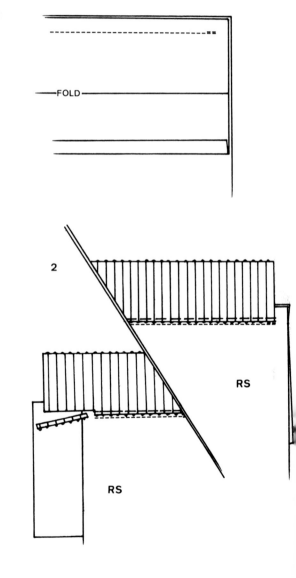

180   *Attaching a straight waistband: stages 1 and 2*

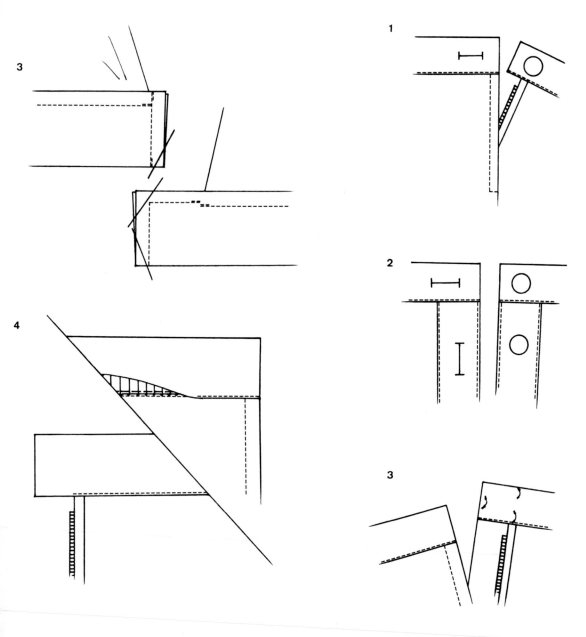

181 *Attaching a straight waistband: stages 3 and 4*

182 *Various waistband finishes showing how wrap is incorporated*

an amount of fabric that is taken up by 'roll', so that the finished lower edge of the wrap will lie exactly in line with the waist seam. The more bulky the fabric, the greater the extra allowance should be. These amounts still, however, remain minimal and experience helps judgement. Minor differences such as this can improve the finish of your work considerably. Trim the seam turnings and turn the waistband ends through.

4 The loose half of the waistband is now edge-stitched down from the RS. The seam turning has already been pressed under to facilitate this. Pull the waistband very firmly around the petersham and, if you wish, pin it down at intervals. The fold edge that is being held by the edge-stitching should just cover the first row of machining so the edge-stitching will, more or less, pass through in the same place as the first row. Hold the fold edge down firmly with the

157

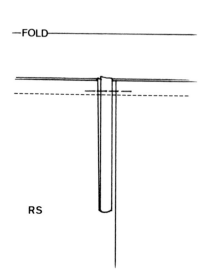

183 *Garment hangers inserted at stage 2 of attaching a waistband*

184 *Attaching a shaped waistband which is cut in two pieces*

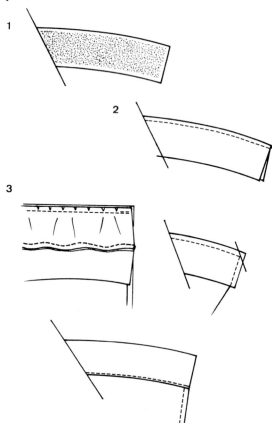

fingers of the right hand immediately prior to stitching, as the waistband will become twisted if the pressure of the machine foot is allowed to push the waistband fabric forward and so distort it. This is one instance where it is preferable to tie the thread ends and darn them in rather than back tack.

The principle of attaching a waistband remains the same but these are various ways that the wrap of the opening can be incorporated in the waistband. Fig. 182 shows three different instances that illustrate how the waistband is finished according to the type of opening.

There may be occasions when you particularly wish to avoid a row of machining showing on the RS of the waistband. Attach the waistband as described above, but place the RSs of the fabric together in the first instance. The loose side of the waistband is then on the WS of the garment and can be caught down by hand.

It is a good idea to stitch garment hangers into the waistband (*Fig. 183*). Use either bought tape or turned through strips of self, or lining, fabric. Narrow hangers of 6 mm (¼ in.) are adequate, cut to about 16 cm (6 in.) in length for a garment with an average waistband of 2.5 cm (1 in.) depth. Complete stage 1. Fold the hanger in half lengthwise. Stitch in place inside the seam turning, machining through all thicknesses as shown. Position the hangers at, or next to, the side seams. When the waistband is stitched down the hangers are automatically caught into place at the same time.

Shaped waistband cut in two pieces (*Fig. 184*)
1   Interface the top waistband.

2   With RSs together, stitch the seam across the top edge of the waistband.

3   Attach the waistband in the same way as given for a straight waistband. When you turn back the waistband to stitch the ends, pull the top seam fractionally over to the WS so that, when the waistband ends are turned through, the top seam lies just to the inside of the waistband. Clip the waist seam turnings at regular intervals, as this is a curved seam. The seam turning of the loose edge must also be clipped at the time it is pressed back, in preparation for stitching it down, whether by hand or machine.

ELASTICATED OR DRAWSTRING FINISH

These finishes are simple and quick to make up and are particularly useful in certain instances. Children's clothing is one example where it is important

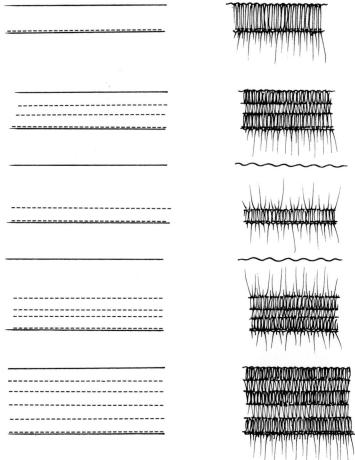

185 *Positioning of casings*

that the garment is comfortable to wear, easy to take off and put on, and, with a fast growth rate, will fit for much longer. Altering the waist size is easy if necessary, too, as a longer elastic is all that is needed.

Straight hem finish
Here, a hem is turned down at the top edge of the garment (which is cut straight, with no waist shaping) on the WS. Several examples are shown where the positioning of the casing is all that varies (*Fig. 185*). Press the hem with a crisp, straight edge. Edge-stitch it down from the WS leaving an opening of about 3 cm (1⅛ in.). Machine the appropriate rows of stitching parallel to the hem row to form the casing(s) required. Leave an opening as before. Thread the elastic through and finish as given on p. 130.

Drawstring waist
The principles of constructing a casing to hold a drawstring are the same as for elastic, with one difference: there must be an opening for the ties to come through to be fastened on the RS. The easiest way to achieve this is to work a buttonhole or a faced slit on the top side of the casing prior to stitching the casing down.

Buttonhole openings(s) (Fig. 186)
Apply a small piece of interlining to the back of the top of the casing as shown. Position the buttonhole vertically with at least 5 mm (³⁄₁₆ in.) of casing depth above and below the buttonhole. Work a reinforced buttonhole by inserting gimp or by machining double vertical rows of zigzag stitches, or just by making a second buttonhole exactly on top of the first.

Faced slit (Fig. 187)
Cut a small facing from a medium- to light-weight fabric. Mark the beginning and end of the slit with small pencil dots and place the facing with RSs together. Hold it in its correct position with a pin.

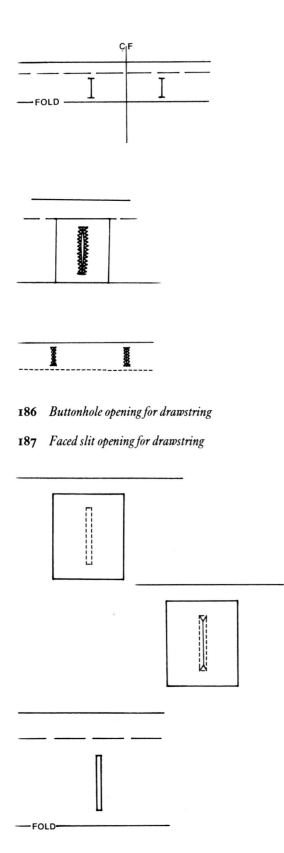

186 *Buttonhole opening for drawstring*

187 *Faced slit opening for drawstring*

Set the machine to a very short stitch and stitch the facing down as shown. With a sharp, pointed pair of scissors cut the slit, making tiny clips into the corners. Poke the facing through the hole to the WS, pull it flat so that the slit appears neatly, and gently press. If the fabric puckers at all at the corners, check that the clipping reaches right into the corners of the stitching. Trim away any excess facing fabric.

WAISTBANDS FOR WRAP-OVER SKIRTS

Wrap-over skirt with button fastening (*Fig. 188*)

It is sometimes impractical to cut the waistband for a wrap-over skirt in one, because of the length of fabric required. Join the waistband with narrow 6 mm ($\frac{1}{4}$ in.) seam turnings first, if it has been necessary to cut in two or more pieces.

Attach the waistband in exactly the same way as given for a straight waistband. There will be no step at each end of the waistband. Finish both ends with suitable fastenings.

Wrap-over skirt with tie fastening

Waistband (Fig. 189)

An opening must be allowed in the waistband for the tie that is attached to the under-wrap to thread through to the RS in order to pass around the waist and fasten to the tie attached to the top-wrap. The waistband is cut in two with seam turnings to press back to the inside. The opening is positioned at the point on the top waist where the under-wrap reaches, and the two fold edges lie exactly together as the waistband is attached with a single row of stitching at the waist seam. The opening is fastened at the top of the waistband with several secure hand stitches, which should be invisible.

Ties (Fig. 190)

Where a tie is cut in a continuous length with the waistband, attach the waistband with the waist seam in the normal way. At the stage where the ends of the waistband are normally stitched up to turn through, fold the waistband and tie, with RS's together, in the same way. Stitch around the tie, trim and turn through. Finish the waistband by catching down, either by hand or machine.

There are numerous possibilities for incorporating skirt fastening in the construction of the waistband of a wrap-over skirt. Consider any other suggestions given on fastenings that might be suitable.

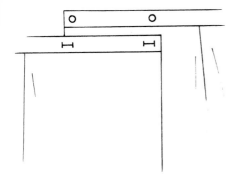

188 *Waistband for wrap-over skirt with button fastening*

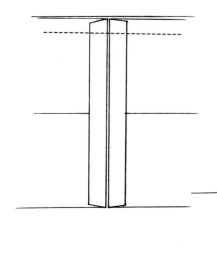

189 *Waistband for wrap-over skirt with tie fastening*

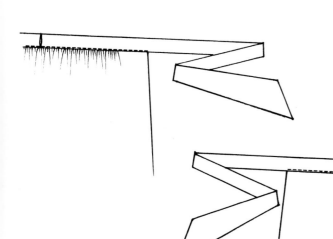

190 *Two-piece waistband for ties cut in one with waistband*

CHAPTER NINETEEN

Collar and neck finishes

SIMPLE NECKLINES WITHOUT OPENING

Check that the opening is large enough for the head to pass through before beginning work on the construction of such a neckline.

A crossway strip is useful to finish a neckline simply, either used as a binding or a facing (*Fig. 191*). Insert a gathered frill or lace to make a feature. Gather the fabric up to the correct neck measurement. Join the frill with a narrow seam. Stitch the frill in place with a row of machining inside the seam turning. For a frill that is to lie flat against the bodice, finish the neck edge with a binding. For a frill that is to stand up at the neck, finish the neck edge with a facing.

ELASTICATED OR DRAWSTRING NECKLINE

The cut edge of a neckline that is to be gathered will be wide and loose. A casing is stitched to contain the elastic or drawstring. Elasticated necklines can be lowered and worn off the shoulder so bear this in mind when determining the finished length of the elastic. A neckline that is finished in this way is rarely cut with shoulder seams, so any sleeve is cut with raglan shaping. (*See Elastic under suppression, p. 129 and Elasticated waistbands p. 61 for suggestions.*)

The three garments illustrated (*Fig. 192*) show how this type of neckline might be finished.

FACINGS (*Figs. 193, 194 and 195*)

1 Interface the neck facing and make it up. Most neck facings are joined with shoulder seams. Stitch a narrow 6 mm ($\frac{1}{4}$ in.) seam turning. Press open. Neaten the raw edge of the facing. (*See Front facing details for finishing suggestions, p. 136.*)

2 With RSs together, stitch the facing around the neck edge. A narrow 6 mm ($\frac{1}{4}$ in.) seam turning

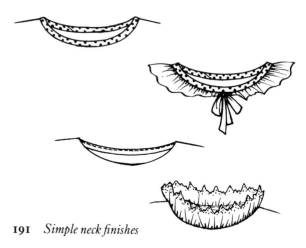

191 *Simple neck finishes*

avoids the need for unnecessary trimming. Match the shoulder seams exactly. Pin in position if you prefer. Clip into the corners of a square neckline and clip into a curved seam turning at regular intervals.

3 Press the seam turnings together towards the facing, turning the facing back. Edge-stitch the facing down through the seam turnings.

4 Turn the facing right through to the WS and press. If the neck edge is to be top-stitched, there is no need to machine the facing to the seam turnings as the top-stitching will hold the facing in place on the WS.

Catch the edge of the facing down on the WS by hand at the shoulder seams. Sew through the turnings only.

A neck facing may be stitched to the garment with both WSs uppermost. The facing is then turned through to the RS and, instead of being neatened, the raw edge is turned under and edge-stitched down from the RS to the bodice all the way round. The examples show instances where this method has been used (*Fig. 195*).

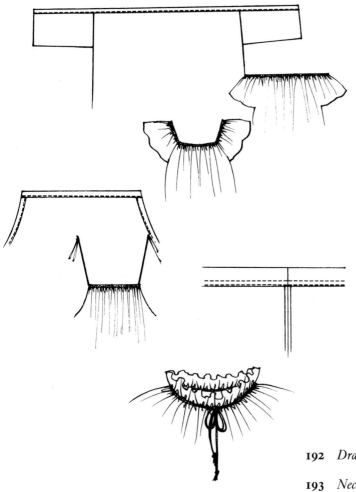

192 *Drawstring/elasticated neck finishes*

193 *Neck facing: stages 1 and 2*

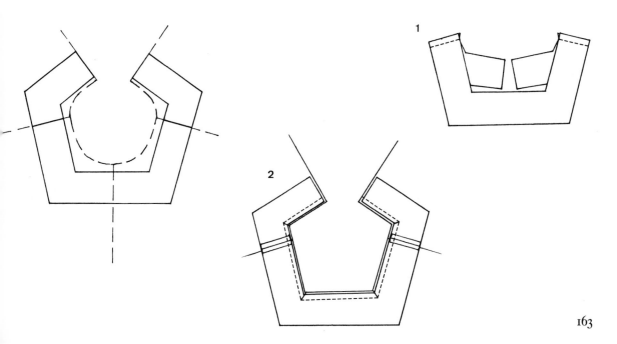

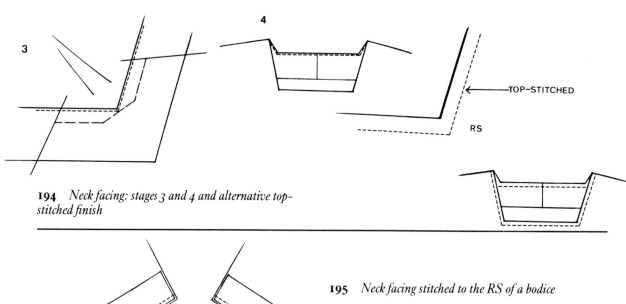

3

4

TOP-STITCHED

RS

194 *Neck facing: stages 3 and 4 and alternative top-stitched finish*

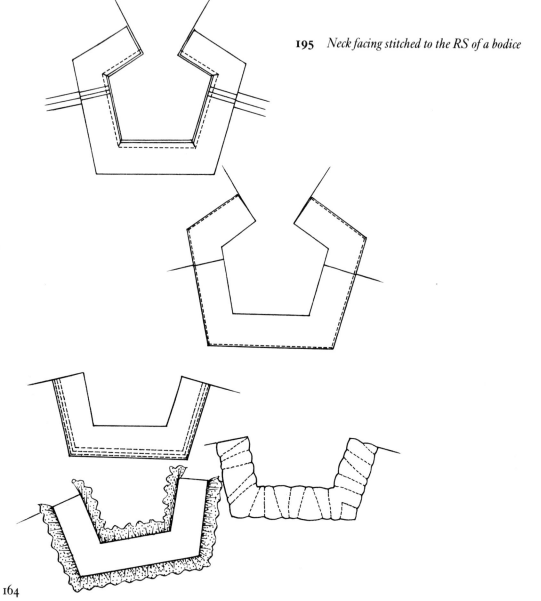

195 *Neck facing stitched to the RS of a bodice*

STAND COLLARS

The method used to attach a stand collar to a neck edge will vary slightly, depending on whether there is a full neck facing, front neck facings only, or no facing at all. The inclusion or otherwise of a neck facing will largely depend on the type of opening the garment has.

No neck facing – collar wraps over when fastened (*Fig. 196*)

1   Interline the top collar.

2   With both WSs uppermost, stitch the under-collar to the neck edge, matching CB and side seam balance nips. Press the seam turnings together towards the collar. Clip the turnings at regular intervals.

3   Press the seam turning at the lower edge of the top collar to the WS. Place the collars with RSs together and machine around outer edges. Trim away all excess fabric at any curves or corners. Turn the collar through to the RS and press.

4   From the RS, edge-stitch the loose edge of the top collar down to the neck edge. It is preferable to tie off the thread ends and darn them in, rather than back tack.

This is the same method that is used to attach a

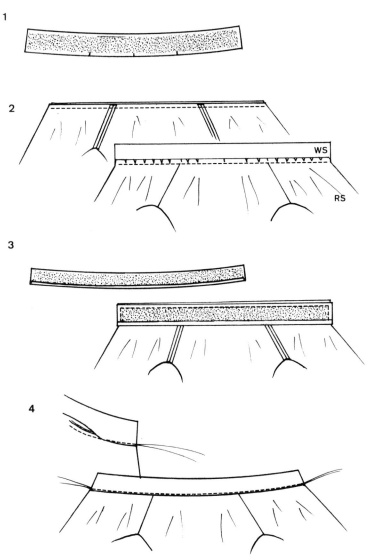

196 *Stand collar with no neck facing*

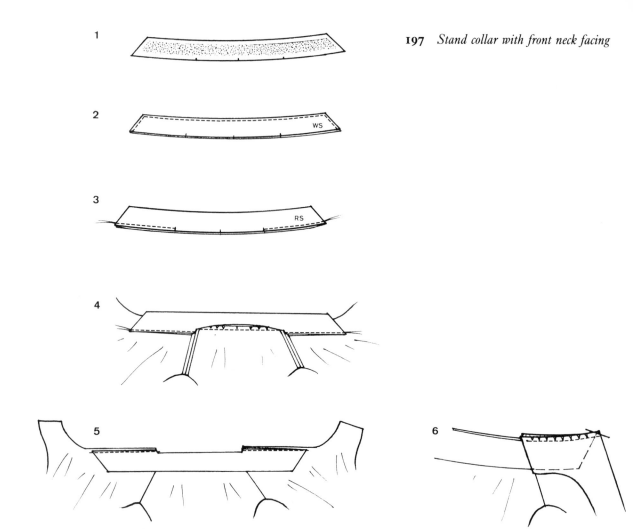

straight waistband. It may be altered in the same way as the waistband so that a hand finish can catch the under collar down on the WS if edge-stitching from the RS needs to be avoided.

Front neck facing – collar meets edge-to-edge (*Fig. 197*)

1   Interline the top collar.

2   With RSs together, stitch the top and under-collar together. Trim the turnings as necessary and turn through to the RS. Press.

3   Pin the collar together and, using a long machine stitch, sew the raw edges together from the shoulder seam nips to the CF, just inside the seam turning. Clip the turnings at the shoulder seam nips right up to the stitching line.

4   Place the top collar to the RS of the back bodice and stitch the collar to the back neck edge only.

Begin and end with a back tack. Press the seam turnings together towards the collar.

5   Stitch the fronts of the collar down to the neck edge, just inside the seam turning, making sure that the collar edges are correctly in line with the CF.

6   Fold the neck facing back with RSs together and stitch the front neck edges as shown, exactly to the shoulder seam. Trim away as much of the excess bulk as possible, nip and turn the facing through to the RS; press.

Turn under the back neck edge of the under-collar and catch down by hand. The top collar can be edge-stitched down by machine from the RS if, at stage 4, the back neck of the under-collar is placed to the bodice with both WSs uppermost. Catch the front neck facing to the shoulder seam turning by hand.

Back and front neck facing (*Fig. 198*)

1 Interline the top collar.

2 With RSs together, stitch the top and under-collar together. Trim the turnings as necessary and turn through to the RS. Press.

3 Pin the collar together and, using a long machine stitch, sew the remaining raw edges together.

4 Place the top collar to the RS of the bodice and machine the collar to the neck edge, using a long stitch just inside the seam turning.

5 Place the prepared facing RSs together and machine in place, so enclosing the collar between the bodice and facing. Trim carefully so that all excess bulk is removed. Clip the neck edge.

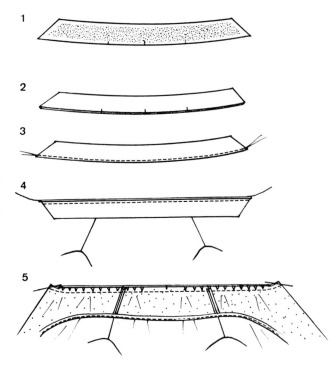

198 *Stand collar with front and back neck facing*

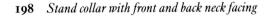

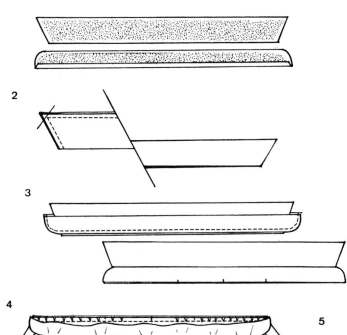

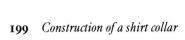

199 *Construction of a shirt collar*

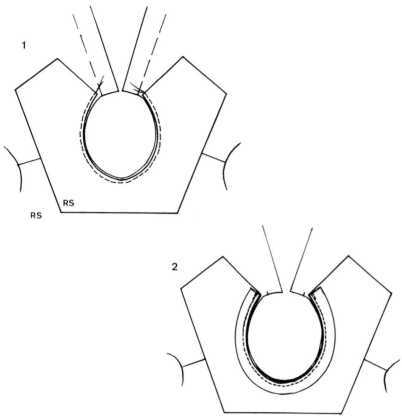

SHIRT COLLAR (*Fig. 199*)

1 Interline the top collar and the top stand. Press under the neck-edge seam turning of the stand.

2 Place the collars RSs together, stitch around with a narrow 6 mm (¼ in.) seam turning, trim away the seam turnings at points or curves, turn through the RS and press. Top-stitch, if required, with the top collar uppermost.

3 Place the stand that is not interlined – i.e. the one that will sit next to the neck with its RS together with the top collar. Now place the interlined stand with its RS together with the under-collar. The collar is now sandwiched between the stand. Check that the CFs are correctly positioned as well as the shoulder seam and centre-back balance nips. Pin as necessary. Stitch right around the stand, enclosing the collar. Trim the curved fronts of the stand, turn through to the RS and press.

4 Place the stand that is not interlined to the neck edge with both WSs uppermost. At the front edges, fold back the seam turnings inside the stand and position that seam so that it lies to the WS of the bodice. Carefully stitch the stand to the neck edge. Clip the seam turning. Press the seam turnings together in the direction of the stand.

5 Edge-stitch down the loose edge of the stand from the RS.

FLAT COLLAR (*Fig. 200*)

A flat collar is first made up completely and the remaining raw neck edge is stitched together just inside the seam turning with a long stitch. Flat collars do not necessarily need interlining.

1 Pin in position on the RS of the bodice and stitch down to the neck edge with a long machine stitch placed just inside the seam turning.

2 Attach a neck facing as described on p. 162. Alternatively, bind the neck edge with a single or double crossway strip. It is also possible to 'bind on' the collar (*see p. 134*). Note that a row of machining will show on the RS around the neck edge. If the flat collar covers this then this method is acceptable. If it does not, consider the finished appearance carefully.

ROLL COLLAR (*Fig. 201*)

This collar can be bound on with a crossway-cut strip and does not, therefore, require a neck facing of any kind. The CF opening is finished with a straight facing.

1 Interline the top collar.

2 With RSs together, stitch the top and under-collar together. Trim the turnings as necessary and turn through to the WS. Press.

3 Pin the collar together and, using a long machine stitch, sew the remaining raw edges together.

4 Place the RS of the top collar to the RS of the garment, matching balance nips. Machine the collar to the neck edge with a long stitch, just inside the seam turning. Clip the neck edge.

Bind the collar on to the neck edge with either double or single crossway strip (*see p. 134 for details*). Leave the ends of the binding raw.

Fold the prepared facing back with RSs together. Stitch the top edge, trim and turn through to the RS; press.

REVERS COLLAR (*Fig. 202*)

1 Interline the top collar.

2 With RSs together, stitch the top and under-collar together. Trim the turnings as necessary and turn through to the RS; press.

3 Pin the collar together and, using a long machine stitch, sew the raw edges together from the shoulder-seam nips to the CF, just inside the seam turning. Clip the turnings at the shoulder-seam nips, right up to the stitching line.

1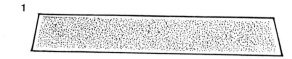

201 *Collar with roll*

2

3

4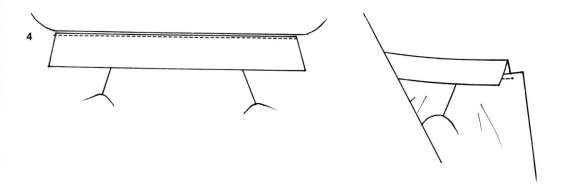

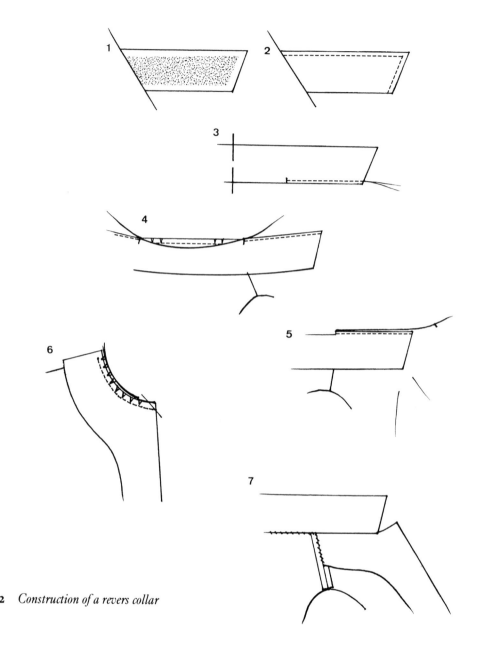

202 *Construction of a revers collar*

4 Place the top collar to the RS of the back bodice and stitch the collar to the back neck edge only. Begin and end with a back tack. Press the seam turnings together towards the collar.

5 Stitch the fronts of the collar down to the neck edge, just inside the seam turning, making sure that the collar edges are correctly in line with the CF.

6 Fold back the neck facing, with RSs together, and stitch the front neck edges as shown, exactly to

the shoulder seam. Trim away as much of the excess bulk as possible, clip and turn the facing through to the RS; press.

7 Turn under the back neck edge of the under-collar and catch down by hand. The top collar can be edge-stitched down by machine from the RS if, at stage 4, the back neck of the under-collar is placed to the bodice with both WSs uppermost. Catch the front neck facing to the shoulder-seam turning by hand.

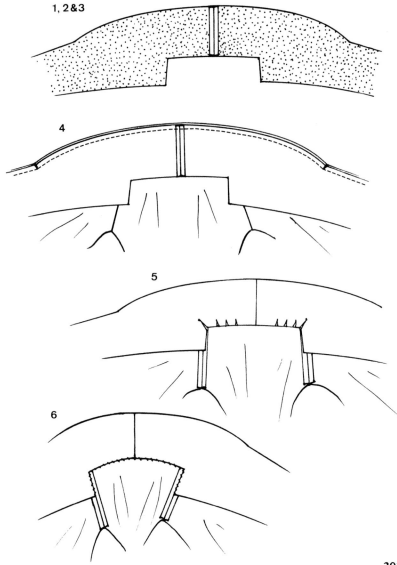

203 *Construction of a shawl collar*

SHAWL COLLAR (*Fig. 203*)

1 Interline the facing and collar.

2 Join at the CB with a narrow 6 mm (¼ in.) seam turning. Press open. Neaten outside edge of facings.

3 Join the CB collar seam (cut as an extension of the bodice) with a narrow 6 mm (¼ in.) seam turning. Press open.

4 Placing RSs together, stitch the facing to the bodice. Clip, trim, turn through and press.

5 Clip back neck of facing right into the corners where the stitching line meets the shoulder seam. Clip around neck edge at regular intervals.

6 Turn under seam turnings and catch down by hand as shown.

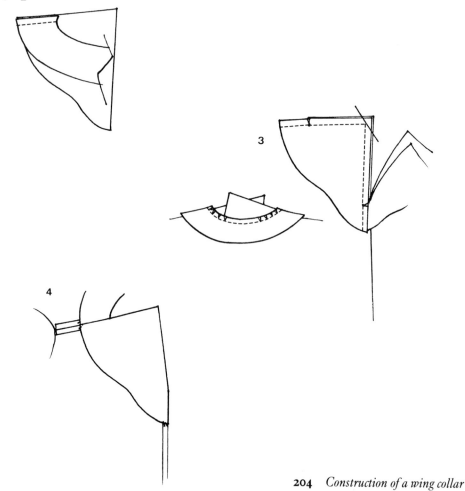

204 *Construction of a wing collar*

WING COLLAR (*Fig. 204*)

1 Interline collar pieces and back neck facing.

2 With RSs together, stitch to back neck facing. Neaten facing edge. Stitch facing together at CF.

3 With RSs together, pin facing to neck at CF, shoulder seams and CB. Stitch together, starting at CF opening. Trim, clip and turn to RS.

4 Catch the facing down on the WS to the shoulder seams and the CF seam.

TIE-NECK FINISH (*Fig. 205*)

1 Place the collar to the neck edge with both WSs uppermost and stitch in place. Clip seam turnings as necessary.

2 Fold the tie RSs together and stitch ends together. This should meet with the first row of stitching at the front neck edge. Trim, turn through and press.

3 From the RS, edgestitch down the loose edge of the collar to the neck seam.

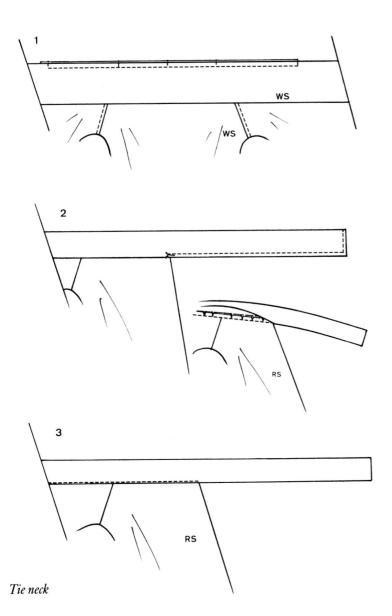

205 *Tie neck*

LOOSE, FLOPPY COLLARS (*Fig. 206*)

First, make up the collar into a tube. Then stitch one side to the neck edge and catch down the other side over the seam turnings either by edge-stitching or by hand.

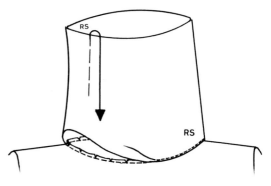

206 *Loose, floppy collars*

CHAPTER TWENTY

Sleeves and armholes

SLEEVE OPENINGS AT LOWER EDGE

All sleeve openings are positioned at the back quarter line of the sleeve. The side of the opening that is to the front of the sleeve wraps over the side of the opening nearest the under-arm seam. Work the opening first, before making up the sleeve.

Simple hemmed opening (*Figs. 207 and 208*)

1 Clip the seam turning (minimum 1.3 cm [$\frac{1}{2}$ in.]) to the stitching line twice. The distance between these clips is the exact width of the finished opening.

2 Fold the seam turning in half towards the WS and press (fold A).

3 Fold the hem along the stitching line (fold B) and edge-stitch down from the WS, back-tacking at each end.

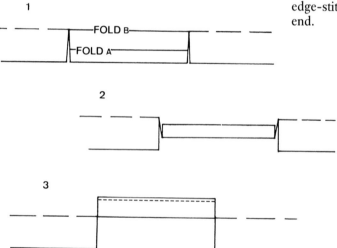

207 *Sleeve opening: hemmed edge*

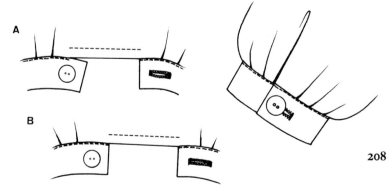

208 *Finished sleeve with hemmed-edge opening*

The cuff is attached to the lower edge of the sleeve as shown in Fig. 215, which may either have a step to include the cuff wrap (*Fig. 208A*) or be finished with two straight ends (*Fig. 208B*), where the wrap has been included in the cut of the sleeve width.

Continuous strip opening (*Figs. 209 and 210*)

1   Cut the slit in the sleeve on-grain and exactly up the back quarter line.

2   Press the continuous strip in half lengthwise with WSs together, and then press one long edge in half to meet the centre crease.

3   With the RS of the sleeve uppermost, position the unpressed long edge of the continuous strip beneath the opened slit with its RS uppermost also, as shown (*Fig. 209*). Stitch to the slit, keeping a narrow seam along the continuous strip straight and positioning the sleeve so that the stitching lies as shown. At the top of the slit, there should be only 2 mm ($\frac{1}{16}$ in.) from its raw edge.

4   Press the continuous strip to the RS as shown, so enclosing the seam turnings. Edge-stitch the remaining long edge of the continuous strip down from the RS.

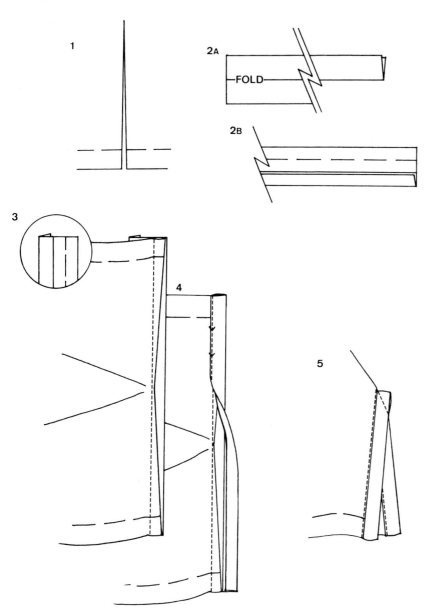

209   *Continuous strip opening*

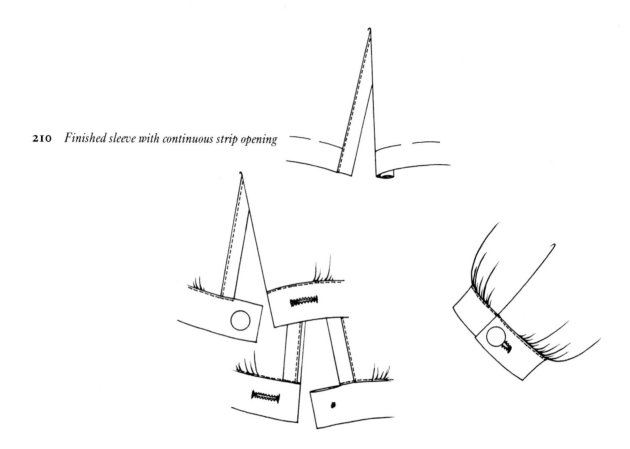

5 With the sleeve opening together, stitch the continuous strip diagonally across the top of the opening from the WS as shown.

The top side of the opening has the strip folded to the WS and on the under-side of the opening the strip remains flat. The cuff is attached to include a step that forms the under-wrap of the cuff.

Dart/hem opening (*Fig. 211*)

1 Cut the slit in the sleeve on-grain and exactly up the back quarter line. Snip 6 mm ($\frac{1}{4}$ in.) across the top of the slit in both directions.

2 Turn back the sides of the opening with two mini-folds to the WS, widening a little towards the lower edge of the sleeve as shown. Edge-stitch these tiny hems down from the WS.

3 Fold the RSs of the sleeve together and stitch a small dart above the opening. Finish the dart with a back tack, meeting the hem-stitching lines worked at stage 2.

4 Press the dart flat. Turn back the sides of the opening at the lower edge to the WS before attaching the cuff.

The wrap is included with this type of opening so the cuff can be finished without a step.

Shirt placket opening (*Figs. 212, 213 and 214*)

1 Cut the slit in the sleeve on-grain and exactly up the back quarter line. Snip 6 mm ($\frac{1}{4}$ in.) across the top of the slit towards the under-arm seam of the sleeve only. Turn back a tiny hem with two folds to the WS and edge-stitch down.

2 Clip the placket as shown and press in half, with WSs together, down the foldline. Press under all the raw edges as shown and, with both WSs uppermost, stitch the placket to the remaining raw edge of the opening with a narrow 6 mm ($\frac{1}{4}$ in.) seam. Back tack at both ends.

3 Press the placket to the RS and pin down in position. Edge-stitch the placket down, starting at point A and working around the pointed placket top and stitching the loose edge down over the seam to complete. Edge-stitch the fold edge of the placket to match, folding back the sleeve to avoid it being caught in the stitching. Leave loose ends to be pulled through to the WS and darned in. This is not necessary at the lower edge of the placket.

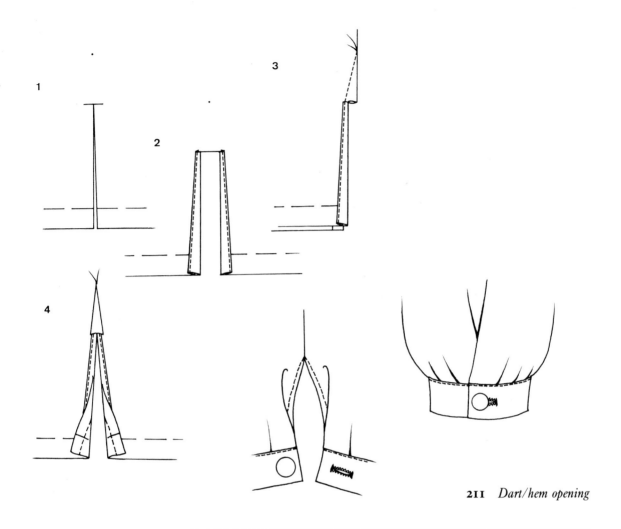

211　*Dart/hem opening*

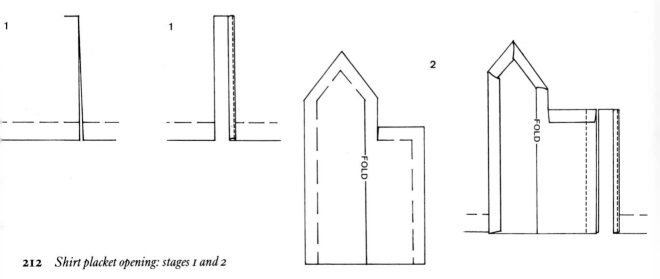

212　*Shirt placket opening: stages 1 and 2*

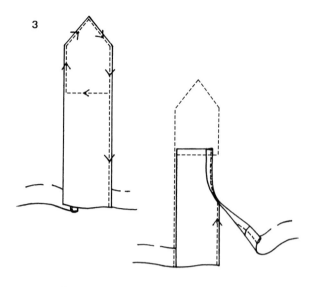

213 *Shirt placket opening: stage 3*

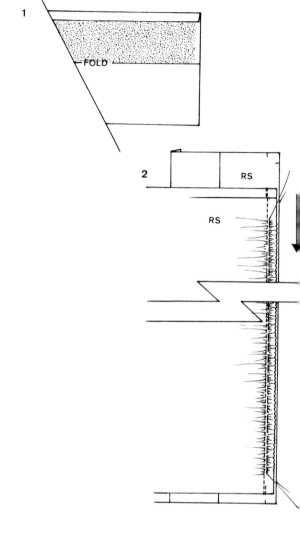

215 *Attaching a cuff: stages 1 and 2*

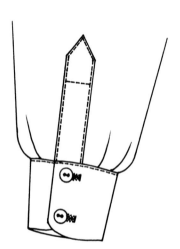

214 *Finished sleeve with shirt placket opening*

The cuff is finished without a step for a wrap, as this is incorporated in this type of opening finish.

CUFFS (*Figs. 215 and 216*)

The sleeve opening is finished and the under-arm seam is stitched and neatened, if necessary, before the cuff can be attached. The principle is exactly the same as that used to attach a waistband to a waist seam. The fullness at the lower edge of the sleeve is prepared and distributed.

1 Apply interlining to one half of the cuff. As a general rule, this will be placed to the top cuff. The edge of the interlining lies exactly along the fold edge as shown. Press the seam turning of the long edge of the top cuff to the WS.

2 The first line of stitching is worked with both RSs uppermost. The easiest way to work is first to turn the sleeve inside-out. Place the under-cuff at the machine in position. Position the corresponding sleeve on top of the cuff. Stitch the seam, 'rolling' the sleeve gradually over the flat cuff as the seam

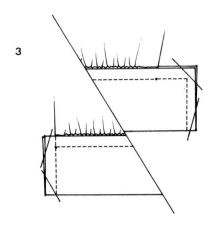

3

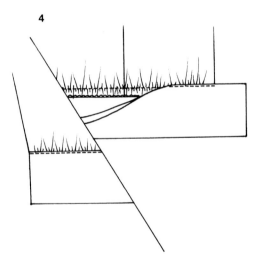

4

216 *Various sleeve hem finishes*

progresses. Match all balance nips carefully. It is easier if this seam is not pinned, so make certain the cut edges lie correctly together all along the seam. Press the seam turnings towards the cuff and trim away any excess bulk from the sleeve turning.

3   Fold the RSs of the cuff together and stitch up the sides in the same way as described for a waistband on *p. 157*, stage 3. If the cuff has a step for a wrap, complete this in the same way also. Trim the corners and turn the cuff through to the RS. Press.₄   Edge-stitch the cuff down on to the sleeve from

the RS so that the fold edge just covers the first line of stitching.

OTHER SLEEVE HEM FINISHES

Fig. 217 shows some examples of sleeve hems finished either without a cuff or an opening or both.

1   The sleeve is loose enough to pass the hand through without the need for an opening. Crossway strip in a contrast fabric is used to bind the raw edge (*see p. 131*).

2   The lower edge of the seam is faced. An opening may be included, if necessary. Join the facing into a ring with a narrow seam and press this seam flat. Neaten the top edge of the facing. Pin the facing to the lower edge of the sleeve with RSs together. Stitch around the lower edge, continuing around the slit as shown. Clip and trim off any corners and turn the facing to the WS. Press. To insert a button loop, *see p. 151*.

3   The cuff is interlined and made up. Place the cuff around the lower edge of the sleeve in its finished position. Machine together the raw edges around the hem of the sleeve to hold the cuff in place. Bind on the cuff (*see p. 134*). When the binding is stitched down to the sleeve over the seam turnings, fold the cuff down out of the way.

4   A wide sleeve may be finished with a casing which carries elastic, with or without a frill (*see p. 159 for various suggestions*).

5   A deep cuff is shaped and is, therefore, cut in two pieces. Attach the cuff in the same way as you would a straight cuff, beginning by stitching the under-cuff (not interlined) to the WS of the sleeve with both WSs uppermost. Join the sides of the cuff in the same way, placing the RSs of the top and under-cuffs together, but continue around the lower edge of the cuff and up the other side in one continuous seam. Trim, turn the cuff through, press and finish in the same way as a straight cuff.

SETTING-IN A SLEEVE

Usually the sleeve is made up and is inserted into the armhole on the bodice. The shoulder and side seams of the bodice, as well as any others that run into the armhole, must be stitched and neatened or completed.

If the sleeve-head has gathers or pleats, for instance, prepare these and stitch them in position with a row of machining inside the seam turning.

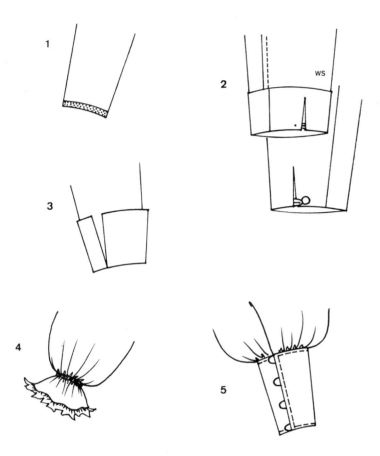

217   *Various sleeve hem finishes*

218   *Setting in a sleeve*

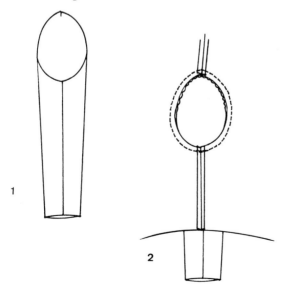

Fig. 218 shows the steps involved in setting in a sleeve.

1   If the sleeve is inside-out, turn it to the RS. Turn the bodice inside-out. With the bodice towards you, reach through the armhole and pick up the corresponding sleeve at the under-arm seam. Bring this to match the bodice side seam and pin with the sleeve facing you, unless you are easing away sleeve-head fullness by hand, when you work with the bodice uppermost and, therefore, will pin with the bodice facing you. Now pin the sleeve around the armhole, matching all balance marks.

2   Begin at the under-arm seam with the sleeve WS uppermost. Stitch a gradual curve, following the cut edge with a minimum width turning of 1.3 cm ($\frac{1}{2}$ in.). Remove the pins as you proceed. Gradually lift the garment as the seam progresses, so the weight of the garment does not pull and distort the seam. Overlap the end of the stitching at least 2 cm ($\frac{3}{4}$ in.) over the beginning.

Ease is distributed around a sleeve-head from the back quarter-line balance nips to the front (*see p. 55*). There is always more ease at the 5–6 cm (2–2¼ in.) across the top of the sleeve-head and then a little more at the remaining back section of head than at the front. Fig. 219 shows this principle in an exaggerated form.

Finish armhole turnings together and always press them towards the sleeve.

Alternative method (*Fig. 220*)

This method is traditionally used for dropped-shoulder shirt sleeves which are made up with flat-felled seams. There is no reason why any sleeve may not be set in in this way and it may be useful if you find the standard method a problem.

1 The bodice is made up, apart from the side seam, which is left open. The sleeve is not joined at the under-arm, but remains flat. Any sleeve opening at the hem may, of course, be made up first, if preferred.

2 Join the sleeve-head around the armhole, matching balance nips. A plain or flat-felled seam can be used, including a reversed flat-felled seam. Neaten a plain seam with both turnings together.

3 Join the sleeve under-arm seam and bodice side seam in one seam, taking care to match the armhole seam at the under-arm exactly.

FINISHING ARMHOLES OF SLEEVELESS GARMENTS

Fig. 221 shows some suggestions for finishing armholes.

1 The armhole is faced. The facing itself will have a shoulder seam and an under-arm seam. Pin the made-up facing to the armhole with the RSs together, matching the seams. Stitch around the armhole, beginning at the under-arm, and press them in the direction of the facing. Edge-stitch the facing to the turnings. Turn the facing to the WS and catch it down by hand to the shoulder and side seams.

2 This shows a 'combination' facing. The neck and armhole are neatened with one facing. Join the facing at the side seams and neaten its lower edge. With RSs together, stitch the facing to the bodice, leaving the shoulder turnings loose as shown. Clip as required and turn the facing to the RS. Turn back the facing shoulder turnings so that the bodice shoulder seam can be placed with RSs together and

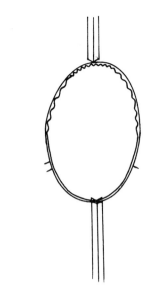

219 *Distribution of ease around a sleeve-head*

220 *Flat method of setting in a sleeve*

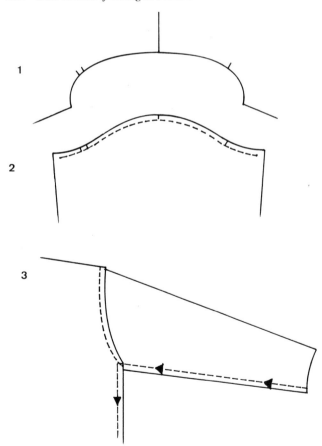

1

2

3

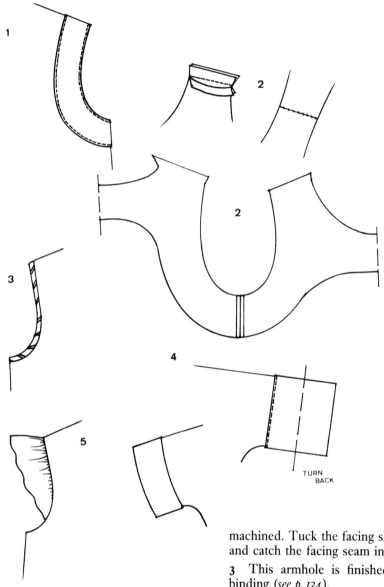

machined. Tuck the facing shoulder turnings inside and catch the facing seam invisibly by hand.

3 This armhole is finished with a crossway-cut binding (*see p. 134*).

4 Turn back a deep hem to the WS and machine. Now roll the hem up on the RS to cover the row of machining. To hold this type of cuff in position permanently, stitch a made-up tab to the sleeve, catching it in the hem. Turn it up from the WS to fasten around the cuff to a button sewn to the sleeve. Catch in place by hand with two or three stitches at the under-arm.

5 A frill is made up and pinned around the armhole with RSs together. The armhole is then finished with a crossway-cut strip, which is turned to the WS, as a facing, and machined down (*see p. 133 for details*).

221 *Various armhole finishes*

CHAPTER TWENTY-ONE

Hems

A hem is usually the final stage of the making-up of the garment. The suggestions included should cover most circumstances. A well-finished hem will give a garment a professional touch.

Press the hem edge to give a smooth, even line. Avoid over-pressing or an indentation of the hem will show on the RS. Pin hems carefully to avoid twisting and distortion, which will affect the hang of the garment. Machine-stitching should be at an even distance from the hem edge, in a smooth line with no wobbles, and should be set at the perfect tension. Hand-sewn hems should really be invisible. Do not pull the thread up tightly, but rather leave it on the loose side so that pulling or puckering does not occur.

Choose the right kind of hem finish to suit the garment type, style and fabric. Consider the following points:

1 Whether the stitching is to be invisible or not. An invisible hem will require a hand finish unless your machine has a blind hem-stitch. Even this may be unsuitable on other than heavier-weight, bulky fabrics or those with some surface texture. Where the hem finish need not be invisible, machine-stitching will show on the RS.

2 Type of fabric. The weight of the fabric will, to a large extent, determine the specific method you choose as a more bulky fabric will not be suitable for folding over twice. A heavier fabric often falls better with a greater depth of hem.

HEAVY-WEIGHT FABRICS

Cut away seam turnings to reduce bulk in the hem as shown (*Fig. 222*).

Finishing off the raw edge (*Fig. 223*)

Machine finish
Use a zigzag or overlock stitch. On more loosely woven fabrics, run a single row of edge-stitching through the single thickness first.

Tape
Stitch a cotton tape to the raw edge. Edge-stitch in place with half the width of the tape protruding

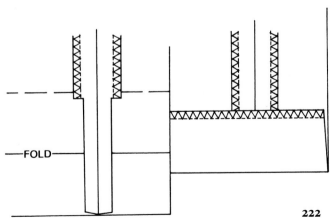

222 *Bulky seam turnings trimmed away inside hem*

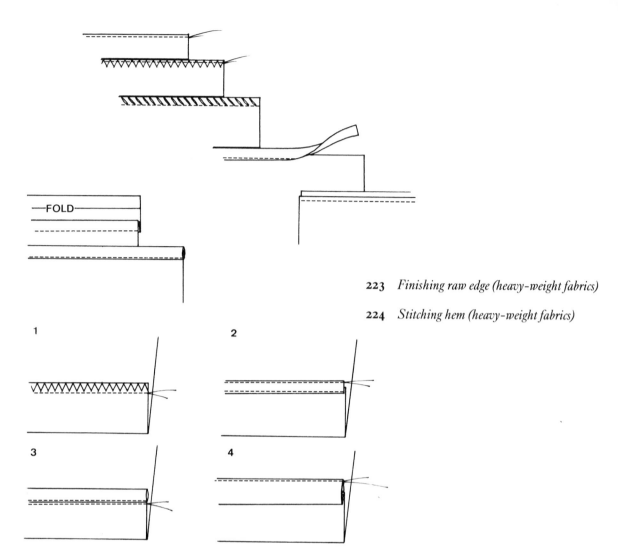

FOLD

223 *Finishing raw edge (heavy-weight fabrics)*

224 *Stitching hem (heavy-weight fabrics)*

1

2

3

4

beyond the raw edge as shown. The tape is then used to stitch through for the hem.

Binding
The raw edge may be neatened with a lighter-weight tape or binding exactly as given for a seam turning finish on page 131.

Catching in place
With a straight hem, it may be suitable to machine in position but test this on a scrap of fabric first to check that the appearance on the RS is satisfactory. Positions for stitching are as follows (*Fig. 224*):

1 The inside edge of machine finish.

2 Along the top edge of the tape, so that the stitching passes through the tape and a single fabric thickness only.

3 Just below the binding or on the fold edge of the binding (4), or both.

On a slightly curved hem, or where you do not consider machining to be suitable, catch the hem down by hand (*Fig. 225*).

1 Where a fabric does not fray readily, or if the garment is lined, the raw edge may be caught down with a herringbone stitch.

2 A machine-neatened raw edge is turned back and caught down by hand underneath.

3 Tape is hand-stitched down.

4 Binding is caught down along the top edge, the thread passing along inside the binding between stitches or is turned back and caught down underneath.

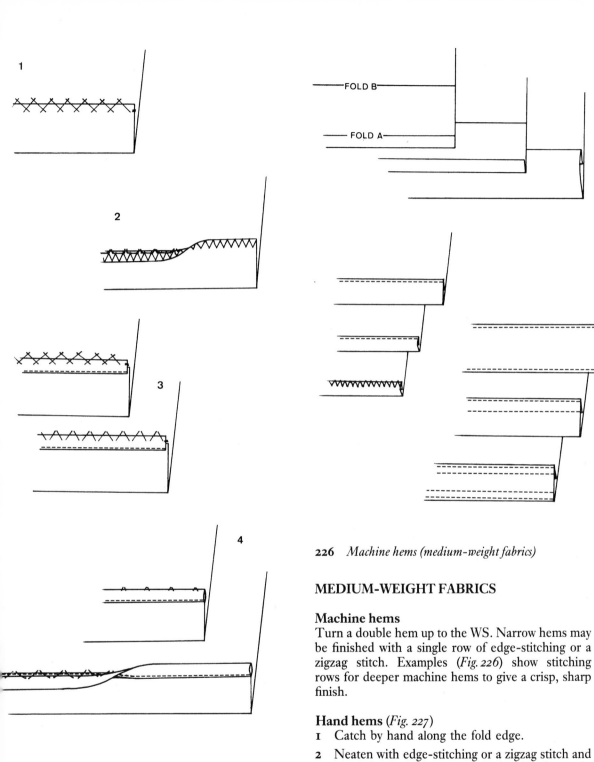

226 *Machine hems (medium-weight fabrics)*

MEDIUM-WEIGHT FABRICS

Machine hems
Turn a double hem up to the WS. Narrow hems may be finished with a single row of edge-stitching or a zigzag stitch. Examples (*Fig. 226*) show stitching rows for deeper machine hems to give a crisp, sharp finish.

Hand hems (*Fig. 227*)
1 Catch by hand along the fold edge.

2 Neaten with edge-stitching or a zigzag stitch and turn back finished edge to catch by hand underneath.

3 Machine a narrow binding and catch down fold edge of binding.

225 *Hand-stitched hems (heavy-weight fabrics)*

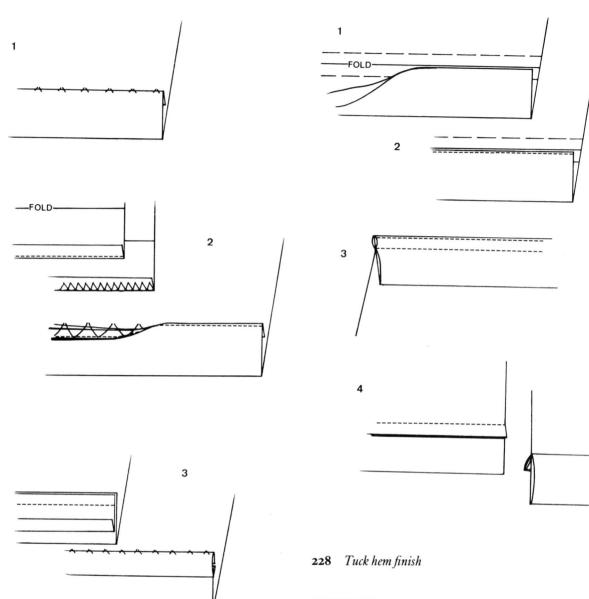

227 *Hand-stitched hems (medium-weight fabrics)*

228 *Tuck hem finish*

LIGHT-WEIGHT FABRICS

Turn under tiny hems and edge-stitch or machine down with a tiny, dainty zigzag stitch.

Tuck hem
This is equally suitable for medium-weight fabrics.

1 Press the hem up to the WS with the raw edge meeting the fold edge of the tuck.

2 Edge-stitch the raw edge down.

3 Fold back the tuck and stitch the tuck at the correct width.

4 Press the tuck down, towards the hem edge.

List of suppliers

Department stores

John Lewis Partnership
Oxford Street
London W1
(and branches)

Harrods
Knightsbridge
London SW1

Liberty & Co Ltd
Regent Street
London W1

Selfridges
Oxford Street W1

Dress fabrics

Laura Ashley
71 Lower Sloane Street
London SW1
(and branches)

The Fabric Studio
10 Frith Street
London W1

H Wolfin and Son
64 Great Tichfield Street
London W1

Strawberry Fayre
Chagford
Newton Abbot
Devon
TQ13 8EN

Whaley's (Bradford) Ltd
Ham's Court
Great Horton
Bradford
West Yorkshire
BD7 4EQ

Netta (Liskeard) Ltd
15 & 25 Fore Street
Liskeard
Cornwall

George Weil and Sons Ltd
63–65 Riding House Street
London W1

Sewing machines and attachments

Elna Sewing Machines (GB) Ltd
180–182 Tottenham Court Road
London W1P 9LE

Singer Sewing Co (UK) Ltd
Unit H Grafton Way
West Ham Industrial Estate
Basingstoke
Hampshire

Bernina Sewing Centre
10 Wardour Street
London W1

Pfaff (Britain) Ltd
East Street
Leeds
LS9 8EH

Aisin (UK) Ltd
Toyota Sewing and Knitting
34 High Street
Bromley
Kent

Husqvarna (Viking) Ltd
High Lane
Stanstead
Essex

Jones Sewing Machine Co Ltd
Shepley Street
Guide Bridge
Audershaw
Manchester
M34 5JD

Frister & Rossmann Sewing
Machines Ltd
Mark Way
Swanley
Kent

Threads and haberdashery

Needle Needs
20 Beauchamp Place
Knightsbridge
London SW1

Tootal Sewing Products
56 Oxford Street
Manchester
M60 1HJ

Perivale-Gutermann Ltd
Wadsworth Road
Perivale
Greenford
Middlesex

McCulloch & Wallis Ltd
25 Dering Street
London W1

J & P Coats (UK) Ltd
Harlequin Avenue
Great West Road
Brentford
Middlesex

Buttons, belts and buckles

Ackerman Buttons Ltd
326 Hackney Road
London E2

Button Queen
19 Marylebone Lane
London W1

Button Box
44 Bedford Street
Covent Garden
London WC2

Harlequin
Lawling House
Stutton
Ipswich
Suffolk
IP9 2SW

The Warehouse
39 Neal Street
London WC2

Molnlycke
Skanthread International
Molnlycke House
Bar Hill
Cambridge
CB3 8EJ

Kincross (Suppliers)
Oakhill Avenue
Pinner
Middlesex
HA5 3DL

Creativity
15 Downing Street
Farnham
Surrey
and
35 New Oxford Street
London WC1

Sewing aids and interfacings

Value House
12 Union Road
Croydon
Surrey

The Vilene Organisation
PO Box 3
Greetland
Halifax
Yorkshire
HX4 8NJ

Pattern Paper

McCulloch and Wallis Ltd
Metropolitan Sewing Machines
321 Ashley Road
Poole
Dorset
BM14 0AP

Index